Praise for Rachel Greenwald and

Find a Husband After 35
Using What I Learned at Harvard
Business School

An International Bestseller

"For the woman who's ready to vault to the altar . . . put yourself on this 15-step plan . . . and you'll have one foot in that Vera Wang gown." —*O: The Oprah Magazine*

"The ultimate single-woman-looking-for-a-man manual!"
—*Palm Beach Post*

"[A]n instant hit." —*USA Today*

"Rachel Greenwald . . . has taught thousands of mature women how to meet Mr. Right." —*People*

"[Greenwald's] new book lends legitimacy to the husband hunt."
—New York *Daily News*

"Greenwald's program is . . . motivational. . . . What I found was that [she] had written the book for me, a smart successful woman . . ." —*New York Post*

"Greenwald . . . has become a national sensation. Unlike the typical pop psychology self-help book, Greenwald's is short on therapy. Her advice is uncommonly blunt." —*San Jose Mercury News*

"*Find a Husband* is . . . perfect . . . for the new millennium, where everything from religion to education to politics comes down to good marketing." —*Chicago Sun-Times*

Find a Husband After 35

Using What I Learned at Harvard Business School

A *Simple 15-Step* *Action Program*

Rachel Greenwald, M.B.A.

BALLANTINE BOOKS
NEW YORK

Author's Note
This book is not endorsed by Harvard Business School, but rather describes many concepts and techniques that I learned there as a student, to my best recollection. In translating these business lessons, I have taken creative license to apply them to the dating world. I am not licensed to practice psychology, psychiatry, or social work, and this book is not intended to replace counseling of any kind. The names of women you will see in this book and certain details of their stories have been disguised to protect their privacy. Some stories are composites of two or three actual experiences. First-person accounts were compiled by paraphrasing file notes. Case studies and examples were gathered from my clients, seminar participants, research with single women, and married women everywhere, whom I always ask, "How did you find your husband?"

www.ballantinebooks.com

Library of Congress Control Number: 2004093497

ISBN 0-345-46626-8

Book design by BTDnyc

Manufactured in the United States of America

First Hardcover Edition: September 2003
First Trade Paperback Edition: September 2004
10 9 8 7 6 5 4 3 2 1

This book is dedicated to my parents, Eleanor and Murray:
My wisest advisers,
My best marriage role models,
And my biggest fans.

Contents

Introduction: Marketing 101   1

On Your Mark, Get Set . . .   13

Step #1: Marketing Focus: Make *The Program* Your #1 Priority   19

Step #2: Marketing Support: Find a *Program* Mentor   34

Step #3: Packaging: Create Your Best Look   43

Step #4: Market Expansion: Cast a Wider Net   68

Step #5: Branding: Identify What Makes You Different   81

Step #6: Advertising: Promote Your Personal Brand   95

Step #7: Online Marketing: Be Efficient   113

Step #8: Guerrilla Marketing: Do Something Different!   144

Step #9: Niche Marketing: "Date" Women   164

Step #10: Telemarketing: Bring Out Your Rolodex   179

Step #11: Mass Marketing: Pump Up the Volume   196

Step #12: Event Marketing: Throw a *Program* Party!   218

Step #13: Product Life Cycle: Recharge Yourself   236

Step #14: Quarterly Performance Review: Evaluate Your Results   247

Step #15: Exit Strategy: "Man"agement   269

Press Conference: Questions and Answers About *The Program*   287

Epilogue: Pay It Forward   305

Business Before Pleasure: A Letter to You   313

Appendix: Online Dating Services   315

Acknowledgments   317

For More Information   323

Find a Husband
After 35
Using What
I Learned
at Harvard
Business School

Introduction

MARKETING 101

Why are you still single? It doesn't matter.

The important question is not why are you still single, but what are you going to do about it? I have created a proven, proactive, assertive program that I simply call "*The Program.*" It will help you find a husband. *The Program* uses powerful marketing tactics that I learned at Harvard Business School, in my professional marketing career, and in coaching single women just like you. It will jump-start your dating life and get you married.

If you're reading this book, you are probably between the ages of 35 and 105 and looking to get married for the first time, or maybe the fourth time. You probably have experienced waves of resignation, thinking that you will never find a wonderful mate. You may be divorced or widowed, or never married after spending time on your career or with the wrong boyfriend. Maybe you've never *wanted* to get married until recently. Maybe you've had weight issues or you've been distracted by a sick parent. Maybe you're shy and have trouble meeting men. It makes no difference how you got here: You're single and ready to make a change.

What this book is *not* is an analysis of all that has gone wrong in your life, who's to blame, or why society is the way it is. You'll see zero quotes from famous psychiatrists, sociologists, priests, or rabbis about the plight of the single modern female.

Women frequently ask me how to change their patterns of the past. They spend too much time on the job, they are attracted to the wrong types of men, they can't get over a lost love, their dates don't turn into committed relationships, their committed relationships always fizzle, or a dozen other common patterns. These are areas that *The Program* does *not* address in its 15 Steps. *The Program* is about action and moving forward: It will help you find a husband, but it assumes that at your stage in life, you have a pretty good idea about why you're still single. (By the way, if you are happy being single and not looking to find someone wonderful, put this book down. It's not for you.)

For some of you, being single has been by choice. You are fundamentally happy except for the frustration you feel about not having met a great partner. You've had other priorities and you have a full life with your friends, family, activities, and career. You have been too busy to focus on getting married. If you are reading this book now, perhaps you're ready to shift your focus.

For others of you, being single has not been by choice for any number of reasons. To understand those reasons, you may have tried therapy, read self-help books, or had friends and family counsel you on your issues. Hopefully, you are now enlightened and ready to break out of any damaging patterns. You want action, not more psychoanalysis.

Of course, you don't want to find just *any* husband. You probably could have done that by now. You want a *wonderful* husband, whatever that means to you individually. This is understood throughout *The Program*. When I say that these tactics will help find your husband, know that I mean "your wonderful husband."

And those wonderful husbands are out there. Every time I go to a new city to teach my seminar "Find a Husband After 35," the seminar registration operator inevitably calls me in advance to ask, "Do you allow men in your class? We've had so many calls from men who want to attend your seminar." I've called back many of those men, and I can promise you they're not looking to "hit on" the single women in my class. They genuinely want to learn how to find a wife. Some are shy, some are busy with their jobs, some are busy with single parenting, and most just don't know where the wonderful single women are. These men are lonely and out there looking for love, too. You're going to learn how to find them in this book.

The Program allows you to take matters into your own hands with 15 action steps. It is designed for women later in life with unique challenges, such as fewer eligible men and more insular lifestyles.

Let me be clear. This is not a program for the uncommitted. At times, you will feel this plan requires too much effort and is too contrived. But reading this book is like dialing "Marriage 911": It's an emergency. And you do what you have to do. You're lonely, maybe your biological clock is ticking, and you want a loving husband more than anything else. If you were searching for a job, you would devote enormous time and effort to finding the right one. Finding the right husband is certainly more important than a job, since hopefully the husband will be with you for a lifetime. If you wanted to lose weight, you'd abide by the required sacrifices and rules. *The Program* is like a combination job search and strict diet: There are commitments, sacrifices, and rules involved.

WHAT IS *THE PROGRAM*?

Throughout this book I will frequently refer to *"The Program."* *The Program* is a simple 15-Step action program to help you find a husband that uses marketing tactics I learned at Harvard Business School and honed in my professional marketing career. You, the reader, are the "product," and *The Program* is a "strategic plan" to help you "market" yourself to increase the quantity and quality of men whom you meet.

When you first hear the words *product, strategic plan*, and *marketing* applied to you and your dating efforts, perhaps you will bristle. This is normal. You are learning about a radical new approach. I assure you that *The Program* will be an empowering experience for you. It will allow you to take control of your unmarried situation and learn how you can do something smart and effective to change it.

You may recognize some tactics in this book that you've already put into practice. But my guess is that you've been doing only a few of these things, and doing them sporadically. Most of the dating activities that women initiate lack focus and coordination. They pull in different directions and don't produce the desired result. The trick is pulling them all together into a comprehensive and systematic strategic program. This is key. Just as in an orchestra, you may have violins and flutes playing, but until a conductor comes along and brings all the instrument sections together, the music doesn't deliver impact.

There are several tried-and-true methods by which 35+ singles meet each other today: fix-ups, organized activities, parties, "chance" meetings, and many kinds of dating services. While several of the 15 Steps advocate these familiar methods, what you'll find in *The Program* is an abundance of new and creative tactics to make them *effective* for you. I don't want to change *you*, I want to change what you *do*.

There are many tactics in this book that are just plain common sense. But I don't assume that you have necessarily been practicing them. Common sense is not always common practice! In any case, what you've been doing so far hasn't worked, so what have you got to lose? Read on.

WHAT YOU WILL LEARN

You will learn a whole new approach to looking for a husband. Your mind-set will change as you practice *The Program Thinking Method* in Step #1 and start looking at the world through *Program* lenses. You will start to see the problem of finding a husband through the eyes of a marketer: a problem that can be solved with creative solutions. You will understand why the scene changes after 35 and why you need to cast a wider net as you search for Mr. Right. When you've finished this book, you will be able to devise and advertise your personal brand, know how to get out of your rut, be able to create a winning plan to increase the volume of men you meet, conduct an exit interview, and much more. So stop obsessing about being single, and let's do something about it!

WHO MOVED MY ALTAR?

It really *is* different looking for a husband after 35. It's as though someone moved your altar: You weren't supposed to be standing here. Maybe you are part of the group of women whom I call the "Lost Cinderella Generation." You broke the glass ceiling, but broke your glass slipper along with it. There are six major differences to take into account now:

1. **Urgency:** If you're over 35 and looking to get married, you probably have a great sense of urgency. Your biological clock is ticking if you want children. Your friends and family are hounding you with: "Why aren't you married yet?" And you're sick to death of floating single in a sea of married couples. If you're divorced or widowed, you have other urgent issues, too: the stress of being a single parent or the burden of loneliness after years of having a partner. Urgent matters require *action*. You can't sit around, feel sorry for yourself, or wait until fate knocks on your door. You need to take matters into your own hands quickly and efficiently, using the proven search tactics from *The Program*. The tactics in this book are probably very different from the ones you used in your 20's.

2. **Fewer single men:** It's a math equation that's hard to grasp. There should be roughly an equal number of single men after 35 as there are women, right? Wrong. There are 28 million single women over 35, but only 18 million single men over 35 (U.S. Census, 2000)! The difference is due to a number of factors, including the fact that many men marry younger women. You must accept the reality you're given and figure out how best to address it. This means no more narrow criteria about what kind of man you're looking for. Accept the possibility that your future husband may have many wonderful qualities, but they may

come in a different package than you've imagined. He may be divorced, he may have kids of his own, he may be shorter than you, or he may work in a profession completely different from that of men you've dated in the past.

3. **Changed bodies:** Another cold reality. You are more likely to have problem body areas after 35. You may have had them *before* 35, but maybe they're worse now. Double chins and cellulite are the enemies. Your friends are talking about botox and plastic surgery. There will always be some perfect older woman out there who looks like she's 25, but for the rest of us, we need to make some changes to keep looking our best to attract men. *The Program*'s Step #3, Packaging, addresses this issue, and it's very important. You don't need to be beautiful and thin to find a husband. In fact, the most important success criterion is your level of commitment to the search. But you need to do some research and figure out what improvements you can make to your overall appearance. As they say, you only have one chance to make a first impression.

4. **Baggage:** By the time you're over 35, you will probably have more "baggage" in your life than you did at 25 or 30. You may have the shadow of an ex-husband or ex-fiancé, the memory of a deceased husband, or worse, a therapist from whom you desperately seek approval. You may have a more demanding job, young children who require all your energy, teenage children who devour your patience, an ailing parent who consumes you with guilt, or a beloved pet who never leaves your side. Maybe you have personal issues with weight, shyness, or self-esteem. *The Program* will show you how to focus on your goal without being burdened by your baggage.

5. **Habits:** The older you are, the more difficult old habits are to break. You may have recurring patterns of choosing the wrong

type of men, or being too picky and not giving new men a chance. You are probably more rigid and set in your ways. You may work too many hours at the office, or have a firmly entrenched routine at home. To really break these habits—which have been forming over many years, and are preventing you from finding a husband—you need a shock to your system. Using *The Program*'s marketing tactics for your dating efforts may be just what you need to help you make a change.

6. **Insular lifestyle:** After 35, your life is more insular. You aren't on a college campus where thousands of single men hang around. You aren't going out all night with your friends to parties and bars where chance meetings with single men are bountiful. Your job may be in a smaller office environment as you've risen higher in your position, or in a smaller city where it seems harder to meet eligible men. Or maybe you've earned the "right" to work at home and you rarely see your colleagues. Most of your friends are married with kids, and socializing means being a third wheel. You're probably in a personal rut, doing the same things over and over with the same circle of people. *The Program*'s Step #8, Guerrilla Marketing, will give you the tools to do something different and change your lifestyle.

THE BOTTLENECK AFTER 35

There are several stages in the process of being single at any age that I have identified through the course of my work. While you may have experienced some but not all of these stages, once or more than once, in a different order, or in varied intensities, they are basically as follows:

THE STAGES OF BEING SINGLE

Freedom > Hope > Love > Loss > Resentment > Reflection > Disappointment > Resignation > Renewal > Searching > Dating > Selection > Commitment

I want to help you with the stage that most women have told me is the hardest one after age 35. I looked at these stages and asked myself, "If these were stages in a business process, where would the bottleneck be?" *Bottleneck* is a term used in business operations to find which area on the production line is not running efficiently and is slowing down the other functions. Most women have told me that "Searching" is the after-35 bottleneck, simply because there seem to be fewer men and even fewer opportunities to meet them. They say they don't know how to find the good ones, they don't have the stamina to continue the search, and they have lost hope. Sound familiar?

Clearly, all the stages in the singles process are daunting and difficult in their own right, but *The Program* is aimed primarily at the biggest bottleneck for women after 35: the Searching stage. Step #15, however—Exit Strategy: "Man"agement—also addresses some of the issues in the Dating, Selection, and Commitment stages. Even though many of you may still have issues with damaging patterns from your past and will have questions about other stages, I believe that you are mature women who can navigate these rough waters. You know where and how to find the help you need (friends, family, therapy, self-help books, and so forth). I want to concentrate on giving you the tools to *find* him first. If you never get up to bat, you can't hit a home run!

NOT WARM AND FUZZY

In teaching you *The Program*, I will be blunt in my advice and tell you things that you may not want to hear. But I will offer the truth. Dozens of self-help books on the shelves offer gentle and coddling advice. This is not one of those books. *The Program* is strict and bold. It will jolt you into action and provide creative tactics to find your husband. So don't be offended as we get down to business.

WHY I WROTE THIS BOOK

I'm a professional marketing expert with an MBA from Harvard Business School. In my former jobs I used to market a wide range of products—everything from bottled water to fashion jewelry. I learned and used classic marketing principles proven effective in selling many categories of products. But ever since my undergraduate days in college as a psychology major, I was always more interested in people than in retail products. It was inevitable that I began to see personal relationships through my "marketing eyes." What I saw was very intriguing, and I came to realize that finding a husband effectively is about applying business principles to the dating process and *marketing yourself*. It's all about using classic marketing tactics such as packaging, branding, advertising, and niche marketing.

So I took my Harvard Business School training and real-life marketing job experiences and applied them to an untapped and growing market segment: single women over 35. I wanted to use my skills and instincts toward the challenge of helping women find a husband later in life. Five years ago, *The Program* was born.

This began as a hobby. I felt so fortunate to have found my own husband, and to be so happy, that I wanted my single friends to have the same experience. I wanted to instill in them the same business thought process that had eventually led me to my husband. I started out working with only one woman at a time and I gave it my all. I acted as Mentor, Advertiser, and Telemarketer for each one until she walked down the aisle. This became my passion. I was constantly on the phone with my latest "project" and always looking for creative ways to fix her up by finding single men who were friends of friends of friends. But I realized that I could have an impact on more than just a handful of single women if I gave them the tools to do it themselves, rather than doing it all for them.

So I sat down and formalized the 15 Steps that now comprise *The Program*. At first, I just had the names of the steps written down on two sheets of notebook paper. I invited a few women (friends of friends) to officially join *The Program*, and my "find-a-husband" consulting business was launched. This small group of pioneer women who first experimented with formal *Program* steps soon discovered that they really worked! I am proud and happy to say that I attended each of their weddings.

Three years ago, I went to a party given by Stephanie, one of my *Program* pioneers. She was then a 40-year-old woman who had joined *The Program* and was on Step #12, Event Marketing: Throw a *Program* Party! She had told many of her party guests in advance about *The Program* and how well it was working for her. By the time I arrived at her party, I was greeted by the single women like a Hollywood celebrity. Stephanie's story had spread. Hordes of single women flocked to me, wanting to learn more about *The Program*. "What is it?" they whispered, as if it were a secret handshake. They were all intrigued and willing to try something new. I knew I was onto something exciting.

My private client base expanded dramatically over the next few years. I am proud that the majority of my clients have met their future husbands within 12 to 18 months of joining *The Program*. I took my message on the road, and I began to teach seminars around the country. I was invited to appear as a guest on several top-rated radio shows. And then someone said to me those five magic words that changed my life: "You should write a book."

On Your Mark,
Get Set . . .

RAMP UP

Before you actually start *The Program*, there are four tasks you should perform to ramp up and get ready:

1. **Value your best customers:** Go buy a few boxes of very nice thank-you notecards. Each card might cost about a dollar. You can never have enough of these throughout your *Program* journey. There are going to be so many people who will help you, support you, and fix you up, and you must be very conscientious about thanking each and every one. Just as in business, you must treat your best customers well to gain repeat sales. What better way to encourage your "best customers" to fix you up again than by sending them a heartfelt thank-you note? If you've ever been a matchmaker for some of your friends, I would bet that few of them have gone out of their way to show their appreciation for your efforts, especially if the fix-up didn't work out. This is

one area where you can stand apart from other women hoping for matches: Simply send a warm, lovely thank-you note after someone has been kind enough to make an introduction for you.

2. **Purge negative influences and triggers:** You must purge negative influences and triggers from your life before you start *The Program*. Stop interacting with people who are not supportive of your quest for a mate, people who facilitate your single status, or even an ex-boyfriend or ex-husband who has an unhealthy emotional hold over you. Put into the back of your closet any objects in your home such as photos of a deceased husband, gifts from an ex-boyfriend, or anything that deflates your mood when you encounter it. To move forward and achieve your goal, you cannot allow anyone or anything into your orbit that is a negative influence or trigger.

3. **Bury your baggage:** Perhaps most important, you need to bury your emotional baggage. This is not something you're likely to hear from a therapist! But since my assumption is that you've been struggling with this baggage for years (we all have it), I'm going to make the bold statement that you should *just bury it*! Maybe you don't feel pretty enough or thin enough to attract a great guy, you're afraid of rejection, you're afraid to trust again, you're a workaholic, your childhood issues still haunt you, your ex-husband cheated, or you think you don't deserve to be loved. Whatever your baggage is, you can't carry it around with you on *The Program*. First of all, you're going to be too busy to think about it. Second of all, it's probably your excuse for why you haven't found a relationship that's worked out, and there are no excuses on *The Program*—only action! So write down all your baggage, your issues, or your hang-ups on a piece of paper and dig a hole to bury it in your backyard or a nearby park. I'm seri-

ous: I really want you to get a small shovel, dig a six-inch hole in the dirt, and bury that piece of paper. It is a symbolic ritual that can liberate you. The "old you" analyzed your issues, obsessed about them, whined about them. The "new you" will have buried all those demons for 12 to 18 months and is ready to move forward. You can always go dig them up after you're married, if you want to!

4. **Splurge:** The night before you start *The Program*, go ahead and splurge! Do something decadent. You are embarking on a regimented plan, and you should treat it like a strict diet. Last year, I joined Weight Watchers and lost twenty pounds. The night before I started my diet, I splurged by eating an entire chocolate cake! Pick something that you consider extravagant, and then splurge. Perhaps relax with a spa treatment, buy a pair of expensive shoes, take the afternoon off from work to see a double matinee, or eat something really fattening and bad for you. This will be your last hurrah before getting serious about the business of finding a husband.

THE PROGRAM IMPLEMENTATION DETAILS

How to Use This Book

You should first read through the entire book to understand the scope of *The Program*. Then return to Step #1 and begin the 15 Steps.

The Program Steps Are Sequential

The 15 Steps are designed to be undertaken in order. Steps #1 through #5 are building blocks. They will give you the foundation necessary to carry out the many tactics advocated in Steps #6 through #15. Each step will add to the skills, confidence, and experience that you will need along *The Program*'s journey. This is a *process*. You cannot truly master the many new ideas and approaches until you've made the required changes described in the earlier steps.

If on any step you meet a man and begin to date seriously, however, you can skip to Step #15, Exit Strategy: "Man"agement. If it turns out that you've found Mr. Right early and you get married, then exit *The Program*. If he turns out to be Mr. Wrong, then return to the last step you were on before you met him.

The Duration of Each Step

Because *The Program* is a process, each step may take longer for some women than for others. It depends on your level of commitment and how enlightened you are to *The Program* mind-set when you start. For some of you, *The Program* will be a 180-degree turnaround from everything you've believed and done in the past; for others, it will involve simply putting structure around principles in which you already believe and behavior that you already (partially) practice.

There is a very wide range of time you can spend on a given step, depending on which step it is, and how difficult it is for you. Some steps might take you only one day to complete (such as Step #1, Marketing Focus), while other steps might take several months (perhaps Step #15, Exit Strategy). Some of the steps are ongoing (such as Step #7, Online Marketing)—you will continue doing them until you meet your husband, even though you've moved on to the next step. The total completion time for all 15 Steps on *The Program* is estimated at 12 to 18 months. The table below shows a breakdown of the approximate duration of each group of steps.

Steps #1–5	Steps #6–12	Steps #13–15
1–2 months	6–9 months	5–7 months

Here's the good news: There is a finite amount of time that you are on *The Program*. Sacrifices are short term and will not be a permanent way of life. If you are on a diet you change your eating patterns to lose weight, but even after you have lost the weight, you must continue making those sacrifices forever or risk gaining back the pounds. With *The Program*, you can take solace that when it works and you find a husband, you can get off *The Program* completely. And no one will be happier for you than I!

The Program Is Strict

Why is *The Program* so strict? Let me answer this by using another diet analogy. If you were five pounds overweight, it wouldn't be critical to find a strict diet plan. But if you were more than a hundred pounds overweight, you might feel a sense of urgency to find an effective diet plan right away and stick to it. This is just like finding a husband. In your twenties, you didn't feel it was critical to get married right away; you had plenty of time and prospects. But after 35 (if marriage is your top goal), you feel more urgency to use your time effectively and make some fast changes.

I was reading an article in *Oprah* magazine (January 2003) that really had a big impact on me. Oprah said, "What I know for sure is that there are no shortcuts. Old-fashioned hard work pays off." *The Program* is a revolutionary approach to dating: it's hard work but it has a big payoff. It takes only 12 to 18 months if you adhere to the strict plan. You cannot make excuses or feel sorry for yourself. It is about meeting Mr. Right. Right now. It is solely for the ultracommitted with only one goal in mind: marriage to a wonderful man.

You Don't Have to Be over 35

The sooner you start *The Program*, the better. The younger you are, the better dating odds and the better attitude you typically have. Usually women younger than 35 don't have the required sense of urgency and commitment to go through this strict *Program*, but perhaps you are "precocious." If you can answer yes to the three Priority Questions in Step #1, go for it!

No Time Like the Present

When is the best time to begin *The Program*? Start as soon as you've finished reading this book. So keep reading and don't waste another day.

Step #1

Marketing Focus:
Make The Program Your #1 Priority

WHAT I LEARNED AT HARVARD BUSINESS SCHOOL

Marketing focus is the foundation of any new marketing campaign. *Focus* means single-minded dedication to the exclusion of all else. Any talented marketing manager worth her salt understands that she needs to completely direct all her energy and resources toward an important new project. The truth is, it's easier to do 50 things halfway than one thing really well. If a marketing program is going to succeed, it needs 100% focus and commitment from its leader.

YOUR #1 PRIORITY

You can't just "sort of" want to find a husband. To get fast results from *The Program*, your husband search must be your #1 priority. Anything less, and you're on a slow boat to China. During the next year, this means that finding a husband is more important than your job, your friends, your beloved pet, your therapist, and anything else that consumes your time. *The Program* requires extreme focus on your goal.

Even before I meet with a client for the first time, I can tell right away whether she will be married within 12 to 18 months. The answer is in the rapid response rate of her correspondence with me. She will learn about *The Program* from attending one of my seminars, listening to me on the radio, or hearing about it from a friend. The women who are ultrafocused on finding a husband will call me to schedule an appointment within 24 hours. They are ready to go. By the time the new client shows up to meet me, she is ready for action. She does not ask me *why* she's still single, nor does she have any desire to talk about past relationships or issues. Instead she asks, "What's the first thing I need to do?" If she has tunnel vision, I know she is a soon-to-be bride.

TESTING, TESTING, 1-2-3

To determine whether you are ready to start *The Program* right now, there are three Priority Questions to which you must answer yes. Be very honest with yourself. You might not think it socially acceptable to admit your answers out loud, but if the answer is yes, have the courage to say it silently to yourself.

Priority Questions:

1. Is finding a husband the *most* important goal in your life right now?

2. Except for something illegal or immoral, would you do *anything* to find a husband?

3. Are you committed to devoting the required time, energy, and money to find your husband?

If you could not immediately answer "yes" to all three questions, this may not be the right time for you to begin *The Program*. That doesn't mean you should close this book; instead, you can continue reading and collect some of the ideas that appeal to you. You are ordering "à la carte." Even if you don't progress sequentially through the 15 Steps of *The Program*, you will still learn many new tactics that can change your single status. You can still move forward, but you're probably not in the express lane.

If you answered "yes" to all three questions, you are in the express lane and should be able to find a husband in 12 to 18 months if you adhere strictly to *The Program*.

WHAT DOES #1 PRIORITY *REALLY* MEAN?

Simply *saying* yes to the above three questions is a good start. But if your #1 priority is finding a husband, your *actions* must be consistent with your *words*. Women often say they want to get married, but then sabotage themselves by creating obstacles to achieving their goal. As Judith Sills wrote in her wonderful book *How to Stop Looking For Someone Perfect and Find Someone to Love*, "Perhaps you have mixed feelings about finding a mate based on old scars, half-understood fears, or familiar angers and disappointments." The next three sections will help you understand if you are truly ready and what you must do if *The Program* is to be your #1 priority.

MARKETING BUDGET: INVESTMENT SPENDING

It costs money to find a husband. I wish it were free, but sadly it's not. There are those direct costs such as dating service memberships, tickets to singles events, hosting a party, and more. And then there are the indirect costs of improving your appearance, such as new clothes, make-up, hairstyling, push-up bras, exercise and diet plans. Depending on your individual situation, the expense can be significant. Maybe you need to buy a home computer to start online dating. Maybe you need to move to a new apartment to be geographically desirable. Don't panic if you're concerned about these costs. As they say in business, you are "investment spending." You are spending more money than the amount immediately coming in, hoping that your investment will pay off in the long run. It's just like you would invest in a job search: you would spend money on printing your résumé, creating a portfolio, and buying a new interview suit. The return on your investment is landing a job. In your husband search, the return on your investment is finding a husband.

So, create a dedicated budget for finding a husband. Of course, each one of you will have a different amount to invest during this process, but I suggest using as a guideline 10% of your annual income. If possible, use 20%. What could be a better use of your money than finding the man with whom you will spend the rest of your life? This dollar amount doesn't necessarily have to come from your current paycheck. Can you take it from your savings account? Most people have some savings set aside for a rainy day. Well, it's pouring!

If you don't have enough in a savings account, consider borrowing the money from family or friends. Would you be able to somehow scrape together the money if you had an emergency? Remember, after 35 it's "Marriage 911." This *is* an emergency!

Create a separate bank account earmarked "Husband Search." Whenever you hesitate to spend $25 to join an online dating service, or $75 for a ticket to a singles charity event, or $100 at the beauty salon for a better haircut and color, just deduct it from your Husband Search account. It's worth every penny.

After you have read through all 15 Steps in this book, be sure to spend time planning *how* you will allocate this budget. In the business world, you would be asked to create a budget forecast. Plan your weekly or monthly expenditures according to which *Program* step you're on, which tactics you think will be most effective, and how much money you have. Some months you might need only a few dollars, while other months you might need hundreds. Later in *The Program* (Step #14, Quarterly Performance Review), you will examine whether your dollars were invested in the areas that delivered the best results.

Following are a few sample line items that you might consider including in your budget and will be discussed further in upcoming steps:

Appearance (Step #3)
- New clothes
- New hairstyle or color
- Weight-loss program
- Gym membership

Dating Fees (Steps #7 and #11)
- Online dating membership
- Tickets to singles events
- Speed-dating events

Other (Steps #6, #7, #9, #12)
- Home computer for online dating
- Direct-mail campaign
- *Program* party
- Thank-you gifts to supporters

IMPROVE YOUR ODDS

Once you have created a marketing budget, you need to focus on improving your odds of finding a husband. *The Program* is first and foremost about playing the odds. Since the odds are not initially in your favor after 35, you want to do everything to *improve* your odds whenever possible. If you have real focus, you will start to make all of your decisions according to which path has the best odds to find a husband. For example, let's suppose you meet a sexy guy and go on a date. If you sleep with him on that first date, what are the odds that you'll have a fun night? Probably 99%! But what are the odds of that man eventually wanting to marry you if you have sex with him on the first date? Of course, no one can say for sure. But based on the stories that women relate to me, I'd estimate it's 5%. To maximize your odds of finding a husband, then you wouldn't have sex on the first date. You'd go with the 95% chance that if this man was someone you could marry, you wouldn't get hot-'n'-

heavy right away. That's betting smart. (Step #15, Exit Strategy, will discuss my "2/2" Rule for dating and sex.)

If you date a married man, what are the odds that he'll leave his wife and marry you? Again, from the stories that my clients have shared, it's about 1%. I heard once about a friend of a client who knew someone's second cousin who left his wife and married his girlfriend . . . but other than that, it pretty much never happens! So if you're smart, you would stay away from the married man based on the 99% chance that he would waste your time and break your heart. This is improving your odds.

There will always be a slim chance that something will happen *against* the odds, like Mr. Perfect will one day randomly knock on your door, but relying on those rare miracles is not efficient and not necessary. Not if you want to find a wonderful husband this year. Here are more examples of areas in your life where you should make decisions to improve your husband-finding odds.

Everyday Decisions

What are the odds of finding a husband if you make yourself a cup of coffee in your kitchen this morning? Maybe 1% (technically, the coffee machine could short-circuit, start a fire, and a cute fireman could rush through your door . . .). But what are the odds of finding a husband if you buy your coffee at Starbucks this morning? Maybe 5%. You could have a chance encounter with a man standing next to you in line or rub elbows with Mr. Right as you both reach for the same coffee cup lid at the condiment counter. You don't need to be an investment banker to know that a 5% chance is better than a 1% chance:

All you have to be is a *Program* woman! So to maximize your odds in just this one of many daily decisions, you'd go out to Starbucks for your coffee.

Free Time

Wednesday night you have nothing planned. Maybe you'd like to take an evening class at your local adult education center. You peruse the catalog and discover only two classes offered on Wednesday: "Make Your Own Greeting Cards" and "Building Log Furniture." The former might be infinitely more enjoyable and useful to you than the latter, but what are the odds you'll find a husband making greeting cards versus building log furniture? If you have *real focus*, go where the men are and improve your odds. Notice that this is really a different (in other words, *focused*) way of thinking: Instead of choosing a class based on what interests you, you will choose a class based on where the men are. Remember, this is a 12 to 18 month program. You can always take the greeting card class next year, after you're married.

It may also be possible to find a class that both interests you *and* is male-skewed. If you're a film buff, opt for the Scorsese film class instead of the Merchant Ivory film class.

THE PROGRAM THINKING METHOD

An ability to truly, genuinely, deeply *focus* on finding a husband, and make it your #1 priority, does not always come naturally. I have the same conversations over and over again with new clients. Women will tell me that they have tried everything possible to meet men, and nothing has worked. So I ask them for examples. One client, Molly, rattled off a long list of activities she had pursued to no avail. She said, "I've gone to parties, I joined a health club, I enrolled in a class . . ."

"Okay, stop right there!" I said. "You enrolled in a class? Which class?"

" 'Real Estate Investment.' " Molly smirked. She was very proud of herself, thinking she had the right approach.

"Great," I replied, "that sounds like a class where a lot of men can be found. But tell me this: Was there a break during the class?"

"Yes," she responded suspiciously, "there was a 15-minute break. Why?"

"Tell me what you did during the break."

"Well . . . I guess I went to the Ladies Room."

"Oh? Was there a long line?" I inquired.

"Yes . . ." She frowned as she suddenly realized where I was going with this line of questioning. Then she confessed, "I waited in the Ladies Room line during the entire break."

So Molly had initially focused her thinking—correctly—on selecting a class where the men were likely to be, but she did not completely make finding a husband her #1 priority. She had squandered the one 15-minute break during the class to stand in a long line outside the Ladies Room (Have you ever seen a Ladies Room that *didn't* have a long line at intermission?) rather than using that opportunity to meet men inside the classroom. That's where the opportunity was, so her efforts were not truly focused. She should have left the classroom while the instructor was still speaking, gone to the empty Ladies Room, and returned to the classroom to circulate during the break. Frankly, she could have stayed in the Ladies Room all night long and just entered the classroom for that 15-minute break!

After hearing enough stories like this from women who believe they've tried many ways to meet men but haven't succeeded, I created a technique called *The Program Thinking Method*. It's a simple, priority-based decision-making tool. It's what you probably haven't been aware of until now. This is learned behavior for most women, rather than instinct. Essentially, this technique offers a new way of looking at everything you do through "husband-hunting glasses." The following chart examines several typical scenarios in your everyday life, and contrasts what may be your *old* way of thinking with the *new*, focused way you must now think (and act) on *The Program*. How do *you* approach these typical opportunities?

THE PROGRAM THINKING METHOD

Opportunity	*Old* Way of Thinking	*Program* Thinking
Party	I arrive with my girl-friend. We stick together the whole night. I quickly decide there is no one in the room who is my type. I look bored and sullen.	I arrive with my girl-friend. We immediately separate, since men find a woman alone easier to approach. I don't pass quick judgments about the men based on appearances, and make eye contact and smile at several of them. I meet women as well as men, since women are likely matchmakers.
Health club	I go when it's convenient for me and the club isn't too busy. I go to my favorite classes: aerobics, Pilates, yoga.	I go when the club is busiest to maximize my chance of meeting someone new. I use the free weights (where the men are). I never wear headphones.
Shopping	I always shop where I'll find items I need: women's clothing, cosmetics, home accessories.	I shop often in stores where men are: hardware, music, electronics, sporting goods.

Opportunity	*Old* Way of Thinking	*Program* Thinking
Adult education classes	I enroll in a class that interests me.	I take a class where the men are (golf, woodworking, fly fishing, computer programming, etc.).
Intermission	When I go to the theater or a lecture, I go to the bathroom at intermission. The line for the Ladies Room is always so long that I barely make it back to my seat before intermission ends.	I leave the room *during* the performance to use the bathroom. I want to be available in the lobby to meet someone new during intermission, not standing in the Ladies Room line.
Jury duty	What a hassle! I try to get out of it.	What an opportunity! I will meet at least 11 new people.
Saturday night	I have dinner with my close friends (a married couple) at their home. Just the three of us.	I go anywhere I am likely to meet someone new.
Newspaper	My home delivery subscription is convenient.	I cancel my subscription. I walk to a newsstand, buy the paper, and read it while drinking coffee at Starbucks. You never know whom you might meet.

Opportunity	*Old* Way of Thinking	*Program* Thinking
Lunch	I eat at my desk because it's convenient during a busy workday.	I walk outside to buy lunch and eat somewhere in public. I don't bring reading material because I'm open to catching someone's eye.
Waiting in line	I feel frustrated. Sometimes I read a book or newspaper to pass the time.	I initiate a conversation to meet the person standing next to me in line.
Car repair	I drop my car off at the dealership and return when it's fixed.	I wait for my car in the lobby of the dealership and meet the person sitting next to me.
Always a bridesmaid . . .	I am a bridesmaid in my friend's wedding. In my speech at the reception, I talk about how happy I am that the bride and groom found each other.	I am a bridesmaid in my friend's wedding. In order to meet more people, I volunteer to be in charge of the guest book and offer to drive out-of-towners around. In my speech at the reception, I talk about how happy I am that the bride and groom found each other and then directly say, "I hope one day I'll meet someone as wonderful as Mike." What an opportunity to prompt the matchmakers in the room!

These examples are just a few of the everyday events and choices in your life. Make sure you are *Program* thinking—that your decisions and actions are based on what will improve your odds of finding a husband.

GOING PUBLIC

In business, when a company "goes public" it announces an IPO (initial public offering) to the world, hoping for maximum media coverage and hype. This is because the more people who know about it, the more people might buy the company's stock. In searching for a husband, the same holds true. You *want* everyone to know that you are looking for a mate because they might be able to help you or might know someone to introduce to you. You don't have to explain your motives for certain everyday activities (like going to Starbucks for a cup of coffee instead of brewing it at home), and of course you shouldn't tell men during first dates about your focus. But you should announce the big-picture goal to friends, family, and acquaintances: "Finding someone special is important to me." Going public is an integral component of many upcoming *Program* steps, and you need to get comfortable with it.

Many women worry that going public with an announcement that they are committed to finding a mate and that they are "on *The Program*" will make them appear desperate. Not seeming desperate has everything to do with your *attitude* in conveying this message, not with the message itself. If you tell a friend that you are serious about finding a mate, but you act embarrassed about it, lower your eyes, or look away while stating your intentions, you will convey the notion that there is something wrong with what you want. Instead, look everyone right in the eye, chin up, and state confidently what you want this year. You are anything but desperate (I really dislike that word!). You are simply *focused*.

You have succeeded with Step #1, and can begin Step #2, if you:

1. Answered "yes" to the three Priority Questions.
2. Created a Marketing Budget outline. Specific line items in your budget will be defined along the way as you read through this book.
3. Opened a separate Husband Search bank account.
4. Are ready to make choices based on improving your odds to find a husband.
5. Evaluated your *old* way of thinking about your actions and then practiced the *new* way: *The Program Thinking Method.*
6. Went public: announced to your friends, family, and acquaintances that you are committed to finding a mate.

Step #2

Marketing Support:

Find a Program Mentor

WHAT I LEARNED AT
HARVARD BUSINESS SCHOOL

A leader is most effective when surrounded by a smart, dedicated, and enthusiastic support team with a range of skills. Usually, the marketing leaders whom I studied had the vision and the drive to succeed but needed resources, ideas, and reality checks from other people to achieve their goals. Most who rose to the top credit having a Mentor on their team as one of their most important career moves. A Mentor is a person behind the scenes who coaches you, gives you honest feedback and advice, helps you network, and is your biggest cheerleader. We concluded in our classroom that a leader's ability to recruit the best support team was one of the most important things that she did during her tenure in a company.

WHAT IS A *PROGRAM* MENTOR?

A *Program* Mentor is someone who is going to help you through the next 13 Steps of *The Program*. This is a bumpy road—a *very* bumpy road. It can be filled with rejection, heartache, depression, and setbacks. But ultimately the road leads to finding a husband and happiness. Your Mentor will act as your coach: someone on the sidelines who will cheer you on, propel you forward, prop you up, tell you the truth, brainstorm with you, and generally support you in every way. Bottom line? This is someone you could call after a disastrous date, when you're convinced you'll never meet the right man, and you know she won't let you give up. A Mentor is not only your marketing support, she may be your *life* support.

THE CRITERIA FOR A GREAT *PROGRAM* MENTOR

Unlike most mentoring relationships in business, your *Program* Mentor is not someone who needs to be "senior" to you. This is someone who is going to support you, regardless of her age. Your Mentor will most likely be female, but can certainly be male. In either case, your Mentor should meet all or most of these eight criteria:

1. **Belief in *The Program*:** As you will see throughout this book, *The Program* is radical. Not everyone will believe in this approach. Clearly, if your Mentor is going to support you on your *Program* journey, she must be a believer.

2. **Genuine fondness for you:** Your Mentor's sole motivation for helping you should be genuine fondness for you—she's someone who truly cares about your well-being and wants to see you find a wonderful husband. People have their own agendas in life. Make sure your happiness is on your Mentor's agenda.

3. **A positive person:** Your Mentor should see the glass as half full, not half empty. A positive, upbeat personality is essential for your Mentor since this process of finding a husband is turbulent. There is no room on this roller-coaster ride for a partner with negativity or pessimism.

4. **Smart:** Who wouldn't want a really smart person on their side? With a *Program* Mentor, this attribute is key because you will have frequent brainstorming sessions to identify new and creative tactics to find your husband. While *The Program* provides you with many tactics, there will always be even more opportunities available in your individual situation and geographic location. Your Mentor should be someone who can visualize these opportunities. If you are not comfortable with computers, think about selecting a computer-savvy person who can help you get online (you may need assistance in Step #7, Online Marketing).

5. **Wise:** A "smart" person is not always "wise." Wisdom comes with maturity and experience, so look for a Mentor who has been there. This is someone who, in your opinion, made good choices in her own life and will offer you a thoughtful and mature perspective on yours.

6. **Candid:** You want a Mentor who will be candid with you. You probably have a lot of people around you who tell you what you want to hear, or what will make you feel better. You need one person on your side who will tell it like it is. You want results, not appeasements.

7. **Married:** Ideally, your Mentor should be married. In my experience, married Mentors are better because they have navigated

your course and found a spouse. She may have a few regrets about her process or outcome, but hopefully she learned from those mistakes and can help you avoid similar ones. Also, a happily married Mentor won't feel competitive with you for men.

8. **Has time available:** Everyone is busy with their own lives, but some people will have a little more time to give you than others. Your Mentor should be able to commit at least two hours per week for you, which may include talking on the phone, editing online profiles, giving feedback, and much more.

HOW TO FIND YOUR MENTOR

Does this list of eight criteria in a Mentor seem daunting? If so, let me assure you that the criteria are attainable, and a little flexible. First of all, get out your address book, Rolodex, Palm Pilot, Christmas card mailing list, and any other resource you have for keeping track of everyone you know. Spend some time studying the list. The ideal Mentor is not always the first person to pop into your mind. Be methodical about considering everyone you know, and really think outside the boundaries of that address book. A Mentor can be male or female, and can live anywhere (even in another city). She can be someone you haven't seen in years, or someone you just recently met. A Mentor could be of your own generation, or even your grandparents' generation. What about your college roommate's mother? What about a sister or an aunt? Or maybe your own adult daughter or your niece? Do you have a Mentor at work? Is there a great Realtor or neighbor in your life?

After you have considered all your options, make a list of finalists. Use the eight criteria to evaluate them. If no one on your list possesses all eight qualities, use your judgment to decide who will best support you (even though someone may only be a "5 out of 8"). Sometimes a single woman can turn out to be a good option because you can reciprocate with each other for fix-ups. I know a few women who met in my seminars, decided to be each other's Mentors, and enjoyed a partnership that worked out beautifully. Or perhaps you have a wonderful married friend who may not be the brightest star in the galaxy, is often cynical and very busy with her own life, but cares about you more than anyone else you know and will be a devoted supporter of your goal. Though not perfect, she could be a good Mentor for you. Make trade-offs here based on your individual list of finalists.

HOW TO ASK SOMEONE TO BE YOUR MENTOR

When you have identified the person whom you want as your Mentor, it's important to think about how to ask her. The seriousness of your tone and words will set the stage for the success of your Mentor–Mentoree relationship. If the person is a close friend or relative, there is even more reason to choose your words carefully. You want to convey that you take this request seriously, have made finding a husband your #1 priority (even if past behavior has indicated otherwise), and that if she agrees to mentor you, there is a time commitment involved.

DON'T SAY: "Hey, Jane, I'm doing this *Program* thing from a book and it said I gotta have a Mentor. Wanna do it?"

DO SAY: "Jane, I recently made a very serious commitment to finding a husband this year. I am following a 15-Step *Program* that has had a lot of success, and requires that I find a Mentor to support me. I've given a lot of thought as to the best person, and concluded that it's definitely *you*. This is actually a really big deal for me. Let me tell you more about *The Program*, and if you're willing to be my Mentor, please let me know honestly if you think you can commit at least two hours per week to helping me."

Of course, you'll be well versed in what *The Program* is all about once you have finished reading this book so you can synthesize the key points for her. You may also want to buy a copy of this book for your Mentor so that she will have all *The Program* information at hand. Add to the conversation with your prospective Mentor anything unique about your own situation. Just remember that if you make your request sound important, your Mentor will take her role seriously.

Make sure your prospective Mentor feels free to say no. Having a reluctant Mentor is not going to be effective in the long run. If someone can't or won't accept the role as your Mentor, no problem! Move to the next candidate on your list. No time to waste.

HOW TO USE YOUR MENTOR

Once you have selected your Mentor, you need to create a formal arrangement. This is a simple one-page written agreement that you will create and sign together. Have an initial conversation about what each of you expects; then you can draft something on paper. You can use the sample agreement here as a template, then edit it to your own needs and expectations. Be sure that both of you sign at the bottom and each has a copy as a reminder of your arrangement. Sure, this is a bit contrived, but it helps clarify both of your roles. This is important to do.

Sample Mentorship Agreement

This agreement is in effect for 18 months beginning _____ [date]. Either person has the right to terminate the agreement at any time should he or she not fulfill the expectations below.

We commit to:

1. Create the time in our busy lives to make this Mentorship a priority (minimum 2 hours per week).

2. Speak by phone, e-mail, or in person at least once per week. A regular time when we will attempt to communicate is _____ [time and day].

3. Be completely open and honest with each other in all communication.

4. Stay focused on the goal of finding _____ [Mentoree] a wonderful husband between _____ [12 months from today] and _____ [18 months from today].

Signed:

_____   _____   _____
Mentor   Mentoree   Date

OTHER TIPS

As in any business relationship between two people, it is important to maintain a positive and productive dynamic. Below are three additional tips for navigating this course:

1. **Be open to feedback:** Having someone on your side who provides you with candid feedback—which will not always be positive—is very valuable in achieving your goal. If you are not receptive to negative (but productive) comments, your Mentor may stop helping you, or may stop telling you the truth.

2. **Don't blame your Mentor:** There will certainly be a few occasions when your Mentor's advice turns out to be wrong. Know that it was probably given with good intent, and that she doesn't have all the answers (no one does, not even me!). The most important thing is that you continue to appreciate her time and support.

3. **Cut your losses:** Not all Mentors are good. It's a big job that not everyone does well, for whatever reason. If your Mentor isn't helping you (isn't giving you enough time, is *repeatedly* giving you bad advice, or just isn't helping you move forward), then you must cut your losses and find a new Mentor. I suggest keeping your first Mentor in the background: There's no need to formally "fire" her, which would certainly create ill will. Just call her infrequently and instead start relying more heavily on your new Mentor.

THANK-YOUS

You need to thank your Mentor frequently because she is doing you a huge favor. Use those thank-you notes you bought before you started *The Program*. Write sincere and heartfelt notes whenever your Mentor has made a particularly helpful contribution. Small, thoughtful gifts, such as books about a topic your Mentor is interested in or a gift certificate for a manicure, are also appropriate now and then. A few of my clients have eventually asked their Mentor to be the Matron of Honor at their wedding.

Information sharing is another form of showing appreciation. Keep your Mentor informed regularly about your successes (and failures). Just like in a company, people feel unimportant if they are the last to know. Short e-mails or voice messages to share information will cultivate your Mentor's support throughout this process.

You have succeeded with Step #2, and can begin Step #3, if you:

1. Understand the importance of having a Mentor.
2. Picked finalists whom you might ask to be your Mentor.
3. Evaluated the finalists against the eight "Mentor criteria" and chose the optimal person for you.
4. Asked your candidate to be your Mentor in a serious manner.
5. Created and signed a Mentorship Agreement with your Mentor.

Step #3

Packaging:

Create Your Best Look

WHAT I LEARNED AT
HARVARD BUSINESS SCHOOL

Packaging may be the most underappreciated marketing tactic. Surprisingly, packaging can be more important than the product itself. At the point of purchase, it is usually the external wrapping on a product that first attracts attention, not necessarily what's inside the package. Research has shown that grocery shoppers view and select a product within five seconds, on average. This fact makes packaging as important as any other element of product marketing. It implies that if you don't have enough money in your budget to invest in every marketing area, then you should prioritize investing in packaging. Given all the competitive products on the shelves, your package must stand out and be appealing enough to prompt a first-time purchase.

WHAT IS PACKAGING?

Packaging is simply how you look on the outside: your "wrapping paper." I wish I could tell you that your inner self is what really counts—and later in a relationship it *is* what counts the most—but the truth is that how you look makes all the difference in getting noticed *in the beginning*. Now the good news: You don't have to be beautiful or have a perfect body to attract men, but you should look your *personal best*. You first need to capture a man's attention visually, and then let him get to know you. As you'll see later in this chapter, looking and acting feminine can also be a big part of the packaging equation. Remember, "You only get one chance to make a first impression." I wish the world wasn't so shallow, but we don't make the rules; we just have to play by them. Here are some of my proven strategies to help you evaluate and make changes to your current look.

MARKET RESEARCH: ASK FOR HONEST FEEDBACK

To create your best look, you first need to do some research and find out how your current appearance is perceived. And sorry, but you need the brutal truth. This is no time to worry about getting your feelings hurt. You are moving speedily toward your goal and need to be efficient. The last thing you want to do is waste time on a great marketing plan if the packaging stops the "sale" right at the beginning.

Select six people (three women and three men) who are going to be your focus group and who will individually give you feedback on your appearance. Most people are too polite or too scared to tell you honestly what they think, so you'll need to figure out which folks are most likely to speak their minds. These are not necessarily close friends or relatives: They may be people who you barely know or who might even dislike you. You can ask your Mentor to be one of these six people. An ex-boyfriend will work. You might even include a personal shopper at a department store or a new hairstylist at a salon, since strangers might be more candid. With six different people, each polled individually, you are likely to get enough varied feedback to create your best look.

Don't fall into the trap of thinking that you already know what you need to change in your appearance. This is a very common problem. Most women, when asked what improvements can be made to their appearance, will answer with issues that are usually their own hang-ups, and not what other people (especially men) actually see. For example, you might answer about yourself: "My thighs are too fat" or "I need to lose 10 pounds" or "My breasts are too small." This is often not what anyone else thinks. You need the objective feedback from outside sources to really understand how you are perceived.

HOW TO ASK FOR HONEST FEEDBACK

To draw out the truth on this very sensitive subject of how you look, you first need to make people feel secure that you will not resent them for being honest, and that the truth is vitally important to you. You need to demonstrate an approachable demeanor that says you are open to hearing anything. No crossed arms, no shifting your feet, no looking nervous when you ask the questions. Then you need to follow these three simple rules for conducting valid market research:

1. Do not combine two questions into one ("What do you think about my hair and make-up?"). Instead, ask about each one separately.
2. Do not ask leading questions ("Do you agree that my hair is too short?"). Instead, ask open-ended questions ("What do you think about my hair?").
3. Eliminate irrelevant questions ("Am I too tall?"). Instead, ask only about what you can change.

Here is a sample script that may assist you when asking the first subject in your focus group for face-to-face feedback. Let's call him "Tim."

YOU: Tim, I really value your opinion. You're someone whom I've noticed over time is very candid and insightful. I hope you won't mind if I ask you something personal? I have decided that this is the year I am going to find someone to spend my life with. Before I start, I want to make some changes to my appearance. This is *really* important to me and I need your sincere opinions. Can I ask you a couple of questions?

TIM: Sure [maybe a little doubtful] . . . I'll try to help. But I think you look fine.

YOU: Now, please be extremely honest with me: I promise you won't hurt my feelings! If I have the ugliest clothes or the worst posture, you've *got* to tell me, okay? So my first question is about my hair. What do you think I could do to make my hair more appealing to men?

[*Note:* Start with one small part of the picture, such as your hair, to get him "warmed up." Try to select what you consider to be your best feature, because if he can tell you something positive first, he will feel more comfortable later on telling you something negative. You also ask for concrete advice ("What could I do to make my hair more appealing?"), rather than baiting him for a compliment ("Do you like my hair?"). You use a third entity ("men") to allow him more comfort in giving an opinion that feels like it's not his own (it's the opinion of "men in general").]

TIM: Well, your hair looks really good! Hmmm . . . maybe it could be a little longer.

YOU: I think that's a great suggestion! I've been thinking about growing it longer, too. Can you show me how long you think I should let it grow?

[*Note:* You are giving him positive feedback on his comment and making him feel insightful. You are also letting him know that you are not sensitive to criticism, therefore encouraging his continued honesty. And you should *want* honesty: This will give you something to change and improve upon.]

YOU: Now, what about my clothes? I'm going shopping next weekend and I'm not sure what style looks best on me. What do you think?

[*Note:* You are asking an open-ended question so that you don't bias his comments with leading questions such as, "Do you think I look good in short skirts?"]

TIM: Hmmm, I don't know much about clothes. I'm just a guy!

YOU: Oh, but you probably know what you like and don't like when you see a woman walk by. How about certain styles you might prefer on me? Or certain colors that look good on me? Or even something you remember that I've worn in the past that you especially liked? Or especially *didn't* like?

[*Note:* Give him some open-ended prompts if he struggles to provide information.]

TIM: I remember you looked great at Joan's party last week.

YOU: Oh yes, I wore my light blue sweater and jeans. I got a lot of compliments that night. Thanks for remembering. I'll wear that outfit more often. What else do you think is important that I should change? What do you think other men notice when they see me?

[*Note:* Continue to give him positive feedback and make it easier for him to say something delicate by using that safe third entity: "What do other men notice?" Keep an upbeat tone to ensure he doesn't think he's insulting you—even if he is!]

Proceed to ask about the rest of your overall appearance, and how you come across to others, in as much detail as you think is necessary. Other items to cover might include:

- Make-up
- Perfume
- Jewelry
- Eyeglasses
- Laugh
- Breath
- Posture

- Manners
- Nervous habits
- Body language
- Conversation style
- Speech volume and speed

- Word repetition
- Shyness
- Defensive comments
- Social situations
- Listening skills

These items can be a big component of your appearance whether you realize it or not. You can look sensational with your coiffed hair and stylish new outfit, but if you fidget with your hair, or slouch, or wear too much perfume, then you might turn off a lot of people. Your conversation style might be an issue, too: Are you a monopolizer, a braggart, a know-it-all, an interrupter, a one-upper, or an arguer? You need to know if you frequently make defensive comments, or you have an annoying word or phrase you repeat constantly, such as "He was, *like*, so funny!" or "She was, *like*, the best tennis player!" What if you are shy, but this trait is misinterpreted by others? Maybe people think you are aloof, arrogant, or indifferent. Maybe you behave very differently in one-on-one interactions versus social gatherings. You need to understand how you are perceived in every realm.

During this research phase, be sure to probe beyond what the eye can see. Listening skills are a particularly important component not only during this research, but also when you are on dates with men. These skills often make the difference between whether someone likes you or not. What does it mean to be a good listener? Signal to someone that you are listening by keeping eye contact, leaning forward, nodding, smiling, expanding on an idea, asking for examples, paraphrasing what you've heard, probing for more details if appropriate, avoiding distractions, and using the person's name.

After you have solicited feedback on these issues from the rest of your focus group, discuss the results with your Mentor to determine which areas of your appearance you should improve, and which areas to ignore or put on the back burner. Begin the change process now, and be sure to commit to a timetable when the changes will be completed.

WHAT IF YOU DON'T GET HELPFUL FEEDBACK?

Getting people to give you honest feedback is very difficult. Even if you manage to convince your six people that you won't shoot the messenger, they might still be reluctant. One problem may be that they simply don't know how to articulate an issue. Another problem could be that you've caught them off guard.

Perhaps if they had time to think about your questions and how to phrase their answers tactfully, they might feel more comfortable offering suggestions.

If you encounter the situation where you are not getting good data from your questions, try these follow-up approaches. Offer some "forced-choice" questions next, instead of the open-ended questions. This is better than getting no data at all. For example, if you asked someone about feedback on your listening skills and received nothing helpful, you could ask, "On a scale of 1 to 10, how would you rate my listening skills? '10' would be excellent and '1' would be weak."

If the forced-choice approach also fails to elicit helpful feedback (for instance, he won't tell you a number on your scale, or he tells you one in the middle and offers no explanation about why he chose that number), then suggest that he think about your questions; you will check back with him in a few days. Try following up by phone, as the person may not feel comfortable telling you a harsh truth in person. The time you offer him to think it over can make all the difference, because sometimes the person might want to discuss your request with a friend or spouse.

One man told me recently that he was asked by a woman for feedback, and he really wanted to help her, but didn't know how to articulate a specific issue without hurting her feelings. He talked it over with his wife who suggested some honest but gentle language he could use during their next conversation. He was later able to communicate to her something that she hadn't been aware of: She came across as insecure. She often made disparaging comments about her own appearance, and repeatedly questioned aloud whether she made good decisions and choices about almost everything. After he told this to her, she made a conscious effort to keep her doubts about her appearance to herself and to stop questioning aloud her decisions.

THE DOW JANE INDEX: CHECK THE BASICS

In addition to the individual feedback you get from your six people, you may want to review my general guidelines, which I call "The Dow Jane Index." In business terms, the Dow Jones Index shows how well things are going in the stock market. The *Dow Jane Index* is a term I use to help clients see how well things are going with their appearance. Because I am not able to peer through the pages of this book and see you, I have compiled my best generic comments on this subject for 35+ women. They may not all be valid for you, so focus on the ones that strike a personal chord.

Clothes

- Are your clothes too tight or too baggy? They should fit just right.
- Are your clothes too sexy? You should look like a future wife, not a hot one-night stand.
- Are your clothes so conservative that you look like a spinster? You should update your wardrobe.
- Are your clothes too "busy"? Bold patterns rarely look good on women. And please don't wear shirts or sweaters with anything sewed onto them (this is either too cutesy or too tacky). Solid colors or small, simple patterns are preferable.

- Are your clothes too fashion-forward? Often the trendiest clothes are not flattering to every figure, even if they are expensive and shown in all the fashion magazines. Beware the clothes that generate compliments from *only women!*
- Do you wear all black? Black pants or a black skirt are okay, but wear a color on top—one that complements your eye and hair color. If you wear too much black, you will not stand out and get noticed. Black is also a severe color and the color people often wear to funerals. You should look "upbeat."
- Are your clothes too businesslike? You should not look too masculine, tough, or unapproachable.
- Do you wear a push-up bra? *Always* wear a push-up bra: After 35 it can't hurt and can only help.

Most high-end department stores have personal shoppers with whom you can make a free appointment and get their advice on what styles look good on you. You are usually under no obligation to buy anything at that store, and if the prices are too high for your Marketing Budget, you can find similar styles at more affordable stores. Remember to specifically tell the personal shopper that you are *not* looking for the most fashionable and trendiest clothes, but rather the styles that are most flattering on you.

Don't think you have to be dressed up all the time, but don't wear your sweatpants with the holes in them or your baggy old clothes as you wander about town. As my grandmother used to say, "There are no ugly women, just lazy ones!" You never know where Mr. Right is, so don't be caught looking dumpy when you suddenly meet him standing in line at the post office.

Hair Length

How long is your hair? Most men prefer longer hair. I didn't invent this: 90% of all men I've ever asked have told me this. Yet most single women I see over 35 have shorter hair. Women get so many compliments from *other women* about their "stylish new haircut" copied straight from the fashion magazines. But this does not mean that shorter hair appeals to men. "Fashion" is not always flattering, it's just the new, new thing. So try growing your hair longer. This doesn't mean that it has to be down to your hips, but longish layers and shoulder-length (or below) hair is usually more feminine and sexy. Just ask men.

Of course, each woman's face is unique, so longer hair may not complement your individual set of features. If longer hair really isn't flattering on you, attempt to create a soft look with your hairstyle (think of the Katie Couric look). Make choices according to what suits you best. In addition to your focus group, you might want to ask at least two hairstylists for their opinions on this issue.

Hair Color

Think hard about your hair *color*. You might be so used to your hair color (whether it's natural or colored) that you don't realize it really needs to change.

- Does it complement your skin tone? Skin tone changes over time, so make sure your hair color complements your current skin shade.
- Is your hair color too harsh? I see some women, especially blondes, who have shockingly horrible hair color.
- Do you color your hair red? If so, make sure it's the right red. Some reds are so phony looking. And never color

your eyebrows the same red as your hair. Not only is it tacky, but having the color red near your eyes makes them look tired. Usually a warm, dark brown looks best on the eyebrows of darker redheads, and a cool, lighter brown looks best on lighter redheads.

❑ Is your hair color natural looking? If you color your hair, be sure to select a color that is as natural as possible, and don't rely on your own judgment. Ask your focus group during your market research phase, and again, ask two hairstylists for their opinions.

❑ Do you color your hair if you are graying? You probably should. If not, what effect does that have on how old you look? I see women with fairly young faces who have gray hair. They are usually proud of being "natural." But this has the effect of making them appear much older than they are and may limit the range of men who could be attracted to them. There is plenty of time to look "distinguished" after you are married!

Hair Texture

Don't use too much hair spray. Men like hair that is soft to touch, not hair that feels like cardboard.

Make-up

1. **Application:** This is usually a challenge for most women. It's hard to apply your own make-up, and harder still to find the time it takes to do it well. I usually recommend (if you can fit it into your Marketing Budget) that you get your make-up professionally applied before significant occasions (such as important first dates or big parties). You can also get it done for free at most make-up counters in department stores, or at least you can buy

one lipstick in exchange for the service. Of course, make-up artists want to sell you lots of products when they apply your cosmetics, but don't feel pressured. You are under no obligation to buy anything at most department stores. Be sure to tell the artist that you don't want to look overly made up. You want a natural look that accents your best features.

2. **Must-have item:** One item that every woman over 35 should own is a magnifying make-up mirror, preferably one that is "7x" (it magnifies your face 7 times its normal image). This is essential for seeing and correcting make-up mistakes and for finding tiny hairs that need to be plucked off your face.

3. **Products:** If you're not make-up-savvy, let me state the obvious: You want to select colors that are right for your skin tone, which a make-up consultant can assist you with. Men don't like to see a lot of make-up on women, so use what you have sparingly. Often wearing too much make-up, especially heavy foundation, can make you look older. Again, the natural look is usually the most appealing.

4. **Mistakes:** The most frequent make-up mistakes I see are:
   • Not accenting your eyes.
   • Not wearing the right lipstick shade for your skin tone.
   • Wearing foundation that looks "caked."
   • Wearing eyeliner that smudges.
   • Wearing mascara that clumps on your lashes.

   To avoid these mistakes, it's a smart investment of your time and budget to do some "research and development" in a department store. Roam to several different make-up counters, ask a lot of questions, and buy good products that work for you.

5. **Eyebrow shape:** While you are focusing on your face, be sure to examine your eyebrow shape. It is relatively easy and inexpensive to have your eyebrows professionally shaped. This updates

your look, and can often give your face a brighter and happier expression. A rule of thumb is that the eyebrow should arch at the point where you could draw an imaginary diagonal line from the outer side edge of your nostril, through your pupil, up to your eyebrow. Of course, don't pluck or wax eyebrows too thin, they are very hard to grow back, and fuller brows (when shaped) are sexier.

Nails

Keep your fingernails looking nice, but not so nice that they resemble a work of art. You don't want to appear "high-maintenance." Nails should be clean and relatively short. If your fingernails make a clicking sound when you press the buttons on your touch-tone phone, they are too long. Long nails can be perceived by men as claws. Avoid fake tips, as you wouldn't want anything breaking off accidentally when a man tries to hold your hand. If you have the time to paint your nails each week, then select a muted color. No bright red, please— you are a future wife, not a hooker. I think the most classic look is the French manicure, but that's a personal choice. If you are too busy to paint your nails each week, just keep them natural (no polish). Chipped nail polish does not project an appealing image.

Toenails should be kept looking nice, too: short and clean. Polish them with a muted color if you have time for the upkeep to avoid chipped polish. Your feet can be quite a visible part of your overall look. If you are invited to someone's house, you might be asked to take off your shoes when entering the doorway, or in warm weather you might wear open-toed sandals. Also, your feet should *feel* as smooth and soft as possible. Apply heavy lotion on them nightly (a lotion containing shea butter works best), and opt for professional pedicures as frequently as your Marketing Budget allows. If you have problem areas on your feet, consult a podiatrist or dermatologist and try to get them fixed. Later on, when you are dating someone seriously, you never know when you might spontaneously be offered a foot massage. You want to "put your best foot forward," so to speak!

Weight

I know very few women who think their body is perfect, and even fewer who don't think they need to lose some weight. Let me assure you that *The Program* is not just for thin, perfectly proportioned women! In fact, I believe an overweight woman who is committed to *The Program* will get married faster than a skinny woman who is not committed.

If you need to lose only 15-20 pounds, or less, to be within the optimal weight range for your height, you should not be concerned. Don't do anything at all: Most men don't even see what you see. Spend your time and energy on doing *The Program* steps, not on weight loss. As I mentioned earlier, I lost 20 pounds on Weight Watchers last year, and do you know what I learned? Only women noticed (and not even that many). Not a single man noticed, not even my husband! At first I thought maybe people were just not saying anything about it, so I asked them directly: "Do you notice anything different about me?" A few said I looked better, but the answer I got most frequently was, "You seem happier." And I *was* happier—but hey, if I'd known then that it was all about my attitude, I could have been ecstatic eating more desserts!

What about women who are 25, 50, or 100 pounds or more overweight? Ideally, try to lose some weight. And try really hard. Still, if you've been on numerous diets over the years and not much has worked, you are not doomed to stay single. The problem is that a depressed or negative attitude often dominates women who are very overweight. They feel bad about their bodies, they feel lethargic, and they too easily get discouraged if men don't respond to them. My advice is: *Lose the attitude, not the pounds.*

It is difficult to speak to a broad audience about weight, as each woman has her own set of circumstances. Joining a weight-loss program and starting vigorous exercise is always a great idea if you are ready for it, and it can open up a whole new world of bachelors to you. But if you have been there, done that, then just spend your energy on *The Program* and work extra hard at it. I would argue that ultrafocus on *The Program* with a positive attitude is equal to losing 50 pounds. As I'm sure you've seen in many instances, overweight women *do* find husbands! There's no reason you can't be one of them.

If you are overweight, find time to read the book *Sexy at Any Size* by Katie Arons. This is a very uplifting read about how larger women can find love without shedding any pounds. I know several women who have experienced a shift in self-esteem after reading this book—which by itself, ultimately made them more attractive to men.

Believe me, there is someone out there for everyone, and you don't necessarily need to lose weight to find him. Rather, you should focus on feeling healthy, which will boost your morale. Eating healthier foods, even if not fewer calories, and getting out for some exercise (an easy 30-minute walk each day) should make you feel better about yourself. And who knows? Maybe you'll meet a great guy while you're out walking. He may be trying to lose weight and get healthy, too!

The most common problem I see among larger women is using weight as an *excuse:* "I'm single because I'm fat," "I'll start dating when I lose weight," or "Men won't be interested in someone my size, so why bother?" Life is short. I urge you to start *The Program* now. No more excuses. I will be honest with you: Overweight women will probably face more rejection than thin women. Still, you must forge ahead. He's out there, and you only need to find *one.*

On the other hand, weight can also be an issue for women who are too thin. While fewer women have this problem, it is still worth discussing because most men find the "anorexic look" very undesirable. If you think you might fall into this category, be sure to probe whether you are perceived as too thin during your market research. You might need to gain 10 or 15 pounds to look healthier. Most men tell me that given the choice, they would prefer a woman 10 pounds overweight than underweight. Why? They say it's the difference between voluptuous versus scrawny.

The bottom line is that no body is ideal, including men's bodies. Men can be paunchy, balding, and more. So what's my point? My point is to do what you can to look your personal best, but not use weight as an excuse to delay your search for a husband.

Specific Problem Areas

We all have problem areas. Maybe you have a large rear end, a big nose, crooked teeth, or bad posture? You may have had a mastectomy after breast cancer. Whatever your issue is, my advice is simple: Try to fix it, and if it can't be fixed, disguise it as best you can. Remember, packaging is important. A fix could involve extensive exercise, cosmetic dentistry, or, in extreme cases, plastic or reconstructive surgery. None of this is inexpensive or easy. *But that's what this step is all about: Create your best look.* Do what you can to fix problem areas, and if that's not possible or desirable, then consult a savvy friend or professional to help you focus on emphasizing your better features while disguising or downplaying a problem area. For example, if you have a large rear end, try wearing long sweaters over a skirt. If you have a double chin, try wearing a short scarf tied at the neck to cover it up, or a V-necked shirt with no scarf at all to distract the eye downward.

Whatever you do, *don't* stop *The Program* while you are fixing any of these areas. You will never be perfect, and if you say to yourself, "I will start the next steps when I fix my problem," you'll never move forward. There will always be something else that you can use as an excuse.

FEMININITY WINS

Part of evaluating your look and how you are perceived by men requires a frank assessment of whether or not you *look* and *act* feminine. I am a devoted fan of femininity. Yes, it's old-fashioned, and many women strongly disagree with this, but I have seen time and again that men are usually more attracted to women in skirts than in pants. I mean that literally as well as figuratively. I believe that *most* men seek women who exude feminine qualities. Of course, there are exceptions out there—as in everything else—but in *The Program* you are doing things to improve your odds.

Now, please don't shoot me as the messenger, but the feminine look that most men tell me they like is longer hair, flowing skirts, soft fabrics, an ever-so-slightly revealing neckline, small-scale jewelry, and manicured fingernails and toenails. They confide that they prefer women who project a feminine image not only with their appearance, but also with their behavior on the first few dates. This doesn't mean they like a giggling Barbie doll; rather, they like a gracious woman who is a good listener. They prefer to take the initiative (they call or e-mail you first, they make the dinner reservations, they pick you up, they pay for the meal . . .). For better or worse, the old-fashioned stereotype that men like to do the pursuing is alive and well. Women today love to bash *The Rules* book, but in this one arena I think the authors are right: Being the pursued instead of the pursuer is more effective in capturing a man's interest.

I have been told by several women that they are offended by this femininity description, but then most admit to me that while they don't like it, it's probably true. To succeed in *The Program*, you do not have to exude a feminine aura. I'm just saying that it helps. It helps *a lot*.

BEND THE FEMININITY RULES ONCE

Even though I believe that men like to do the pursuing, I'm going to make one tiny exception here and bend the femininity rules just once for post-35 women. Because there are fewer single men around for you now, I think it's okay to make one initial, low-key contact with a man you'd like to date but who has not shown interest in you yet. The post-35 dating reality is like a typical supply-and-demand situation in the business world. When there is less supply (single men) than demand (single women wanting to meet single men), you might have to resort to slightly less "feminine" behavior—the kind that is a bit more assertive—to get what you want. I say "a bit more" because I don't want you to go overboard and start aggressively making all the moves. I've seen too many relationships that started this way and ended up failing. What I'm advocating is a one-time-only gesture (with each man), and I'll demonstrate what I mean with my friend Lynne's example. Lynne is 51 and lives in Phoenix, Arizona. This is what happened after she bent the femininity rule only once:

> I met a man named Ward at a party and we spoke for about 15 minutes. I was really attracted to him. He was there with a man I knew through work, who introduced us. But Ward never asked for my phone number or made any mention about seeing me again. I didn't even know if he was single, although I didn't see a wedding band.
>
> Two weeks after the party, I was still thinking about him and knew that I'd probably never see him again unless I tried to initiate contact myself. I decided to call his friend, the one I knew through work, and after he told me Ward wasn't married, I invited them both to a dinner party at my house. I asked him to call Ward to extend the invitation for me. If they could come, then I'd find a few more guests to invite so it wouldn't look too obvious that it was just a ploy to see him again. Luckily, they both said yes. They came to dinner, along with 4 other guests I corralled, and Ward and I had a chance to interact for several

hours. I knew I had used up my one "femininity rule-breaker" move by inviting him and his friend to dinner, so if Ward didn't call me after that, I would have to forget him.

In Lynne's case, Ward did call her after the dinner party, and they have been dating for two months as I write this. But of course I also know many cases where the woman made a low-key first move, and the man didn't respond. It can go either way. The important thing is not to break the femininity rules twice. A man knows you're interested after one attempt, and if he doesn't reciprocate, then consider yourself lucky that you won't waste any more of your time and can move on.

Many men experience a sudden popularity after age 35 because they are in short supply, and they start to expect it. They become used to being pursued aggressively by women who think there aren't any good men left. I had dinner last month with a group of people. One single man at the table, who is 50, told me that he had dated two women recently who were in their early forties. He had enjoyed the dates but became turned off when the women began to call and e-mail him aggressively after only one or two dates. He knew that at their age they probably wanted to find a husband and have a baby fast. He backed away because he felt pressured. Women can panic when they meet a "good one" and react by becoming the pursuer. But we've all seen again and again that men usually want the one they can't have. Be the elusive one. Stand out by doing the unexpected: Let him pursue you (after you've used up your one femininity rule-breaker move, if necessary).

Consistency

Consistency is very important. If you look and act feminine with men but other details in your life aren't consistent with that image, your feminine aura won't be effective. For example, what does the outgoing message on your answering machine sound like? This is often the first point of contact that a blind date has with you, so it creates the first impression. I've heard many women's messages that announce, "You know what to do at the beep," or something similar. This sounds hostile, not warm and alluring. Often the tone of voice I hear is not inviting and certainly doesn't project a welcoming image. Call your own answering machine today (including your home, cell, and work numbers) and listen objectively to your message and your voice. Have your Mentor do it, too, and make any appropriate changes. We'll talk more about "brand consistency" in Step #6, Advertising.

Businesswomen

One of the most common problems I see is the single 35+ career businesswoman who is projecting a masculine aura. She has the short hair, the power suits or jackets, and the sturdy, black leather briefcase. She's aggressive at work and is used to taking control in her personal life as well. While some men do find this attractive, I think it's a small percentage. When I have a client who fits this mold, I tell her bluntly that she comes across as too masculine. To my great surprise, very few of these women have heard this before. Maybe they know they are "bold," "assertive," or "intimidating," but they didn't quite see themselves as "masculine." Usually, looking more feminine is an easy fix for a businesswoman: It's about growing her hair a bit longer, getting sexier eyeglasses (including sunglasses), wearing more feminine clothing (not business jackets with structured shoulders), and replacing the black briefcase with a less austere, preferably colored tote bag.

Renee, a businesswoman, called me with this interesting dilemma:

> I am going on a second date with a man I really like. I can't decide what to wear. I wore a pretty dress on our first date, but I am so nervous about this next date and I want an outfit that will help me feel confident. I'm thinking about wearing my expensive black-and-white suit that I bought with my bonus check last month. It's fabulous! Whenever I wear it to work, I always feel like I can conquer the world. I wear it when I'm giving a big presentation and it makes me feel very self-assured. What do you think?

I told her to keep that black-and-white suit in her closet! You don't wear a power suit on a date, no matter how confident it makes you feel. She was thinking like a woman who wanted a promotion, not a husband. I helped her select a dress that made her look soft and feminine. She told me later that when her date arrived to pick her up, she opened the door, and the first thing he did was smile and say, "You look beautiful."

Finding a Husband but Not Losing Yourself

In every seminar I've ever taught, I always have a woman in a power suit emphatically raise her hand and say, "This is who I am! If a man finds my look and attitude too intimidating or masculine, why would I want him anyway?" And I answer simply, "I've learned from my marketing career that if you want to succeed, you have to sell what customers want to buy."

I mentioned in the introduction to this book that *The Program* is not about changing *you*, it's about changing what you *do*. It's also not about pretending to be someone you're not; rather, it's about highlighting your most desirable qualities. Many women feel a tension during this step between wanting to stay who they "really are" versus making some significant changes to themselves to find a husband. Understand that my advice is about redesigning your exterior look and behavior (not changing your inner self) to attract men initially. Marketers do this successfully all the time with "new and improved packaging" for the exact same product.

But it's important that *you* feel comfortable with your new packaging if it's going to be effective. Often it's a matter of time: You just need to get used to it, and see how many compliments you receive. But sometimes an element of your new packaging is making you so uncomfortable or self-conscious that it is actually doing more harm than good. In that case, do what it takes to feel good about yourself.

In the end, a man will get to know all of you. Being smart and strategic to meet more men upfront is what this step is all about. I want to empower you by giving you as many choices in men as possible. My job is to get your foot in the door, and the rest is up to the "real you."

You have succeeded with Step #3, and can begin Step #4, if you:

1. Conducted your market research by asking three men and three women for honest feedback about your appearance.

2. Evaluated the feedback with your Mentor and prioritized the most important areas for change.

3. Reviewed the Dow Jane Index guidelines for clothes, hair, make-up, nails, weight, and problem areas, then integrated any relevant items into your priorities for change.

4. Began the process to create your best look, and committed to a timetable when the changes will be completed. (*Note:* Do not wait to complete any major changes before moving to the next step.)

5. Evaluated whether your appearance and behavior are consistently feminine.

6. Did not get discouraged by any worries or negative feedback about your appearance, and did not allow any of these issues to become excuses for procrastination of your goal.

Step #4
Market Expansion:
Cast a Wider Net

WHAT I LEARNED AT
HARVARD BUSINESS SCHOOL

A key marketing goal is to sell your product to as many customer segments as possible. Marketers usually define customer segments based on demographics (gender, income, age, education, race), psychographics (social attitudes, degrees of adventure seeking or risk taking), and geography. For example, BMW might target a new car model to affluent women ages 35–55. Customer segments considered likely to buy a product may be further grouped into one of two categories: Primary Buyers (those who are perfectly targeted to your product) and Secondary Buyers (those who are likely to be interested in your product but perhaps not a perfect match). A marketer's goal is to expand the market and sell her product to as many customer segments and buyers as possible.

Motorola originally designed cell phones for the business market. On-the-go businesspeople were the most logical consumers (Primary Buyers). But the folks at Motorola soon realized that cell phones were valued by other types of people as well. So they expanded their market to target nonbusiness segments (Secondary Buyers): yuppies, soccer moms, teenagers.

You always want to increase the chance of selling your product by expanding your market—by targeting as many relevant customer segments as possible.

WHY CAST A WIDER NET?

As I discussed in the introduction to this book, the odds of finding a husband change after age 35. There is a smaller pool of eligible men, both in reality (remember, the 2000 U.S. Census reported 28 million single women over age 35, but only 18 million single men over 35), and in perception ("The good ones are all taken"). But there's no cause for alarm, because in this step you are going to make a crucial shift in looking for Mr. Right that will unveil many new eligible men. You are going to cast a wider net.

HOW TO CAST A WIDER NET

Phase One: Accept the Reality

Casting a wider net means looking for a husband who may not be the type you've always imagined. Judith Sills observes in *How to Stop Looking for Someone Perfect and Find Someone to Love* that men (and women) over 35 are *real* people. When you are in your twenties, you select a man for *potential*. But later in life, you select a real person who comes with more history, simply because he has a longer past. He has more failures and problems, and has a complex web of "long-term relationships into which you must fit . . . life leaves its mark . . . and most eligible men will be a lot further from your ideal picture" of the mate you dreamed about in your 20's. There is a silver lining to all this: Older men are (hopefully) more seasoned and mature. But *accepting this reality* is Phase One of learning to cast a wider net.

Phase Two: Forget Your Type

Most women, when asked what type of man they are looking for, will rattle off a list of five, ten, or fifteen criteria: He has to be at least six feet tall, have a great sense of humor, be smart, sensitive, love my cat, be a good skier, not have kids from a previous marriage, live within twenty miles of my home, practice my religion, be nice to his mother . . . I hope you are smiling with recognition as you read this typical list. Here's your next task: Throw out your criteria and forget your type.

I admit this action doesn't come naturally. You've had many years of thinking about "your type." The details of this type may include both external traits (height, hair color, age, profession) and internal traits (attitudes, beliefs, behaviors). Even when clients tell me that they don't have "a type" and are attracted to a wide variety of men, they usually mean men with a variety of external traits (they come in all shapes, sizes, and colors). While these men may look different on the outside, often they have similar internal patterns (especially negative ones). When women repeatedly date men with the same negative internal traits (say, needy, selfish, and arrogant), it's no wonder their relationships don't work out again and again. If this describes you, *now* is the time to break out of this pattern.

Let me be *very* clear that I am not telling you to "settle." But

I am telling you to be flexible. Your future husband may stand five feet eight rather than six feet tall. He might not know how to ski. He may be twenty years older. And horrors, he may be allergic to your cat! But if he is a wonderful person and you could fall madly in love with him, should you really overlook him?

I had a 47-year-old client named Julie who was a smart, successful vice president at a top Wall Street firm. She was also very active in Jewish organizations, so her religion was important to her. All her life she had looked for her male counterpart: a smart, successful, Jewish investment banker. This was clearly her "type." For years, she dated men who fit that profile, but she never fell in love. And as the years passed, the number of guys who were her type, and were eligible and interested in her, decreased drastically (they mostly wanted to date younger women). So when she joined *The Program,* I coached her extensively on Step #4. Truthfully, I never thought she believed in this step; she kept reverting to her "type."

Then one day she went to return a broken cell phone at Radio Shack, and asked to see the manager. When the manager came over to ask how he could help her, she looked right at him: right into the eyes of her future husband. She actually married the Radio Shack manager 12 months later! He wasn't Jewish, he certainly wasn't the Wall Street type that all her former boyfriends had been, and he was even 9 years younger than she. But this guy was a gem, and she fell madly in love with him. He connected with her on an emotional level in a way no one else ever had. He loved her so much that he later converted to Judaism. She has never been happier, and in fact, they adopted their first child last month.

I'll never forget their wedding. When Julie stood up to give the bride's toast after the ceremony, she said, "I was looking for someone like Paul my whole life . . ." Then she paused and smiled at the puzzled looks of her guests, who knew that she had certainly *not* been looking for someone like Paul. And then she resumed, ". . . but he came in a completely different package than I'd ever imagined."

Look, finding and marrying someone outside your "type" won't happen to everyone, but with the statistics stacked against you, it pays to be open. Remember, all you have to do is find one great guy, whatever his type may be.

Phase Three: Spread the Word

So how do you break out of your habit and forget your type? Start by "talking the talk." The next time someone asks you what kind of man you're looking for, spread the word and answer simply, "Someone wonderful." That's it. Just two words. If an acquaintance mentions fixing you up on a blind date and asks you to describe your ideal man, restrain yourself from giving your old list of criteria. See what happens when you respond with those two little words and let someone think outside your box.

What about all those friends whom you've already told over the years that your type is a passionate artist from Italy with big, brown eyes? Call them up and take it back!

This phase is not only verbal, but written as well. When you start online dating in Step #7, you will create a profile for the man you are seeking. And guess what you're going to write about the type of man you're looking for? Two words: "Someone wonderful."

Phase Four: Practice the *Program* Scan

There are two simple exercises I want you to practice. These exercises use a technique that I call the *"Program* Scan" to help you realize how small your net has been in the past and what possibilities open up when you expand the size of that net.

The first exercise is simply about color. The next time you enter a crowded room, whether it's a party, a restaurant, or an auditorium, scan the room for only the people wearing the color red (it can be anywhere on their body: red shirts, red hats, red jackets). Let your eyes quickly dart around the room, passing over anyone without red. Give yourself 30 seconds to identify your red targets. Perhaps you counted 10 people in the room. Now, repeat this scan looking for only people wearing black, which is a more common clothing color. You probably counted 50 people this time. The people in your "red group" represent your old type. The people in your "black group" represent your wider net. This basic color exercise begins to highlight how changing one element that you look for can open up a whole new world of opportunity. There are a lot more fish in the sea when you cast a wider net.

Now repeat the *Program* Scan exercise with more meaningful criteria than color. Look around the crowded room for your "opposite physical type." If the type of man you've always been most attracted to physically is tall and blond, scan the room for short, dark-haired men. Make a point of focusing on them, positioning yourself closer to where they're standing, catching their eye, and initiating a conversation. This is just an exercise. While none of these men may turn out to be Mr. Right, you are deprogramming yourself and opening up your mind. Maybe the short, dark-haired man will make you laugh with his sharp wit, or impress you with his brilliant mind. You never know what is underneath the external disguise!

Pop Quiz

SITUATION: A friend approaches you at a party and says she'd like to introduce you to some of the single men in her office. She asks, "What's your type?"

QUESTION: What do you say?

ANSWER: "Someone wonderful."

Phase Five: Three Blind Mice

The practice exercises above were intended to open your mind. Now you're ready for the real thing: I want you to deliberately go on three blind dates with men who are definitely *not* your type. First you need to clarify who *is* your type, and then you'll cast the widest net possible away from that type to select these three dates. In the *"Program* Expansion Grid" on the following page, I have listed the parameters by which most women develop their type. Next to these parameters are three empty columns. Fill in the first column (My Type) with your preferences for men you used to seek prior to reading this chapter. In the second and third columns (Cast Wid*er* Net and Cast Wid*est* Net), fill in an expanded version of those preferences, going further away from your favorite type in the two columns. The sample grid below was completed by one of my clients named Anne (a 53-year-old divorcée).

ANNE'S *PROGRAM* EXPANSION GRID

Parameters	My Type	Cast Wid*er* Net	Cast Wid*est* Net
Age range	50–55	48–60	43–68
Height	6'0"+	5'8"+	5'6"+
Race	Caucasian	Caucasian or Hispanic	Any
Physique	Athletic/fit	Slightly overweight	Any weight
Personality	Funny, outgoing	Funny, quiet	Serious, quiet
Profession	White-collar professional	Small-business owner	Blue-collar worker
Income	$150,000+	$100,000+	$50,000+
Education	Master's or professional degree	College degree	High school degree
Religion	Protestant	Atheist	Any
Marital status	Never married, or divorced with children not living at home	Divorced with children living at home part-time	Divorced or widowed with children living at home full-time
Geography	In my city	In my state	Anywhere
Interests	Hiking, travel	Reading	Watching TV

MY *PROGRAM* EXPANSION GRID

Parameters	My Type	Cast Wid*er* Net	Cast Wid*est* Net
Age range			
Height			
Race			
Physique			
Personality			
Profession			
Income			
Education			
Religion			
Marital status			
Geography			
Interests			

After completing your grid, circle one parameter on which you are most willing to compromise in the Wid*est* Net column. Then select at least two parameters from the Wid*er* Net column. The circled parameters on Anne's grid demonstrate where she was willing to compromise. For the truly open-minded, challenge yourself to select more from the "Wid*est* Net" column, if you can. The circled selections reveal your new cast-a-wider-net type.

For many women, the most critical parameter to expand is

"Age." This will provide the best windfall of additional bache-lors for your consideration, especially if you expand *upward* in age. I know, I know: You don't want to marry a sickly, old man. Ditch the stereotype and keep an open mind. For women *under* 50, I recommend seeking men in the range of five years younger and fifteen years older than you are. For women *over* 50, I recommend a range from ten years younger to fifteen years older.

By the way, I see a lot of women looking for younger men these days. That's great, if you can find ones who are interested in you, but beware those men who are seeking a mother figure or a "sugar mama." Most of the older woman/younger man re-lationships that I see are short-term, do not result in marriage, and serve to break your heart and deflate your ego. There are always exceptions, so just keep your eyes open.

Now you are ready to go on the blind dates with three single men who have at least one of the characteristics you circled un-der the Wid*er* or Wid*est* Net columns. For example, Anne cir-cled Height and Interests under her Wid*er* Net column and Age under her Wid*est* Net column. She traditionally preferred men who were very close to her age, tall, and outdoor and travel enthusiasts. So she set out to find three dates who represented her cast-a-wider-net type: one who was much older or younger (10 years younger or 15 years older), one who was shorter (five feet eight or taller), and one with more sedate interests (reading).

How to Find Not-Your-Type

How do you find your three wider- and widest-net dates? Look around you. Now that you are looking for different types, you may notice someone who was previously invisible to you. Maybe it's your plumber, your neighbor, or your Salsa dancing teacher. Ask your friends and your Mentor to help you identify them, then strike up a conversation with each one and see what ensues. Maybe they'll ask you out if you show some interest. If you're already online, it's easy to search efficiently for three dates using your new parameters with just a few taps on your keyboard. If you're not online yet, we'll talk more about that in Step #7, Online Marketing.

Normally, I don't advocate women asking men out (the femininity thing), but if you've identified your three men and they haven't asked you for a date after about two weeks, then go ahead and ask them first. This will not count as "bending the rules once." This is really just an experiment, so you have nothing to lose. There may be a low chance that one of these three men will become your future husband, but what you will learn from this experience is worth all your time and energy here.

The point of these three dates is to show you that there is more to someone than meets the eye. Maybe you think you already know that, but what you know in theory is different from what you know in practice. Spending time out on a couple of dates with three men who are completely out of your typical realm of possibility will not only help you open your mind, but could even spark a small, unexpected attraction that can occur when you get to know someone better. This is all part of a foundation you are building that will be vital in subsequent steps on *The Program*.

Anne's Result

What happened to Anne after she completed her *Program* Expansion Grid? She went on her three "against-my-type" dates, and really didn't have a bad time. But there was also no chemistry: just a few evenings with seemingly nothing to show for them. She was an outgoing, active 53-year-old who always looked for spirited and adventuresome men. It was essential to her that her dates or boyfriends love outdoor activities (especially hiking), were willing to travel anywhere, and have a sense of adventure. She dated these types of men for years after her divorce, and none of her relationships ever progressed toward marriage. When she joined *The Program*, she started dating a few men during this step whom she called "boring." She swore to me that she'd rather live her life alone than marry "some old boring guy." I actually wrote her quote down word for word in my notes. About four months later, she called me with this update:

> I started Step #7 (Online Marketing) three months ago, and began corresponding with a 64-year-old man named Phil whom I met on Match.com. He wrote that his interests are reading, watching sports on TV, and visiting his grandchildren. Ugh! He sounded too sedate. But I kept an open mind, we had some good phone conversations, and finally somewhat reluctantly, I decided to accept a face-to-face date with him. It turned out that he was anything but boring! His lifestyle is certainly less active than mine, but he makes me laugh. And, I have to confess, he is an extremely passionate lover.

Anne had successfully cast a wider net, but of course that didn't mean Phil was perfect. They have been together 3 months now. She wishes that he would go on hikes with her, take swing dancing classes with her, or run off to Las Vegas with her for the weekend. Occasionally he joined her on adventures and enjoyed them, but when he didn't want to, she persuaded one of her girlfriends to go and had a great time without him. He was always waiting for her when she happily returned. This situation with a man she now loves doesn't fit the old formula she had been looking for: What she thought was essential turned out not to be.

You have succeeded with Step #4, and can begin Step #5, if you:

1. Understand the importance of casting a wider net.
2. Forgot about "your type."
3. Learned the answer to the question: "What type of man are you looking for?" (Answer: "Someone wonderful.")
4. Practiced *The Program* Scan.
5. Completed your *Program* Expansion Grid.
6. Selected three parameters on which you were willing to compromise, then went on three dates with men who represented wider or widest nets in each of those areas.

Step #5

Branding:

Identify What Makes
You Different

WHAT I LEARNED AT
HARVARD BUSINESS SCHOOL

A well-defined, memorable brand is absolutely essential for any successful product. Brands serve four main functions:

1. To help customers remember the product.
2. To convey a complex message quickly.
3. To help customers distinguish the product from similar products.
4. To create positive appeal to entice someone to buy the product.

Today there is an explosion of product choices: We have many, many options. For example, 30 years ago there were only 16 brands of bottled water. Now there are more than 300 brands. Marketers must differentiate their products from other similar products because customer selection will inevitably be based on product *differences*, whether implicit or explicit.

Brands that are memorable and distinctive have been very successful. The Federal Express brand is "Overnight Delivery," the Wheaties brand is "Breakfast of Champions," and The Four Seasons brand is "Luxury Hotels." I learned two important things from examples like these. First, a product *needs* a brand (without a brand, it will be perceived as generic and won't sell). And second, if the brand is too vague (trying to be all things to all people), it usually ends up being nothing to everyone.

WHAT IS A PERSONAL BRAND?

A "personal brand" is what makes you different from everyone else. It is a set of distinguishing features and characteristics that makes you stand out in a crowd and makes you memorable. People have brands just like products, but usually they cannot be communicated by only one word or concept. Madonna's brand might be: "Outrageous, Sexual, Pop Singer." Mother Teresa's brand might have been "Noble, Selfless, Charity Worker." People are complex and multifaceted, but we often look for a shortcut (a few words or phrases) to sum them up quickly.

How do your friends and acquaintances describe you when you're not listening? You want to know this because you rely on them to fix you up on blind dates and portray you in a unique and favorable way. It's important how they summarize you. You can help them communicate your complex set of qualities to other people by suggesting which facets about you to highlight. You will also want to highlight these same areas when meeting someone for the first time, since people will make snap judgments about you during the first few minutes. In this step you will learn how to select three adjectives, phrases, or identifiers that will become your personal brand.

This brand will quickly communicate who you are and will distinguish you from other women.

WHY YOU NEED A PERSONAL BRAND

A personal brand is a must-have for every woman who is single and over 35. Here's why:

- You need to stand out in the crowded arena of 28 million single women to get noticed.
- It will help you target your ideal customers. A woman whose brand includes "Intellectual" is likely to attract a smart man, or at least a man who appreciates a smart woman.
- If you don't create one for yourself, someone else will do it for you (and you may not like it). I bet you'd be surprised how your friends and acquaintances describe you when you're not listening. It may not necessarily be bad, but it can be either incorrect or just different from how you see yourself.

Your future husband may be someone you meet on a chance basis whereby he will take only a few moments to decide if you are someone he wants to get to know. It's better that you help him see what you want him to see—your brand—than allow him to make snap judgments that may not be in your favor.

A TEAM EFFORT

Creating a personal brand will require a lot of thoughtful reflection about yourself, but you cannot do it alone. It's a team effort. Your brand has to ring true not only to yourself, but to others as well. As you did in Step #3, Packaging, you must again seek feedback. You want to solicit impressions from both those who know you well and from those who barely know you at all. These may or may not be the same people you spoke with earlier. In Step #3, your goal was to talk with people who would be candid with you. You still want candor, but what you are after now is what makes you different. That is, "different" on both a superficial level (impressions from those who barely know you) and on a deeper level (those who know you very well). Your goal here should be to find insightful and creative people to help you.

Your personal brand should be a combination of your outer and inner qualities. But the most distinctive qualities are not always obvious or easy to identify. The three-phased explanation below will take you through your personal brand creation process.

HOW TO CREATE YOUR PERSONAL BRAND

Phase One: Make a List

Take out a sheet of paper and make three columns on the page. Label the columns: "Physical," "Personality," and "Other."

Under the Physical column, write down adjectives or phrases that you think describe your physical appearance. For example, you might write: tall, stocky, cute, overweight, thin, blond, voluptuous, Rubenesque, fit, Asian, elegant, or beautiful smile.

In the Personality column, write down as many adjectives or phrases that you think describe your personality. For example, you might write: witty, serious, artsy, well-read, shy, gregarious, assertive, gentle, feisty, low-maintenance, honest, or kindhearted.

In the Other column, write down as many adjectives or identifiers that you think are relevant to who you are, but that don't fit into the first two columns—perhaps your profession, religion, interests, geography, marital status, special talents, etc. Here you might select: accountant, Buddhist, avid skier, New York Yankees fan, from Ohio, single mom, divorced, or bridge champion.

PERSONAL BRAND TIPS

- The adjectives and phrases you write down don't have to be all positive ones. Some may be negative or perceived as weaknesses. Make them *honest*.
- Take your time in creating this list and use your imagination. A complete picture of yourself is usually not on the tip of your tongue, even if you pride yourself on knowing who you are. You should revisit your list several times over the next few days before finalizing it.
- Be as specific as possible when choosing your adjectives and phrases. Avoid broad adjectives. Instead of *pretty*, are you cute, gorgeous, all-American, exotic, or big-blue-eyed? Instead of *smart*, are you intellectual, well-read, educated, street-smart, or an expert in European history?
- Try to select words that are not ordinary. Bring out a thesaurus. For example, an ordinary word like *tall* could become *statuesque*; or a common word like *funny* could become *sharp-witted* or *David-Letterman-funny*. You want to ensure that your attributes are memorable to other people.

Phase Two: Seek Feedback

After you are comfortable with your list, seek feedback from four people: two men and two women. You learned in Step #3,

Packaging, how to conduct good market research, so practice those skills again here. Also, you don't want to show these four people your list. It is for your own use to compare how you perceive your attributes against what others say. The most important piece of data you're after is what makes you unique and different from other women.

You might start the conversation like this: "I am reading an interesting relationship book. It suggested that I try a personal exercise to help me understand how other people see me, especially in ways that make me different from other women. Could you tell me several adjectives or phrases that describe me physically? Please be very honest!" After each person has given you some physical descriptors, ask next about your Personality and Other attributes. Remember *not* to give prompts like, "Do you think I have a good sense of humor?" But it's okay to help explain what kind of information you're looking for with comments such as, "Is there anything unique about me in the realm of my appearance? Personality? Profession? Interests?"

After you have collected all four opinions, call your Mentor to discuss your original list and the feedback from your four people.

Phase Three: Choose Your Personal Brand

Once you and your Mentor have discussed all the data you've collected, select just three adjectives or phrases that *make you different*. These three items do not have to be chosen from separate columns on your list: They could all come either from one column or from different columns. Look for a unique set of three positive attributes that, when they're all combined, create an intriguing and alluring personal brand. The four criteria to judge whether the brand you select is a good one are:

1. The brand rings true to who you are, both as you see yourself and as others see you.
2. The brand will appeal to a wide range of men.
3. The brand is memorable and unique.
4. The brand positions you as "marriage material."

We are all complex people, a compilation of many personality traits, moods, and abilities. It will be difficult to select only three attributes to highlight, especially since we wear so many faces depending on whom we are with and what circumstances surround us at any given moment. While your choices should be honest, they don't have to attempt to describe you at all times.

Remember that your three choices are not necessarily your three best attributes, nor the ones with which you are most comfortable or familiar. They should be selected so that when they are combined, they will make you stand out *favorably* in a pool of marriage-minded men. For example, a brand like "Pretty, Smart, California" is too generic. A brand like "Divorced, Homebody, Overweight" is too negative. A brand like "Sensual, Adventurous, Babe" portrays a woman who wants a one-night stand rather than a serious relationship.

Once you have identified a brand that you believe meets the four criteria above, be sure to consult your Mentor as a final checkpoint. If your brand passes the "test"—it meets the four criteria above—then you should be in good shape.

The following case study from one of my clients, Sarah, should help you with this phase.

CASE STUDY:
CREATING SARAH'S PERSONAL BRAND

Sarah's Master List

Physical	Personality	Other
Age 42	Outgoing	Travel agent
Red hair	Fun	Catholic
Freckles	Adventurous	Irish descent
Petite (5'1")	Spontaneous	Tennis player
Sexy clothes	Good listener	Boston native
Skin blemishes	Temperamental	Great chef
	Sensitive	Divorced
	Bored easily	No kids
		8 siblings

→ *Personal Brand Selected:* "Red Hair, Adventurous, Great Chef"

After getting feedback from two men, two women, and her Mentor, Sarah created her final list as shown above, and selected for her personal brand: "Red Hair, Adventurous, Great Chef." She thought these were the right three attributes for her personal brand because:

1. **They ring true:** They describe her quite accurately. All are attributes she had written down herself as well as ones her four people had mentioned.
2. **They include qualities that are likely to appeal to many men:**

"Adventurous" suggests that she is someone with whom you could have an exciting life. And who wouldn't want to be married to a "Great Chef"? Maybe a man on a strict diet, but to everyone else, it's a huge bonus.

3. **They include something memorable and unique:** Red hair is the least common hair color and it's a striking physical attribute of Sarah's.

4. **They position her as marriage material:** None of the attributes suggest that she is just out for a good time.

How you *combine* your attributes is the key to a great personal brand. Individual words are usually not unique until you bring them all together into one package. Sarah's package is distinguishing and alluring.

What Sarah Did *Not* Select

Following are some sample combinations and single attributes that Sarah and her Mentor considered using for her brand but decided against:

- **"Red Hair, Temperamental, Irish":** Why not? This combination is a stereotype ("the Irish are redheaded and temperamental") and too predictable. You want to create a brand that is *intriguing* so men will want to learn more about you, not assume they already know what you're like.

- **"Boston Native, Tennis Player":** Why not? This combination was too boring for someone like Sarah. She's a dynamo, and her brand should ring true. This set doesn't suggest anything exciting about her.

- **"Adventurous, Spontaneous, Travel Agent":** Why not? This combination is not a marriage-oriented image. It may suggest *fun, good-time gal,* rather than *wife, mother-of-my-child.* It could attract the wrong men: those looking for short-term fun rather than a commitment.

- **"Sexy Clothes":** Why not? Having a reputation for wearing sexy clothes might suggest that she is a one-night stand and not a future wife. Again, you want your brand to appeal to marriage-minded men.

- **"Petite":** Why not? Although this adjective has a nice ring to it, and it might attract a large number of shorter men (a good thing for your wider net), Sarah has better choices to make her unique.

- **"Sensitive, Good Listener":** Why not? Sarah has a history of ex-boyfriends with emotional issues who expected her to understand their problems and console them. She deliberately wouldn't want to highlight these traits, in the hope of attracting more stable, self-assured men.

- **"Temperamental, Divorced":** Why not? This sends out a warning signal. "Divorced" reveals some baggage (which you shouldn't do with your brand), and "Temperamental" suggests that she might be a difficult person to live with.

- **"Catholic":** Why not? While Sarah is Catholic, she is not very religious. She only occasionally goes to church, and is very open to meeting men of any faith. She wouldn't want her brand to limit her options.

- **"Tennis Player":** Tennis is a sport that Sarah plays, but she is not a superstar in the game. This would have been a wasted descriptor in her brand because it is not a big part of her life— nor is she a better tennis player than the average person.

Okay, you get the idea! Select your combination carefully using the above examples as guidelines.

YOU MAY BE WONDERING . . .

• *Can I change my brand over time?*

Yes, but you should make changes only if your brand is not working for you (if it's not memorable, for instance, or it's not attracting appropriate men). The consistent message of one brand throughout this time period while you are single is what makes it effective. When you are married next year, your lifestyle and goals will be very different, so your personal brand will certainly change as you evolve through life's different stages. But on this fast and efficient *Program*, you should change your brand immediately if you find that it's not working.

For example, I had a 54-year-old client from Wyoming named Lisa who had been a teacher for 20 years. She then switched careers to become a barrel racer at the rodeo. When we first created her brand, I encouraged her to select as one of her attributes "Rodeo Professional" since it was so unique. She created the brand "Kindhearted, Blue Eyes, Rodeo Professional." She posted an online profile, and this is what she told me during our next session:

> I selected the screen name "RodeoSweetheart." I thought that was catchy and unique. But I had a bit of a shock when the first responses came in. This brand attracted the wrong kind of men! I received several lewd e-mails, including one from a man who called me his "Little Heifer" and said he wanted to tie me up!

We made some fast changes to her brand, substituting "Teacher" for "Rodeo Professional," and changed her screen name to "TeacherSurprise." Lisa soon started to receive responses from much more appropriate candidates.

• *If I have a dominant attribute that could be perceived as negative (such as being very overweight, or a single mom with six kids, or a workaholic), shouldn't I incorporate that into my brand so it will screen out the wrong people and not waste my time?*

Since the definition of a brand is something that makes you stand out favorably in a crowd, the answer would be no. Everyone has qualities that can be perceived as negative or as baggage, but one man's problem is another man's jackpot. If you are 50 pounds overweight, you would still select three attributes that will be viewed as positives by most men because you want to accent your best features. You want men to see you as more than a number on the scale. While some men may be turned off by your weight, there will certainly be men who won't be, and those are the ones you want to target. Giving them three unique, positive attributes about you is vital in helping them see beyond your outer shell.

Single moms have a similar issue. I often hear complaints from women such as "When he found out I had 3 small children, he ran the other way." Again, what is perceived as a problem by one man will be considered an asset (or at least a neutral attribute) by another. There are certainly men out there who love children and who may have young ones of their own from a prior marriage. They are specifically attracted to single moms who understand the commitments and sacrifices involved in raising and loving a child. One man (a 48-year-old divorced dad) told a client of mine (a 43-year-old single mom) that the only reason he went out with her in the first place was that he knew she had children of her own. He didn't want to start over again with babies, and knew that most women between the ages of 35 and 45 would want children of their own. She did not use "Single Mom" as part of her brand, but "Does she have kids?" was a standard question he always asked any would-be matchmaker who attempted to fix him up on a date. If it's important to someone, he will ask up front.

Of course, whether you want to live with *his* kids—if he's a single dad—is a whole other topic. What I'm trying to do is put the ball in your court. Once you know he is open to helping you raise *your* kids, you can evaluate *his* situation and decide if you can tolerate it. Many of my clients tell me that integrating another man's children into their own family is a huge struggle and the source of endless friction, but the bottom line is that they are willing to work it out for a wonderful man.

WHAT TO DO WITH YOUR PERSONAL BRAND

Now that you've developed your personal brand, what do you do with it? You have built another critical piece of the foundation that you will use in upcoming *Program* steps. You will learn to advertise your brand, make your brand consistent in all details of your packaging, and reinforce your brand with online dating and other dating activities. You will extend your brand across your entire "product line" going forward. From now on, everything you do and wear and say and write about yourself should be consistent with your brand. You will no longer risk being viewed as generic if you effectively communicate and advertise your new personal brand . . . which are the next tactics in Step #6.

You have succeeded with Step #5, and can begin Step #6, if you:

1. Spent time reflecting upon your Physical, Personality, and Other attributes, and then compiled them into a master list.

2. Selected attributes for your list that are honest, specific, and memorable.

3. Sought feedback from two men and two women to help you refine your attributes with objective input.

4. Selected three adjectives or phrases and created a unique personal brand.

5. Tested your personal brand with your Mentor to ensure that it rings true about you, projects an image that will appeal to a wide range of men, differentiates you from most other women, and positions you as marriage material.

Step #6

Advertising:

Promote Your Personal Brand

WHAT I LEARNED AT
HARVARD BUSINESS SCHOOL

A product can be the greatest item in the world, but unless it has an effective advertising campaign behind it, it can fail in the marketplace. No one except the Marketing Department will ever know about the product's incredible attributes unless that message is effectively communicated to consumers. Many companies think of advertising as a necessary evil: It's expensive, time-consuming, and promotional. But it's the only way for consumers to learn about the product. Consumers need to be educated and guided toward making the right selections.

Two important advertising lessons stand out:

1. **Brand consistency** is absolutely key in any form of advertising: The brand image of the product must remain the same every time the consumer is exposed to it.

2. **Brand recall,** a measure of how easily people remember what the brand stands for, is essential to an effective advertising campaign. If your advertising doesn't make your brand memorable, it is wasted. If I say "FedEx," you immediately think "Overnight Delivery." If I say "Rolls-Royce," you immediately think of a luxury car. The Rolls-Royce brand is and always has been consistently advertised as the "most luxurious car." Without brand consistency and high brand recall, advertising messages just create confusion and are ineffective.

While many forms of expensive advertising exist (television, magazine, newspaper, billboard, and so on), some of the least expensive methods such as direct-mail, word-of-mouth, and image advertising can deliver the most impact.

WHY IT'S IMPORTANT TO ADVERTISE YOUR PERSONAL BRAND

Now that you have created a personal brand in Step #5, Branding, you need to advertise it. Consider your brand as if it were a new name: Everyone needs to know what it is. It doesn't do any good to have defined your personal brand in your mind or leave it written on a piece of paper. You need to make sure everyone around you knows it. This is not abnormal. Whether you are aware of it or not, you advertise yourself all the time. People form opinions about you every day: in casual conversations, on dates, at parties, in job interviews. You tell people what you want them to hear about yourself—even if you do it subconsciously. Since they can only really evaluate what you show them, it's possible to take control over situations simply by being conscious of the messages you're sending.

There are two key groups of people who need to be aware of your brand: those who can fix you up on dates, and your dates themselves. What follows are tactics you should use to help these two groups describe you and perceive you in the terms of your personal brand. This will help you find and attract men who are intrigued with your unique points of differentiation.

Many women tell me they are uncomfortable promoting themselves and their unique qualities. This is mainly because most of us are raised to be modest and demure about our assets. Braggarts are never well liked. But all you are really doing here is communicating what makes you *different*, not what makes you *great*. This is not bragging or acting smug, but rather helping people frame you in their minds. You need to get comfortable with the fact that advertising is okay. Still, reaching this comfort level doesn't happen overnight. The more you tell people about your new "label," the more at ease you'll be with it. Your advertising efforts will be very effective, but only if you enact them with confidence.

You are about to launch the "new you" advertising campaign. But it is important to understand that I'm not saying you should lie about yourself or use "bait and switch" tactics. Your advertising campaign is about putting your best foot forward to get the initial attention of as many men as possible. Once you start to meet and date these men, your full picture will emerge. That's what dating is for. Then, either you'll hit a home run or you won't, but at least you'll have gone up to bat.

CAVEAT EMPTOR: "LET THE BUYER BEWARE!"

Through branding and advertising, you are highlighting only certain aspects of who you are. Of course, you are still the same person as before you first heard the term *personal brand*, and it's up to the men you date to get to know over time your many qualities, both positive and negative. Similarly, it's up to *you* to unravel the many complexities of a man with whom you're contemplating a lifelong commitment. Everyone tries to put his best foot forward in the beginning, so just beware of what advertising *can* do (distinguish you initially) and what it *cannot* do (substitute for really getting to know each other eventually).

HOW TO ADVERTISE YOUR PERSONAL BRAND

Don't worry, I'm not going to suggest that you produce a real TV commercial or rent a billboard to advertise your personal brand. I advocate instead three other (less expensive) forms of advertising that are better suited to this process: direct-mail, word-of-mouth, and image advertising.

DIRECT-MAIL ADVERTISING

Direct-mail is a form of advertising that delivers targeted, individually addressed communication through the mail. With this method, you can efficiently contact everyone you know in writing and thus advertise your new brand image. This is also a great opportunity to ask for fix-ups.

I want you to create and send a clever *Program* holiday card. First, pick any holiday *except* Christmas or Hanukkah. You don't want your card to compete with the dozens of others arriving in mailboxes during December. Perhaps your card can offer tidings for a Happy New Year (mailed after January 5, when people are back from vacation), Happy Bastille Day, Happy Halloween, or Happy Thanksgiving. You can also select an occasion for your card that is not a holiday, such as an announcement of your latest change of address. Pick the nearest non-December holiday or event for this Step #6 activity.

Second, pick the message you want to deliver. Your goal is to communicate, somewhat subtly, who the "new you" is. So you want to create a card that showcases your personal brand. For example, Anita, age 44, selected the brand: "Witty, Easy-to-Talk-To, Golfer." She created a "Happy Thanksgiving" card. She chose three photos of herself (two of them had to be taken specifically for this card): One showed her laughing with friends (to convey wittiness), another revealed a nice, warm smile (which made her look like someone easy to talk to), and a third depicted her on the golf course.

She took the photos to a graphic artist at a local Sir Speedy copy store. The artist cleverly arranged the photos as tee flags on a golf course and typeset HAPPY THANKSGIVING inside the card. She had 150 cards printed for her friends, family, acquaintances, and co-workers. She added a typed letter folded inside the card describing what had been going on in her life over the past year, making sure to highlight some recent activities that related to her brand (such as participating in a local charity golf tournament). She added some witty lines to the letter, in keeping with her sense of humor.

But she wasn't ready to mail the card yet! Most important, she added a personalized message on the inside of each card, spending about an hour each night for three weeks working through her list of 150 names. The personalized note asked the recipient of the card directly for fix-ups. It looked like this:

Dear Sandy,

Are you still enjoying your new job? It sounds wonderful! I have a special favor to ask you. This year, I would like to find someone wonderful to spend my life with. Do you know any single men you could introduce to me? If so, I would truly appreciate your help. Please call me at xxx-xxx-xxxx.

Happy Thanksgiving, Anita

Another woman, Joanne, sent out a Happy New Year's card showing a series of photos as she grew up—at age 3, age 13, age 21, and her current age, 38, although she didn't actually print any of the ages on the card. In each photo she had a big smile, since part of her brand was "Vivacious." Over her current photo was the caption: THIS IS MY YEAR! and the personal message she wrote inside each card began with "This is my year to find a wonderful man . . ."

If you do not have the time or money to find a graphic artist to create your direct-mail campaign, or your creative juices aren't flowing, or you do not feel comfortable putting your own photo on a card, you can take another route. Get preprinted cards at a stationery store or on the Internet. You can select an image of an object or concept suited to your brand. Online, try www.cardsupply.com, or search on www.google.com for other greeting card sites. You can also find more ideas on my web site: www.FindAHusbandAfter35.com.

Sending out cards in a direct-mail campaign like this accomplishes two important goals: effectively communicating all or part of your brand and prompting your friends to fix you up.

Another woman, Cynthia, had a great idea. This is how she described her direct-mail card to me:

> Most people I know are so busy. I wanted to make it quick and easy for them to fix me up, if they knew anyone. So I included a reply card with a self-addressed stamped envelope inserted inside the larger envelope containing my holiday card. It looked like one of those small RSVP cards you get in wedding invitations. I created a checklist on the reply card that looked like this:

_____ Yes! Please call me. I know someone whom I'd really like you to meet. He is my:

❑ Doctor	❑ Neighbor	❑ Ex-boyfriend	❑ Spouse's co-worker
❑ Dentist	❑ Cousin	❑ Instructor	❑ Friend
❑ Plumber	❑ Hairstylist	❑ Co-volunteer	❑ Friend's friend
❑ Accountant	❑ Realtor	❑ Father	❑ Other

_____ No, I'm sorry I can't think of anyone right now, but I'll keep my eyes open for you!

Not only did this reply card make it easy for someone to fix me up, but the diverse checklist demonstrated the wide net I am casting. I mailed 90 cards, and within three months I got 14 yes replies sent back to me with fix-ups. It worked—I was thrilled!

WORD-OF-MOUTH ADVERTISING

Word-of-mouth advertising is a powerful marketing technique, but it's not something you can create *directly*. It requires more indirect methods. Word-of-mouth advertising happens when one customer tries a product, has a good experience with it, and then takes the initiative to tell friends about it. On *The Program*, as in business, you can't force this mode of advertising, but you can certainly do your best to ignite and encourage it. How? First, select ten people you know who have large social networks so your message will have the farthest reach. These ten people (friends, family, co-workers, acquaintances, etc.) should be a subset of your direct-mail campaign list, and they should have already received your card. So this method is an attempt to *reinforce* in person what many of them have already seen in print.

This tactic is especially useful for people with whom you might feel uncomfortable *directly* asking for fix-ups, such as colleagues at work. The idea is to project your brand to them in a subtle way, and strongly hint that you are open to being fixed up. Allow yourself approximately two weeks to communicate with these 10 people. Your hope is that they will be influenced and encouraged to repeat your message to other people, which may in turn facilitate direct fix-ups with single men, or indirect fix-ups via their friends who may know single men.

The best way to illustrate this word-of-mouth tactic is to show you how one woman, Ellen, did it.

CASE STUDY:
A DAY IN THE LIFE OF ELLEN'S WORD-OF-MOUTH ADVERTISING CAMPAIGN

Background

Ellen is a 39-year-old woman who selected the personal brand: "Architect, Charming, International." She chose "Architect" because this was her profession and it is not your run-of-the-mill job. "Charming" was chosen after feedback from four people in Step #5, Branding, suggested that it was her most appealing personality trait. She could comfortably talk to anyone, always made a good impression, and made people feel that their conversations with her were easy and engaging. She chose "International" as her third attribute because she had lived in four different countries in South America and Asia, which is unusual for an American woman. This also served to cast a wider net by attracting men of different nationalities.

How Ellen Conducted Word-of-mouth Advertising

First, Ellen identified ten people who were most likely to have large social networks and might be able to introduce her to single men. They were mostly work colleagues. She set a goal for herself that every day for two weeks she would tell one of those ten people about her personal brand. She allowed herself a four-day "grace period" during the two weeks in case she couldn't make contact with one of her targets. Of course, this advertising had to be a subtle endeavor: She couldn't just walk up to someone and announce her personal brand out of the blue. Ellen's approach was to drop hints into casual conversations. For example, one day she and a "targeted" co-worker were walking back from lunch, and they admired a stylish leather purse in a store window. Ellen remarked, "When I lived in Argentina, I saw purses like that for half the price." "Oh?" her co-worker said. "I didn't know you lived in Argentina." "Yes," Ellen answered, "I've actually lived in three other countries, too. I'm quite the international gal!"

Later in the conversation, Ellen referenced a phone call that she'd had with a friend the night before. Her subtle advertising to the co-worker sounded like this: "I was talking to my friend Melissa last night, and she said, 'I want to introduce you to this guy I met in my writing class. I've told him that you're a charming architect with an international background.' He said I sounded like someone he would really like to meet, so I'm excited to hear from him." This "casual mention" showed the co-worker how Ellen is described by others in one clear sentence. "By the way," Ellen continued, as an afterthought, "can *you* think of a nice single man to fix me up with?"

By the end of Ellen's exchange with her co-worker that day, she had used word-of-mouth advertising for her brand: She explained her international background and offered her friend Melissa's summary of herself as "International, Charming, Architect." Ellen had also hinted that she is open to fix-ups when she referenced Melissa's intent to introduce her to the man from the writing class. She then attempted to "close the sale" by asking outright whether her co-worker personally knew any nice single men.

If Ellen's co-worker knows a single man, or meets one in the future, and attempts to introduce him to Ellen, she will now have some seeds planted in her mind about how to describe her. Of course, we can never totally control what other people say about us, especially when we're absent, but Ellen has done her best to ignite word-of-mouth advertising via subtle conversation hints.

This is certainly contrived behavior that I'm advocating here, but if you can't just blurt out your brand, how else are you going to solidify it in the minds of the most influential people you know? The goal is to look for opportunities in conversations with them to communicate your three unique attributes.

Your 30-Second Commercial

Another exercise for successful word-of-mouth advertising is to create your own "30-second commercial." No, not a real TV commercial, but just a verbal practice session with yourself (or maybe with your Mentor) to describe yourself in the most appealing manner. Just like companies use 30-second TV commercials to pitch their product to viewers, you need a ready-made pitch about yourself for potential dates or friends who might fix you up. Practice in front of the mirror. Give yourself only 30 seconds to highlight your best attributes and incorporate your brand. Practice sounding engaging and upbeat. This is not a brag session, but a sincere, thoughtful, catchy, perhaps even witty description of how you'd hope to be described to a potential blind date. Now the next time someone asks you, "So, tell me about yourself?" you'll have a great answer on the tip of your tongue.

IMAGE ADVERTISING

As you learned in Step #3, Packaging, the image that a product projects with its packaging is important. You are now ready to focus on brand consistency by fine-tuning your packaging and making all the elements *consistent* with your personal brand. Without consistency, you risk sending mixed messages and confusing "the customer" about who you are. Use the following checklist to craft an effective image advertising campaign.

Consistency Checklist

- **Clothing style:** Do you dress like a jock? An artist? A nurse? Is that consistent with your personal brand? For example, if your personal brand is "Intellectual, Catholic, Nurse," you might *not* want to wear leather miniskirts and a see-through blouse, but it would be consistent if you wore conservative black pants and a soft-fabric sweater set.
- **Eyeglasses:** What does the style of your eyeglasses or sunglasses say about you? Conservative? Sassy? Creative? For example, if your personal brand is "Creative, Redhead, Graphic Designer," you might *not* want to select glasses with big, round Harry Potter–style frames, but it would be consistent if you wore trendy, red speckled cat's-eye frames.
- **Accessories:** What kind of shoes, hat, jewelry do you wear? For instance, if your personal brand is "Blue-eyed, Colorado, Horse Breeder," you might *not* want to wear 4-inch stiletto-heeled sandals, but it would be consistent to wear snakeskin cowboy boots.
- **Props:** Are your car, your keychain, the photos in your wallet, and your tote bag consistent with your brand? For example, if your personal brand is "Spontaneous, Sassy, Runner,"

you might *not* want to drive a safe, conservative Volvo, but it would be consistent to drive a sporty, convertible Jetta.

- **Conversation topics:** Do you initiate conversations that reinforce your image? If your personal brand is "Adventurous, Brazilian, Doctor," you might *not* talk too much on a first date about baking cookies and watercolor painting, but spend more time talking about your trek through the Amazon rain forest and your latest mission to bring medical supplies to São Paolo.

- **Answering-machine message:** As you did in Step #3, Packaging, to verify a feminine tone, call your own voice mail (on your cell phone, office phone, and home phone) and listen to the recorded outgoing messages. Are your words and tone upbeat? Intriguing? Witty? For example, if your personal brand is "Witty, Georgia, Teacher," you might *not* want your message to include bad grammar and a dull, matter-of-fact tone, but it would be consistent to record a quip about why you're not available to answer the phone, spoken in your warmest southern accent.

- **E-mail address:** What image does your e-mail address project? Use your address as an opportunity for brand reinforcement. If your personal brand is "Fun, Quirky, Librarian," then you could leave your e-mail address as MaryJones@xxxxx.com, but it would be more consistent to create a new address such as BookGoddess@xxxxx.com.

CUSTOMIZE YOUR IMAGE ADVERTISING

Although you should be consistent in advertising your personal brand, there is one caveat. It is okay to adjust or customize your message to make an emotional connection with men you date. A good marketer first researches what the customer wants, then designs a product to meet those needs. We all have our own unique sets of emotional needs, and while a man may be attracted to you early on for your personal brand, it is often an emotional need that determines whether a lasting connection is made. For example, a divorced man whose wife cheated on him probably needs a new wife who embraces fidelity—someone he can trust. Therefore, as you get to know a man better and learn his important emotional needs, you can fine-tune your advertising message to highlight a fourth attribute that is also true about yourself. Here you would pick "Faithful" or "Trustworthy" if it rings true for you, which is the key emotional need of the divorced man in this example. The fourth attribute you select will change with each man you date. This is basic marketing strategy: "Find a need and try to fill it!"

Of course, be honest with yourself and with him about whether you can truly deliver the emotional pieces you both need. If you're the bossy type, and the very reason that the man you're dating left his last girlfriend was because she was too domineering, you are not likely a good match for him. He probably needs someone more accommodating or passive. Practice "truth in advertising" because true colors always shine through. If you create false advertising, ultimately you will waste your time in a doomed relationship and probably break both your hearts.

It's helpful to think about how to customize your image advertising before practicing it with your next date. Try making a list of three men: previous dates, ex-boyfriends, or even ex-husbands. Then identify one key emotional need that each man had. Look back at the list of attributes that you compiled in Step #5, Branding, to see if any of your personality attributes would fill the key emotional needs of the three men you wrote down. My client Nora's list looked like this:

His Name	His Key Emotional Need	My Attribute (if any) to Fill His Need
Colin	Someone who loves him for himself, not his money	Not materialistic
Michael	Someone who is stable, not irrational	Mature, grounded, consistent
Sam	Someone to "mother him," take care of him	None (I'm not the nurturing type)

For example, once Nora detected that what Colin needed most was someone to love him for himself, not his money, she could have made a concentrated effort to "advertise" to him that she was not materialistic. Often this can be accomplished with a series of small gestures. When they spent time together, she could have suggested going on picnics or hikes, rather than having him take her to expensive restaurants. She could have mentioned that her favorite candy was Twizzlers, rather than a gourmet box of Godiva chocolates. It would have been easy for her to emphasize these things, because Nora was genuinely not very materialistic, and she could have highlighted this fact. She told me she thought it would have made a difference early on in their dating if Colin had known this. Unfortunately, Colin stopped calling Nora before she communicated this about herself.

The lesson here? Try to identify his emotional needs or sensitivities as early as possible, decide if you can meet them, and—if you can—then customize your image advertising right away. I believe that a marriage-minded man is on the lookout for a woman who fits with him emotionally, and will make quick decisions about whether or not to call her back based on early and perhaps random data points: the little actions or comments he observes that may or may not reflect her actual personality.

After viewing Nora's list, compile your own list of three men from your past with their key emotional needs. Spend some time reflecting on this list. Then the next time you have a date, try to practice this new skill of customizing your image advertising—trying to let him know how you can fill his key emotional need. It may require the skills of a detective to identify what his key emotional need is. Often a man's need arises as a reaction against his last girlfriend, mother, or ex-wife. These types of needs can also stem from positive relationships experienced with previous women in his life. Or sometimes these needs arise out of his own insecurities. But most men do have a predominant emotional need that you should try to identify early on (in the first few dates). If you can fill that need, advertise it. If you honestly can't fill his need, let him know. You don't want to waste your time.

THE BRAND RECALL TEST

When you attempt the advertising methods in this chapter, you will quickly see whether you have chosen a good personal brand or not. People should be able to remember your brand easily and repeat it accurately to others. Of course, your brand has to ring true to people who hear it. If you've chosen an attribute that is a disconnect between how you see yourself and how others see you, you will find out early in this step. Your first clue will be if others seem surprised by your brand description or cannot remember it. You might have the right attribute *concept*, but maybe you chose a word that is difficult to remember. If you chose the attribute "Statuesque" as mentioned earlier, for instance, but you realize that people are describing you as "Tall," this word may be too esoteric.

If you discover during this step that your brand is in distress (people have low recall of your advertising message), go back quickly to Step #5, Branding, and make the necessary changes before continuing with the three advertising tactics I have described in this chapter.

How Do You Know When Your Brand Is Working Well?

You know when a brand *isn't* working well because people seem surprised by it or can't remember it, or if it's attracting the wrong kind of man. You'll know it *is* working well when the reverse starts to happen: People express enthusiastic recognition when they hear your brand attributes, they remember your brand easily, and the brand is attracting quality men. You'll start to notice that people will think to invite you to particular events or include you in certain conversation topics relevant to your brand.

For example, my client Anne (profiled in Step #4, Market Expansion) selected "Hiker" as part of her brand. She called me excitedly one day (before she met Phil) to tell me this story: "I was walking down the hallway at work today and saw a few colleagues talking together. One man called over to me and said, 'Anne, come listen to this. We were just talking about Joe's recent trip to climb Pikes Peak. You'll be interested in hearing this.' " She said to me on the phone, "It works! No one at my office knew about my passion for hiking until I started advertising my brand last month. Apparently they've been listening to my advertising and now think of me when they hear a story about hiking. Maybe someone will invite me on a future hiking trip, and I'll meet some interesting new friends."

You have succeeded with Step #6, and can begin Step #7, if you:

1. Achieved a solid comfort level with promoting your personal brand.
2. Created and sent personalized cards in a direct-mail campaign to advertise your brand and specifically asked for fix-ups.
3. Mastered the art of subtle word-of-mouth advertising and promoted your personal brand to ten targeted people over the course of two weeks.
4. Evaluated your image advertising efforts with the consistency checklist in this chapter.
5. Practiced customizing your image advertising message on your next date.
6. Passed the Brand Recall Test.
7. Perfected your 30-second commercial.

Step #7

Online Marketing:

Be Efficient

WHAT I LEARNED AT HARVARD BUSINESS SCHOOL

f you want to succeed in business, you have to sell your product *efficiently*. This typically means making your product and your message available quickly and cost-effectively to as many prospects as possible. Businesses have found that the Internet is a very efficient sales tool. The online marketplace offers an enormous audience quickly and at low cost: It is too big to ignore. Where else can you target specific groups in mere seconds for pennies? Where else can you create virtual storefronts in numerous locations with immediate control over the image of your store displays, take orders 24 hours a day, and send different messages to different audiences (and immediately know which ones work and which ones don't)? Online, you can leverage your business savvy and marketing budget more effectively than in any other arena. Yet success isn't guaranteed in this cyberworld of vast potential. As always, you have to use smart marketing tactics customized for the nuances of online transactions.

WHY ONLINE DATING IS CRUCIAL AFTER 35

To some of you, I'll be preaching to the choir: You've been dating online for some time, and already know the advantages (and disadvantages). For others, you might consider the Internet a scary or geeky domain. Or maybe you consider those who post personal ads online to be "losers" or "desperate." Or perhaps you have avoided it because your friends reported negative stories to you about their online dating experiences.

But I am here to tell you that you are foolish if you don't start online dating. It's the single best thing you can do to maximize your odds of finding a husband, despite the inherent pitfalls. Online dating is now socially acceptable, hugely popular, and used by all ages and types of men and women. In April 2004, more than 25 million adults in the United States logged on to an online dating site (as reported by Nielsen/Net-Ratings), and that number is rising fast every month. Approximately half of those online today are over 30 years old. And importantly, approximately 53% of users of online personal ads are looking for a "serious relationship." It is a *must* for any single woman over the age of 35! In fact, if you are only going to take one step in *The Program*, this should be the one. That's how strongly I feel about it. You're reading this book because you want to change your situation, right? Online dating is a powerful catalyst.

I can't even calculate how many women have come to me and said, "I tried online dating, and it didn't work out." In each and every case, I discovered that the reason was because she wasn't doing it *correctly*. You'll learn in this chapter how to do it correctly.

First, for any of you online dating resisters, let me tell you why this is a crucial activity:

1. **High volume:** Dating is a numbers game, and the sheer volume of different types and locations of men whom you can quickly reach online is unparalleled. If you live in a major city, a large online dating service is likely to have twenty thousand or more single men within 25 miles of you . . . all lined up and ready to meet you!

2. **Fast:** For anyone who is in a hurry to meet someone and has a busy life outside the dating realm, online dating is *superfast*. You will be able to quickly meet and interact with many eligible men.

3. **Inexpensive:** Currently, it costs only about $25 per month for an online dating service—that's compared to spending hundreds or thousands of dollars for other dating services such as matchmaking or video dating.

4. **Convenient:** If you're tired after a long day at work (either in the office or as a stay-at-home mom), you can relax and see who's out there from the comfort of your home. And you're not confined to meeting men only on the weekends. You can meet and interact with men during the day, even at work. Online dating is open 24/7. You can wear your comfy sweatpants to do it! Can you believe there is even a way now to use your cell phone to date online? For the busy *Program* woman, you can get matches and exchange text messages in traffic jams or in the boardroom (check out www.mobile.match.com for more details).

5. **Wide net:** Talk about casting a wide net (no pun intended)! Online dating gives you the opportunity to tap into new groups of men outside your regular social circle. You can use the anonymity of the Internet and the ease of e-mail to explore new types of men.

6. **What counts:** It's actually an old-fashioned way that has come full circle. Men and women use the written word to get to know each other first. Sure, you usually see a small photo of each other in the beginning as a screening mechanism, but total physical appearance is not a barrier to learning what really counts about one another. You have a chance to connect with someone on a deeper level (thoughts and feelings) rather than only on a superficial level (appearance).

7. **Better ratio:** Did you know that more men than women are dating online? It's true. This is bound to change in the future, but the ratio currently is 55% men to 45% women online. Since the total ratio of women to men is not ideal for you in the over-35 general singles pool, you'd be crazy to miss this opportunity to improve your odds online.

8. **Anonymous:** Men can e-mail you, but the online dating site never lets the men know your real name, actual e-mail address, or anything else about you that you have not put into your profile. This is called "double-blind" e-mailing. Some dating sites now have a double-blind voice system that allows you to set up anonymous telephone dates. Of course, posting your photo doesn't keep you truly anonymous, but at least someone can't track you down without your permission. You can decide *if* you want to reply, *what* you want to reveal, and *when* and *where* you're ready to meet someone.

NO EXCUSES

I've given you eight good reasons to start online dating. Excuses are not accepted. As I mentioned in the Introduction, there is no room for excuses on *The Program*. You don't have a home computer? Use your Marketing Budget to buy an inexpensive one, or stay late at work, go to the library, visit a friend's house, or check out an Internet café. You don't know how to scan a photo for your profile? There are easy, step-by-step instructions on every site. I'm not a tech-savvy gal, and I did it in five minutes for one of my clients. Ask someone to help you, or simply send a photo through regular mail and most sites will post it for you.

Do you still think it's a "desperate act" to post an ad online? I understand that you may feel an initial reluctance to try it because it doesn't sound natural, but once you've started, you'll quickly forget that notion and realize that it's just a way of life these days. The interesting men whom you can meet also decided to go online, so you're all in the same boat. My clients all tell me that it's a great ego booster to have e-mails arrive in their in-box from men who want to know more about them.

Still hesitant? Go back to Step #1 and ask yourself if you are willing to do anything that is not illegal or immoral to find a husband. As tactics go, this one isn't outrageous (wait until you get to Step #10, Telemarketing!). As *USA Today* reported, "The only reason it has taken this long for online dating to catch on is that we as a culture [believe] love is serendipitous—that it happens haphazardly and is not something you do intentionally." Well, welcome to *The Program*!

THE GOALS FOR ONLINE DATING

There are five main goals that you must focus on to succeed with dating online. Remember these as you venture into cyberspace:

1. **Be unique:** Because there are many other women dating online, you must strive to be unique and stand out in the crowd.

2. **Create intrigue:** Men surf through profiles quickly. You must create intrigue to entice them to spend more time to learn about and contact you after a quick glance at your photo.

3. **Create volume:** The more men who write to you, the more choices you have. You want the ball in your court. The last section in this chapter will address whether or not it's okay to e-mail men first.

4. **Be efficient:** Dating online can be a huge time commitment. You must create systems and strategies to quickly weed through the volume of men and make smart choices. Use a dating site that offers the easiest and most advanced tools for efficiency. And start online dating when you have relatively more free time in your life. Don't post your profile during your busy season at work, for example.

5. **Find a husband:** Of course!

MARKET RESEARCH

Yes, this again! I hope you're not tired of investing time in good research, because it's always a crucial phase of any business initiative. You must perform new research to gain important competitive intelligence. You need to understand the online marketplace. See what's out there—what's good and what's bad. This means spending a significant amount of time on your computer (perhaps 2 hours or more), surfing the existing profiles of both men and women on online dating sites.

I would suggest starting with a large online dating site that will provide the biggest pool of people for you to research. Your research is all free, by the way. You can explore profiles on most online dating sites without paying a penny; usually fees are charged only for corresponding directly with members. First log on as a "man looking for a woman." You want to check out other women's profiles to assess the competition. Indicate an age range of 10 years older and younger than yourself, and type in your zip code. Spend about an hour perusing the female profiles that emerge on your screen. If you were a man, what do you think you would like and dislike? What makes one woman stand out from the others? What compels you to read a profile more in-depth? Write down what you learn.

Repeat the same research in a different zip code: Try large city zip codes to view the most profiles (New York 10001, Los Angeles 90001, or Chicago 60601), and try searching within a hundred or more miles. You want to learn if there are any creative approaches that women in other regions are taking.

Then return to the home page and log on again as a "woman looking for a man." Now you need to focus on what the men are hoping to find. I think you'll be surprised, but see for yourself. Do the men market themselves in the same way that the women do? What are the differences? How do men describe the type of woman they want? Spend another hour reviewing the male profiles and write down what you learn.

Even if you've already been dating online, it is important to develop and keep current your knowledge of this dating medium. It changes so quickly, and there are many subtle nuances for success.

HOW TO GET RESULTS ONLINE

One of the core principles of *The Program* is to generate volume, so naturally you want to be where the most men are. Since

Match.com is currently the largest online dating site (there are 8 million singles who use it), and it is focused on bringing women and men together for serious relationships, it's a good service to try first. You are maximizing your odds to find a husband by placing yourself where the highest quantity of marriage-minded men are looking (Match.com reported 2.75 wedding announcements *per day* in 2002!). To sign up, you need to create your "profile" and include the monthly fee (currently $25) in your Marketing Budget.

Your profile will consist of a screen name, a photo, a description of yourself, and a description of the type of man you are looking for. The key strategy here is to post your information in such a way that you get noticed when men are surfing. Most men to whom I have spoken are fairly consistent in how they go about searching on an online dating site. They describe a simple scanning process that they use to figure out which women to contact: They type in the age range and location of women they want to meet, glance at the photo ("Am I attracted to her?"), then glance at the screen name and headline ("Am I intrigued enough to read more?"). If they've answered yes to both questions, they'll read more about the woman (her profile and "his" profile—what she's looking for) and decide from there whether to initiate contact via e-mail. Getting results, then, all comes down to how well you market yourself via your photo, your screen name and headline, your profile, and his profile.

YOUR PHOTO

Let's start with the most important element: your photo. Again, I wish it weren't true (so please don't shoot the messenger), but men are very visual, and your appearance is critical. Your photo is the first screening mechanism when a man is searching.

You already know about the importance of appearance from Step #3, Packaging, and from life in general. What are you going to do about it? Well, after you justifiably decide that men are shallow, you are going to make sure that you use the best damn photo of yourself possible! You may not have a great, recent photo of yourself, so invest the time and money (dig into your Marketing Budget again) to have one taken. You can hire a professional photographer (expensive), go to a Sears Portrait Studio (less expensive), or have a camera-savvy friend snap your picture (practically free).

For the photo shoot, I want you to wear something fabulous and feminine (soft shoulder lines; no business-type clothing), choose a vibrant shirt color that accents your hair and eyes (don't wear white or you'll blend into the background), and have your hair and make-up done professionally (or at least spend a full hour doing them yourself). A head shot of you smiling warmly and confidently is perfect. Don't use a full-body shot, because it will be difficult to see your face clearly. The whole photo will appear on a man's screen initially in a one-inch by two-inch box, so if you use a full-body shot, your head will not be much larger than a speck of dust! Even if you have a great body, this is not the place to show it off (you're looking for a husband, not a "quickie")! So no "come hither" facial expressions, and no revealing or vampy poses and clothing.

All these elements are vital to an effective online photo. You need to convey a quick and positive impression, because as men surf they are likely to spend about three seconds deciding whether or not to read further. You certainly don't have to be beautiful to create a great photo ("There's a lid for every pot," as they say), but invest the time to make it your personal best.

I can hear the protests now: "But what about looking *real*? I don't want to post a 'perfect' photo of myself looking too good, the way I look only a few days per year. I don't want to see disappointment in his face when we meet for the first time and he sees my everyday look." Well, you're right! That's why you're not going to use just one photo, you're going to use two or three. Most sites have a "front" photo position (that's where you're going to post your fabulous photo described above), along with a "Click for More Photos" feature. Here you're going to add a second or third photo that represents a more casual, everyday look for you.

But of course you still need to make a favorable impression, so make these backup photos good as well. While you don't need to have your hair and make-up done professionally for these other photos, make them count. If you're overweight, you should consider a full- or partial-body shot here to manage his expectations. Of course, no red eyes or blurry photos. You can generate the most "qualified" responses from a mixture of flattering and realistic photos of yourself. And don't forget your personal brand. Your photos should be consistent with your attributes: Having photos taken of yourself on the tennis court is great if you're a "Tennis Player," photos on a snowy mountain work if you're a "Skier," or pictures next to your bookshelf make sense if you're an "Intellectual."

I would not recommend using photos with your kids or pets. Remember, you want to cast a wider net and generate a high volume of qualified responses so that you have the most men from whom to choose. Kids and pets don't appeal to everyone at first glance. What if you post a photo of yourself with your dog, and the most wonderful man in the world sees it, is attracted to you, but doesn't really like dogs? You might respond, "Then he's not for me!" But in reality, once he gets to know you and falls in love with you down the road, he is likely to grow fond of your dog, too. He might not like dogs in general, but he can learn to like *your* dog. Don't create initial barriers that may be keeping Mr. Right elusive.

A SUMMARY OF DO'S AND DON'TS FOR YOUR ONLINE PHOTO

Do:
- Use a fabulous photo for the front profile slot.
- Use 2nd or 3rd back-up photos that are "real," but still good.
- Have your hair and make-up done professionally for the front photo.
- Look feminine.
- Smile warmly and confidently.
- Wear a vibrant shirt color.
- Integrate your brand into your back-up photos, if possible.

Don't:
- Wear business-type or masculine-looking clothing.
- Wear revealing or vampy clothing.
- Portray "come hither" facial expressions.
- Include kids or pets in photos.

- ❑ Use full-body shots.
- ❑ Post blurry photos.
- ❑ Show red eyes.

YOUR SCREEN NAME AND HEADLINE

In case you're new to online dating, a screen name (or "user name") is the name you give yourself online to protect your privacy and to receive e-mails. Your headline (or "tag line") is a phrase or set of adjectives that appears above your photo on most sites and is supposed to quickly summarize who you are or convey something about you. Most dating sites have a maximum number of characters that can be used in a screen name (usually 15) and headline (usually 125), so you'll have to be concise.

Since you're a graduate of Step #5, Branding, you understand the importance of being different. This is perhaps more vital in online dating than in any other venue because men are scanning hundreds of profiles at once and quickly making distinctions. It's a sea of vanilla online: bland, basic, and boring. I'm going to teach you how good marketing can make you stand out during the male scan.

What Is Bad Marketing?

Or, better said, what does *not* intrigue good men? Screen names that are too basic ("JaneSmith24"), too obscure ("MiesVanderohe"), too sexy ("NiceCleavage"), or too saccharine ("SpecialHarmony"). And headlines that are too boring ("Good woman seeks good man"), too cynical ("Are there any honest men left?"), too marriage-minded ("Looking for Mr. Right"), too weird ("Bring the shoe horn"), too cocky ("I'm the one for you"), or too trite ("Smart, nice gal"). By the way, all of these are real screen names and headlines that I have seen online!

What Is Good Marketing?

Or, what *does* intrigue good men? Screen names that are unique ("Starpepper"), intriguing ("DenverAllure"), and appealing ("AquaEyes"). And headlines that are catchy ("5 Foot 2, Eyes of Blue"), upbeat ("Fresh-brewed life"), humorous ("What do you get when you mix Katharine Hepburn and Lucille Ball?") and sassy ("Groovy, electric, curvy").

Don't rush the creative process just to get it done. It may take several days to create something really good. Keep thinking about your brand, ask for input from clever friends, and refer back to your online market research notes. Maybe you can create a new twist on someone else's screen name or headline that you admired.

YOUR PROFILE

A profile is the essay section of your ad that asks you in some form to "Describe Yourself." You want to accomplish several things with your profile. Usually there is a 100-character minimum required, but I think about 250 characters is just right (not too detailed, not too abrupt). You'd be surprised how many women use 1,000–3,000 characters! This is not the place to divulge your innermost feelings, list all your likes and dislikes, and (especially) disclose all your baggage. I've seen more than a few profiles in which women write, "I have a few pounds to lose . . ." or "If you can handle my teenage daughter . . ." or

"I've had many disappointments in my life . . ." Don't create a barrier that few men would want to cross. There's time for that later, after you're in his heart. Also, don't write what *women* want to hear ("I love sunsets and cuddling . . ."): If you're looking for a husband, write for the *male* audience.

So what's the best approach? Just be brief, positive, and unique. Most of all, strive to create intrigue so that men will want to learn *more*. Here's a sample profile I like:

> *Describe Yourself:* I am not your typical San Diego woman. I'll take an afternoon at the theater instead of the beach, or spend Sunday morning reading rather than biking. Though it may surprise you that I was once a hula-dance champion! Men have called me "Alluring," "Creative," and "Worldly." Friends trust me to keep their secrets.

This profile accomplishes many things. It sets the woman apart from the pack: She isn't typical, she states, but her interests are not so outrageous that she'll turn off a lot of men (for example, she *didn't* say she likes sumo wrestling or playing with her pet iguana). She focuses on being unique in her region (theater and reading interests stand out in San Diego, though they'd be commonplace in Manhattan) with interests that sound substantial, not flaky. Then she throws in a twist: Not many women can claim a hula-dance title. She uses third person referencing effectively to "modestly" convey some of her unique attributes ("Men have called me . . ."). And she ends with an endorsement that she is trustworthy, which is reassuring when meeting someone on the Internet and a trait you'd like to have in a life partner (but it's not too saccharine). Overall, she is positive about herself. I don't know about you, but I'm intrigued and would like to know more about her!

Always try to avoid sounding generic. If your interests are somewhat generic, like reading or exercising, you can make them more memorable by divulging a few more details. Instead of saying simply that you like to read, reveal which books or authors you're most passionate about. But remember that your target audience is male, so don't tout Virginia Woolf or Danielle Steele. (*Note:* The San Diego profile above used "reading" specifically to set her apart from an outdoor stereotype in her city, so in this instance she didn't need author details.)

Make your own assessments of profiles that you think are effective, and those that aren't, when conducting your market research. Each of us has a different personality and will need to find a style with which we're comfortable. But do make sure to highlight the three attributes of your personal brand. Like a good marketer, just leave them wanting more when they're done reading.

"HIS" PROFILE

"His" profile is the essay section of your ad that asks you to describe what you're looking for in a man. The most common mistake I see is women composing a fantasy list of the man they're looking for. As you learned in Step #4, Market Expansion, men later in life are "real" and have baggage, failures, and imperfections, just like you. Why would anyone post a fantasy list when there's only a 1% chance that such a person exists? You won't get many replies if your list sounds intimidating or you set the bar too high. You'll only block out a lot of great men who could potentially capture your heart. If you are looking for love and happiness, you have to search for an emotional connection with someone, which may come in a completely different package than the one you're dreaming about. If your strategy is to create volume, you will be able to evaluate many options and still be able to hit the "delete" key later if you want. Here's a sample profile I like:

> *What you're looking for:* I am looking for someone wonderful. I am open to many possibilities about the type of package inside which he is wrapped. Kindness and strength of character are traits I admire. When buying a car last month, I chose a Ford Explorer over a Corvette.

This profile is destined to attract a solid man, don't you think? It casts a wide net and should garner a high volume of appealing responses. It's brief—about 200 characters—but illustrative. It has a catchy writing style so it doesn't seem dull or generic. Men can relate to the car analogy: You chose sturdy over flashy. And it portrays the woman as someone of substance (therefore encouraging *men* of substance to apply). I think with this profile a woman can generate many responses that will include good options. So be brief, creative, and don't turn away potential candidates. Remember, you don't have to date everyone who e-mails you.

MORE TIPS

You have seen in this step that dating online is not just something you should begin on a whim. Like most things that matter in life, you need to make the effort to prepare for it and do it well. Here are a few more tips you might find useful as you prepare (or revise) your cyber debut:

- **Take your time:** I have clients who tell me that they "sat down Sunday night and joined a dating site." Immediately I know that what they posted is probably ineffective. When you start dating online, it should be a strategic, thoughtful, coordinated effort. A screen name that is unique, alluring, and appealing usually doesn't just pop into your mind. Ditto for the headline and great profiles—not to mention the preparation necessary for your photos. Be sure to review your ad with your Mentor and maybe with a few male friends.

- **Clear your calendar:** When you first post your ad on a site, you will usually have a NEW symbol displayed next to your profile for a few weeks. Many men sort each week for the new women coming online. This typically brings a sudden windfall of responses for you, especially if your photo is attractive. I had one client who received 40 e-mails in her first two days, and that's not even counting the many direct matches that dating sites sent her automatically—profiles of men who fit the criteria she listed. For most women, the volume surge lasts for one or two weeks, then becomes a more manageable trickle. You'll need time to screen these men, respond to some of them, and then hopefully meet a few of them in person. The volume can be overwhelming, so make sure you clear your calendar and time your debut according to what else is going on in your life.

- **Diversify:** You never want to put all your eggs in one basket. As you get more comfortable with managing your e-mail volume, or if you simply want to expand your options, select additional online dating sites to join (see the listing in the Appendix for some choices). You never know which site your future husband has joined, so look in more than one place. Being on two or three sites simultaneously is desirable. At about $25 per month per site, you might find yourself spending $50 to $75 a month on this tactic. Keep deducting it from your Marketing Budget. And if you meet someone wonderful and start a serious relationship, you can always "hide" your profile (request that the dating service temporarily take you off the site) so this won't turn into an expense over a prolonged period of time.

- **Don't hype:** While you should strive to be unique and appealing, you don't want to hype yourself so much in your photos or in your writing that a man will actually feel disappointed when he meets you in person. Also, no one likes a braggart. Try to create a balance—you want to sound appealing without comparing yourself to Jennifer Aniston or Audrey Hepburn. The best thing that can happen when he sees you on "date zero" (a term used to describe the first meeting between two people who have corresponded online) is that he is pleasantly surprised. This reaction will set an upbeat tone for your date.

- **Use all available tools:** Online dating is evolving faster than the speed of light. Top sites are constantly adding new tools and features that make it easier for you to get and track accurate information as quickly and efficiently as possible. Be sure to invest the time when you join a site to learn about all the tools available to you, and to compare and contrast features when selecting a new site to join. For example, some industry experts say that the "video dating" feature is the future of online dating. Video profiles are now being offered on a few sites to augment a person's photo. If you see that a man's profile includes a video, be sure to check it out. This will give you more information about his demeanor and voice to help you sort through a large volume of responses. (But be cautious not to make snap judgments!) Other advanced features such as mobile phone dating and double-blind voice calling can help you maximize your efficiency in this medium.

- **Seek professional help:** Professional services are available to help improve or create your online dating profile. www.e-cyrano.com or www.profiledoctor.com will help you write an enticing profile to attract more potential dates. And to improve your photo, www.lookbetteronline.com, www.soulmatepics.com or www.singleshots.com will provide photo sessions for online profiles in many U.S. cities, often certifying the date that the photo was taken.

- **Keep a journal:** It's hard to keep all this online volume straight! Since you will have many communications with numerous men (including e-mails, phone calls, and dates), it's a must to get a journal. A standard ruled notebook is fine. Print out each e-mail to which you respond, staple it to a page in your journal, and add your handwritten notes after every phone conversation you have and every date you go on. Track the information by his screen name and list his basic background, general conversation topics you've explored, anything unique you've learned about him, and any of your likes and dislikes about him. There's nothing that makes you look more insincere than confusing one guy with another. For the truly organized, you can create a file system instead of a journal with color-coded labels and folders by screen name. If you're on Match.com, you can also use the "Favorites" tool, which allows you to keep track of the profiles that appeal to you and log any communication received and sent.

HIGH RISK, HIGH RETURN

While online dating provides many great opportunities, it is certainly not a perfect world. There are many risks along the way. You need to understand and anticipate them in advance, and adapt your strategies accordingly to avoid these pitfalls:

- **Safety comes first:** Although you are on a mission to find a husband, please exercise caution and common sense at all times, especially on the Internet. Guard your anonymity until you feel comfortable with a man with whom you're corresponding. Give him your cell phone number instead of your home phone number, since someone could find your address from your home phone number. Consider changing your phone listing to "private" so it doesn't reveal your number on the man's Caller ID. Tell friends or family where and when you're going on date zero with a man, and give them all his details in advance. Meet in a public place. Pay attention to red flags such as signs of anger, disrespectful comments, or inappropriate behavior. Most online dating sites include a section about safety; please read this carefully for more details on being safe.

- **Not everything you read is true:** Just as you would when meeting someone for the first time at a party or bar, you should be hopeful but leery about what someone first tells you about himself. You'll need to watch out for men who exaggerate, who are calculated liars, or who believe in a fantasy version of themselves. Look for inconsistencies, portraits that are too good to be true, and stories that are too coincidental to be real. Men who are reluctant to send you a photo or meet you in person in a public place are usually hiding something (maybe a wife, or a hundred pounds!). Once you learn someone's real name, you might try "Googling" him (go to www.google.com and type his name in the search box), or go to a site such as www.ValiDateUSA.com, which specializes in criminal background checks and other information. Try to learn anything about him that does or doesn't verify what he has told you.

One woman I know started to correspond with "a successful doctor" she met online, but when she Googled him, she discovered via an old newspaper article that he had been involved in a malpractice suit and had lost his license. He no longer practiced medicine, but told her in detail about the patients he supposedly saw every day!

- **Not everything you see is true:** A good photo of a man is not always accurate, but then again neither is a bad photo. Men haven't read this book to learn the importance of posting a fabulous photo.

I know about bad photos from personal experience. Although online dating didn't exist when I was single, I first saw my husband's photo in a business directory. We had spoken once on the phone, and since I liked his voice so much, I decided to try to find a picture of him. So I flipped through a business directory I found that included thumbnail photos. When I located his photo, my face dropped. I could *never* be attracted to someone who looked like that (I guess I hadn't grasped the wider-net concept yet)! It was really an awful photo. And immediately I forgot about him . . . until we met almost a year later on Step #12, Event Marketing, and he was so cute! He looked *nothing* like his bad picture, and sparks flew.

- **Love at first type:** It is easy to fall in love with an online fantasy man. You're attracted to his photo, you adore his e-mails, and he says all the right things. This goes on for weeks and months and you've never even met FTF (face-to-face). This is a waste of your time, especially if you want to be married in 12 to 18 months. Remember that dating online is a tactic on *The Program* because it's efficient. Your goal should be to meet men in person (even if it's just for coffee) as quickly as possible once you determine a good connection via e-mail and phone contact. Suggest a meeting within two weeks if he hasn't asked you first (your one femininity rule-breaker with this man). If he stalls the FTF meeting, move on. If you do meet him, and he's not right for you, move on.

  If you start dreaming about your future together before you even meet him, you will want to stay home just to be near your computer rather than going out and productively meeting new men. He may be Mr. Wonderful, but if he hasn't arranged to meet you within two weeks after you receive the first e-mail, move on to the next man.

  When you do finally meet him, the most important thing you can do is not make snap judgments during the first few minutes when he walks in. And I always recommend giving a man a second date if he appears to be a nice guy during your first date, even though you don't feel any chemistry. Chemistry can build!

- **Don't put all your eggs in one basket:** Men appear and disappear online all the time. You should be e-mailing and talking to several men at once, if you have the option. That way, the risk that one of them will disappoint you should be mitigated by the others. Don't put all your eggs in one basket.

- **Don't give up after one (or a few) bad experience(s):**
Many women are reluctant at first, but eventually start online dating. Then they have a bad experience and swear off the entire online medium: the man was a liar, he looked much worse than his photo, he was charming and solicitous but then never called back, he never showed up for the date at all, no one appealing even replied to the ad. Well, it doesn't make sense to give up altogether, does it? You have been warned about these risks in advance. You're bound to have disappointments in any medium but you have to persist. This certainly happens offline, as well, and you don't decide to become a nun! I know so many women who have found great relationships—and several who have found husbands—online. There may be a hundred frogs out there, but one of them is your prince.

BENCHMARKING

How do you know if your online dating is a success? Of course the answer is easy if you're engaged to a man you met online, but prior to that you should be getting the following results:

- You should be receiving a minimum of 2 e-mail responses per week from "decent" men—those who are appealing enough that you would like to learn more about them.
- You should be writing back to a minimum of 2 men per week.
- You should go on a minimum of 3 dates per month with men you meet online.
- You should have a second date with one man you meet online per month, which attests to how good you are at the screening process.
- You should always leave from a bad date with something good that came out of it: maybe a recommendation for a good book

to read, or a suggestion for a new service or party for singles that you should try, or simply a nice man to keep in your address book who wasn't right for you (but who can be invited to attend your *Program* Party in Step #12 with his single friends). By the way, this guideline applies to all bad dates, not just the ones from the Internet.

- You're learning and becoming more efficient with the process after each new online experience.

WHAT TO DO IF YOU'RE NOT GETTING THE EXPECTED RESULTS

If you're not getting the expected results, you should quickly go back and make changes to your profile. This is the beauty of the online medium. Nothing is written in stone. The issue may be something simple: Perhaps your profile appears at the end of a long list of search results that a man requests. Many sites will put you in a higher rotation of search results when you merely change or update your profile (sometimes if you change only one word). Therefore, you should regularly update your profile (once or twice per month).

But the issue may be deeper. Make sure you solicit feedback from your Mentor and candid friends (especially male) about your ad. You may come across as generic, cold, needy, too serious, too sexy, or any number of things that you may never have considered. Your photo may not be flattering. You need help figuring it all out, so ask people you respect for input.

Also, like a good marketer, you should use the trial-and-error technique for troubleshooting. Try one photo for a week and see what kind of replies you get. If they're bad, then switch the photo the following week using different poses, clothing, or backgrounds and see what happens. Change your headline, change the age range you're seeking, or change the description of what you seek in a man. If you are getting lots of "first" e-mails, but men stop replying after your response, show the correspondence to your Mentor to evaluate whether you're doing something wrong. Keep trying different approaches until something clicks.

YOU MAY BE WONDERING . . .

There are so many different elements to discuss about online dating that I could write a whole book just on this subject. You may want to read a book solely dedicated to online dating if you need a more comprehensive understanding beyond these marketing tactics. But here are five questions most frequently asked by women in my seminars:

• *Is it okay to search for male profiles and write to the man first?*

Usually not. The same dating rules apply online as offline: Femininity wins. Men like to do the pursuing. Statistics show that 80% of male online daters make the first move. If the man doesn't pursue you first online, any relationship you might initiate will be skewed in his favor. You want to be adored in your relationship and ultimately in your marriage, and if you're chasing him—even with the simple gesture of writing to him first—this doesn't bode well for the dynamic between the two of you in the long run. Any "normal" man who has posted a profile online is also searching for women on that site. So if you haven't caught his eye during *his* search, chances are he isn't interested.

There are, however, two exceptions. First, many dating sites regularly send "direct matches" to your in-box, which is an automatic feature that searches men's profiles for the criteria you listed (age, height, religion, and so forth) and finds new members for you who match. The wider the net you cast with your criteria, the more matches will be found. If you receive a profile directly from the dating service that appeals to you, it's okay to send a short, low-key e-mail to the man because technically you're not initiating anything—the dating service initiated it, and you're just following through. You can write something short like, "The computer sent me your profile and it says we might be a match. Who am I to tempt fate?"

And there is another feature I've seen that could be described as an online version of flirting. Some dating sites allow you to "show interest" in a man by sending him a symbol. The symbol (which can be a "wink," but varies by site) indicates you are interested in his profile and would welcome an e-mail from him, but it's not quite as bold as sending him an actual text message. Think of it as making online eye contact, where the man can still respond in the traditional dating role and write the first text e-mail to you. This is similar to seeing a man you like at a cocktail party, and smiling at him as an invitation to come over and say hello. I especially like this feature in large cities, where there are thousands of profiles and a man might have missed yours during his search.

Secondly, for women who experience a low volume of responses to their ads from good men, and have dutifully gone back and revised their profile according to the feedback they received, you can bend the rules once as discussed in Step #3, Packaging. You can actively search men's profiles and send one low-key e-mail to each man who appeals to you. This is an attempt to spark connections and generate some volume. Perhaps pick one line from each man's profile that intrigued you, and send a two-sentence e-mail to him such as, "I'm intrigued. Stephen Frey is my all-time favorite author, too." A link to your own profile will automatically be attached to your e-mail so he can check you out.

But be prepared when you initiate contact: The man may not respond, so keep your ego intact. You don't want his lack of interest to send you into a tailspin that makes you give up online dating altogether. Never write to him more than once if he doesn't respond, and allow him to initiate all contact going forward in the early stages of correspondence and dating.

• Should I lie about my age online?

You never want to lie about anything. It always catches up with you. But age is a tricky subject, both online and offline. On an Internet dating site, men will type in certain age parameters to use in their search process, and if you fall outside the age range by even one year, your profile will not be shown to them. And then there are the stereotypes associated with certain ages. Men assume that women in their late thirties and early forties want to get married and have babies right away. Men want to date younger women, no matter what decade you or they are in. So what should you do?

Go back to your goal: You want to find a husband. And you don't want to waste your time in the process. If you lie now about your age (either online or off), you risk wasting your time in a relationship that could ultimately end because it is based on something false. So find men to whom your age *does* appeal. If you are in your thirties, you sound young to men in their forties.

If you are in your forties, you sound young to men in their fifties. If you are in your fifties, you sound young to men in their sixties. And so forth, up the line. As long as *you* are willing to cast a wider net in the age category, you'll be fine admitting your true age.

Women over 50 especially worry about revealing their age. But tell the truth if you want a mature man. Mature men are looking for someone like you: They want an equal partner, they don't want a woman who reminds them of their own daughter, they probably don't want to start a second family, they don't want to explain who Gracie Allen is, and they don't want to hold in their stomachs all night on a date. If you're still concerned about your age, though, you can always add something in your profile such as, "I'm a young 61" or "I'm 73 years young" to emphasize your youthful spirit and interests.

• *What is the best approach to completing the multiple-choice sections of the online dating questionnaires?*

When posting your profile, you will be asked to select answers to multiple-choice questions regarding such areas as your profession, your income, your social habits, and your lifestyle. You should be honest, but review the tips and suggestions noted in earlier sections of this chapter regarding creating your screen name, headline, and profile. Much of that discussion can be applied to these multiple-choice sections as well. The important part that my clients always forget is to stay consistent with their brand. If your brand is "Elegant, Intellectual, Antique Collector," then it would be consistent if the favorite type of music you selected in the multiple-choice section was "classical" rather than "rap." If you don't quite know what to put down, you can always select the "I'll tell you later" option, which is perfectly acceptable.

• *Should I respond to e-mails from men in whom I'm not interested?*

It is certainly not required that you respond to e-mails from men in whom you're not interested, but there can be a big advantage to doing so! It is a nice protocol to reply to anyone who has selected you and taken the time to write you a note, even if the man does not seem like he's for you. Not many women do this, so your gesture can really make you stand out.

To save time, you can draft a standard reply for such occurrences, and simply cut and paste it into your reply. Send something short such as: "Thank you for taking the time to write to me. It doesn't look like we're a match, but I really appreciate your message." If you have other women friends who are also dating online, and you think he might be interesting to one of them, suggest at the end of your standard reply that he check out your friend's profile. You can then say directly, "If you have a friend who may want to meet me, please forward my profile as well." You have accomplished three things with this response. First, you have been polite to respond at all. Second, if your girlfriend is interested in this man, you have created goodwill with her, and she may return the favor in the future by introducing you to someone else. Third, if this man forwards your profile to a friend of his, you might just wind up meeting someone wonderful. Stranger things have happened!

• *If you start dating someone, when should you take down your online profile?*

Most sites allow you to take down your profile and not pay membership fees during this time. Your relationship should be classified as "exclusive" for you to decide to do so. You should always keep your options open until you are quite sure he may be The One. You're not on the slow boat to China, remember? You are moving quickly and efficiently through this searching and dating process, and you don't want to miss any opportunities that may arise. The man you're dating may be Mr. Right, in which case you'll gladly drop all other options and convert that relationship into a commitment, but until you have every indication that the same intent is on his agenda as well, keep your profile up and continue screening the replies that you receive. No need to tell him you're doing this unless he specifically asks and indicates he'd like to be exclusive. If he sees your profile posted and hints that he's unhappy about it, but doesn't ask you for a commitment, then he is being unfair. He needs to "put his money where his mouth is." You will learn more about this in Step #15, Exit Strategy. And what was he doing surfing women's profiles in the first place?

You have been successful with Step #7, and can begin Step #8, if you:

1. Conducted market research to assess the online marketplace.
2. Carefully prepared and posted a fabulous photo of yourself, plus one or two more back-up photos that are realistic but still good.
3. Strategically created your screen name, headline, and profiles before posting them.
4. Verified with your Mentor and friends that your ad is appealing, makes you stand out, and creates intrigue.
5. Understand the pitfalls of online dating.
6. Registered with a large online dating site.
7. Are getting the expected online dating results.

Step #8

Guerrilla Marketing:

Do Something Different!

**WHAT I LEARNED AT
HARVARD BUSINESS SCHOOL**

Guerrilla marketing is the use of nonconventional, cost-effective, out-of-the-box tactics to reach your prospective customers. It's a technique primarily designed for small businesses that don't have large marketing budgets but need to compete against giant companies. Guerrilla marketing uses many small tactics to regularly and consistently reach the customer and achieve a big result.

There are many examples of these nontraditional marketing tactics. For example, a small record label company might pay "cool" inner-city teenagers a small fee to hand out samples of cutting-edge rap music to their friends in school, hoping to start a trend. Or a microbrew beer company might give bar owners free plastic table caddies that display the appetizer menu hoping customers will then order the beer featured on the caddy as they select what to eat. You can successfully market a product simply via lots of small, effective tactics like these.

Most businesses employ only the standard, same-old marketing methods; they don't use all of the creative, low-cost marketing tools available to them. The companies that try different, street-smart approaches can have a competitive advantage. At its core, guerrilla marketing subscribes to the idea that persistence and cleverness are more important than big budgets.

SHAKE IT UP!

Are you doing the same things over and over again by force of habit? Are your routines familiar and comfortable? You may be in a personal rut. When it comes to finding your husband, you have to get out of that rut and do something different. Probably the reason you haven't found him yet is because he isn't in the small orbit of your office, apartment building, local Starbucks, or circle of friends. Many people don't even know they're in a rut because they *like* what they do, where they do it, and with whom. But getting out of your rut has the power to change your single status. A rut isn't necessarily a bad place, but it is something that makes your life insular and prevents you from achieving your goal of finding a husband. In this step, you're going to shake it all up with many different, street-smart guerrilla marketing tactics.

THE RUT QUIZ

Look closely at everything you do and when you do it. Examine everywhere you go, and everyone who surrounds you. Is there justification for it all, or merely force of habit? Take the Rut Quiz to determine if you're in a rut:

1. Do you go to work via the same means of transportation every day?
2. Do you get your coffee at the same place every morning?
3. Do you eat lunch at a handful of the same places every day, or—even worse—at home or at your desk?
4. Have you been using the same dry cleaner for years?
5. Do you have a few favorite restaurants, bars, or hangouts that you frequent?
6. When you buy a book, do you always buy it from the same store (or Web site)?
7. Do you have one hobby or sport that occupies most of your free time?
8. Do you have a few close friends who comprise the bulk of your social life?
9. Have you had similar *types* of friends over the years, even though the names and faces may have changed?
10. When someone asks you "How are you?" or "What's new?" do you usually give the same response, more or less?
11. Do you rarely initiate conversation with a stranger?

If you answered yes to five or more of these questions, you are definitely in a rut. And your future husband probably isn't there in the rut with you. The good news is that it's easy to fix, and making changes will greatly improve your chances of meeting Mr. Right.

THE EMERGENCY EXIT

A successful marketer doesn't do things because that's the way they've always been done before. You need to closely examine everything in your life and methodically make changes to get out of your rut. You want a *strategic* approach to your life now as you're looking for your husband. Everything has a purpose, even your errands! Nothing is sacred. Find the "emergency exit" in the building and escape your rut.

Get out three pieces of paper. On the first page, write down where and when you go for your errands, basic needs, and social life. For example, you might have a list like this:

Where I Go (and When)

- **Groceries:** Safeway on Main Street (Saturday mornings).
- **Dry cleaning:** Executive Cleaners on 3rd Avenue (Thursday after work).
- **Hardware store:** Ace Hardware (no regular time).
- **Drugstore:** Walgreens on Main Street (Saturday mornings).
- **Gas station:** Exxon on 6th Avenue (no regular time).
- **Health club:** Downtown Athletic Club (Wednesday and Friday after work).
- **Coffee:** Starbucks on Main Street (weekday mornings before work).
- **Dinner with friends:** Mel's Café or Pasta Haven (Saturday nights).
- **Deli:** Joe's Deli (Sunday mornings).
- **Dentist:** Dr. Smiley (no regular time).
- **Dog walking:** Regent Park (weekdays after work; weekend mornings).

- **Vacations:** Cape Cod or home to Chicago (last week in August; Christmas).

... et cetera. You will probably have a list of at least 25 places that you go to regularly when you really think about everything in your life.

Now, on the second page, make a list of everything you do for work and fun. For example, your list might look like this:

What I Do
- **Job:** Mortgage broker.
- **Exercise:** Treadmill or yoga class (at Downtown Athletic Club).
- **Sports:** Tennis.
- **Friday night:** Rent a video or meet friends at Le Bar.
- **Hobby:** Writing poetry.
- **Adult education:** Spanish classes.
- **Volunteer:** Meals on Wheels.

... et cetera. You will probably have a list of at least 10 things you do regularly.

On the third page, make a list of everyone who actively surrounds you in your life:

Who Surrounds Me
- **Work:** Megan, Sally, Jim.
- **Phone pals:** Carol, Sheila, Brenda.
- **E-mail pals:** Adam, Erin, Molly.
- **Weekends:** Jane and Paul, Carol, Bonnie.
- **Exercise:** Susan.
- **Travel:** Susan.
- **Shopping:** Bonnie.

- **Spanish classes:** Sarah.
- **Family:** Mom, sister Gina.

. . . et cetera. You will probably have a list of 10 to 20 people who surround you in your immediate circle.

Take a few minutes to examine your lists. You may see how insular your life has become if you are always doing the same things, and how few chances you really have to meet Mr. Right in such a small orbit. The *quantity* of places, activities, and people you recorded is not the issue; the problem is the *repetition*. After age 35, we have all developed more ingrained habits. Imagine how many more "chance meetings" you could orchestrate if you simply changed your daily route!

If you need inspiration to make these critical changes, let me tell you what happened when a 36-year-old woman named Alison did one small thing to get out of her rut. For years, she had been going to a Starbucks near her office every morning to get her favorite coffee—a tall half-caf vanilla latte. She was addicted to it and absolutely *had* to start her day with this concoction. When I looked at the patterns of her everyday life in Step #8, I asked her if there were any other coffee shops near her home or office that she could try. She almost went into cardiac arrest. Her coffee was sacred! But this is the e-mail I later received from her:

Last Thursday, the line at Starbucks was really long and I was in a huge hurry. I remembered your suggestion about changing my routine, so it seemed like a good time to try something different. I went across the street to this shop called Peaberry Coffee. I doubted they would even have my half-caf vanilla latte on the menu, but they did. I was just about to leave, and I was at the condiment bar putting a packet of Equal in my latte, and I noticed this man standing next to me. He had spilled part of his coffee and was looking for napkins. So I grabbed a handful of napkins and gave them to him. This may sound odd, but I liked the way he was so calm about spilling his coffee. He didn't get frazzled. Ironically, I was carrying a book called *Don't Sweat the Small Stuff*, and he asked me if it was any good. We started to talk and I really liked him! His name is Ron. But he left after a few minutes without even asking for my last name or where I worked. So I went back to Peaberry Coffee at the same time on Friday, hoping to run into him, and there he was! He was reading a newspaper, and I think he was hoping to see me too!

Alison and Ron had coffee together that day, began dating, and have now been married for 2 years. At their wedding reception they served half-caf vanilla lattes to pay tribute to how they met. Alison can't imagine what her life would be like today if the line at Starbucks had been shorter that Thursday!

BLUEPRINT FOR CHANGE

So the first part of your guerrilla marketing plan is clear: Get out of your rut and get into new opportunities to meet men. Consider everything you've written on your lists about where you go, when you go, what you do, and who surrounds you . . . and change it *all*, over and over again. Be strategic about making changes by going through your list methodically and setting daily goals for yourself. Don't just make spur-of-the-moment decisions to do something different now and then. While spontaneity may happen, and I encourage it when an opportunity arises (as in Alison's example above), sporadic changes are not really going to get you out of your rut. You need an organized plan of attack.

Set an initial goal for yourself to make one change per day. You can gradually work up to three changes per day as you get more comfortable with this step. For example, your weekly planning calendar might look like this:

- **Monday:** Grocery shop at Whole Foods rather than Safeway (after work).
- **Tuesday:** Try new dry cleaner on Fifth Avenue rather than Executive Cleaners (during my lunch break).
- **Wednesday:** Get coffee at Bob's Deli rather than Starbucks (30 minutes earlier before work). Call cousin Joel whom I haven't talked to in a year to say hello.
- **Thursday:** Invite new co-worker out to lunch. Attend adult education class on dog training (in the evening).
- **Friday:** Take subway to work instead of driving (in the morning). Stop by Happy Hour at Downtown Athletic Club after evening weight conditioning class instead of taking yoga class and then rushing home.
- **Saturday:** Walk dog in Central Park rather than Regent Park (30 minutes earlier in the morning). Buy lightbulbs at Home Depot (instead of Ace Hardware). Grocery shop at King's Mart rather than Safeway or Whole Foods (in the afternoon).
- **Sunday:** Buy bagels at Einstein Bagels rather than Joe's Deli. Invite Jenny my neighbor for brunch instead of best pal Susan.

Continue to cycle through your lists each week again and again, changing your routine. While the many decisions you make, like grocery shopping at Whole Foods on Monday and

King's Mart on Saturday, may appear random, at least it's *something different*. You have just created many new and different opportunities to meet men. And that's the point! And in keeping with guerrilla marketing techniques, this couldn't be a less expensive step, right?

CONVERSATION STARTERS

Props

So there you are grocery shopping at Whole Foods on Monday night, dutifully getting out of your rut and placing yourself in a new environment. And you see an intriguing man in the frozen food aisle. What do you do? There is a great guerrilla tactic that can be used to leverage this chance meeting into a connection: Carry a "conversation starter." This is a physical item that is designed to prompt curiosity and provoke interaction. You take it everywhere to trigger spontaneous conversations with interesting strangers. The idea is that a man might see your conversation starter and have an easier time initiating contact with you. Many men are shy, and all men don't want to look or feel stupid. So your conversation starter may provide him with an excuse to talk to you so he doesn't have to come up with some trite pickup line. You should select a signature item that is consistent with your brand, and keep it visible everywhere you go.

For example, books are great conversation starters. One woman, Diane, was living in Maine but was originally from Texas. She developed the brand: "Texas, Spontaneous, Photographer." The "Texas" attribute really made her unique in Maine. She carried a photography book with her titled *Texas on My Mind*. Be sure the book has a big picture of something obvious on the cover, or large and legible words. If the man can't grasp the subject of the book quickly or read the title easily, it's useless! If one of your brand attributes is "Aspiring Writer," you might carry with you the book *Nonfiction Book Proposals Anyone Can Write*. If your brand includes being from New Hampshire, maybe you could wear a large button on your coat that says LIVE FREE OR DIE (the state motto). If your brand includes "World Traveler," you might *not* want to carry the latest issue of *Fitness* magazine, but it would be consistent to carry the latest issue of *Travel* magazine.

Another idea for a great conversation starter would be to wear something (a T-shirt, a hat, or a pin) with a foreign slogan on it. A man who wants to meet you can ask you to translate the slogan. Or you could wear something with a sports team logo, university logo, or another city name. All of these are easy prompts for a man looking to initiate conversation. Women should always carry or wear a conversation starter whenever they're in public to capitalize on chance encounters.

Be sure to look for *other* people's conversation starters, too. Maybe someone sitting next to you on an airplane or standing next to you in line at the car wash isn't *intentionally* carrying a prop, but most people have something in their possession that could provoke an interesting question from you.

Ice-Breakers

What if that intriguing man back in the frozen food aisle just doesn't see your big, obvious conversation starter? Or he sees it, but doesn't say anything? In this case, it's time to take a more active approach and initiate some dialogue yourself. The actual words you use are almost irrelevant. A man who looks up and is attracted to you usually won't pass judgment on your words. He will decide based on nonverbal cues whether or not he wants to engage in dialogue. You've got to love men for that! Perhaps you can quickly think of an ice-breaker and say light-heartedly, "What's your favorite frozen dessert here?" or "Wow, why do you think the store is so crowded today?" *The important thing is to ask a question that requires more than a yes or no answer.* You want to build a bridge to more conversation.

If you're really too shy to ask a stranger a question, whether you are at the grocery store or at a party, then there's always the tried-and-true standby line where you simply say "Hi" and smile. This might lead to a dead end, especially if he's shy, too, and he answers back only with "Hi." But this standby approach is better than saying nothing.

You'll quickly find out by a man's responsiveness if he is not at all interested in conversing with you (he may be married, in a hurry, gay, or simply not attracted to you), and you'll continue on your way. Nothing ventured, nothing gained.

Always be looking for an opening to start a conversation with an intriguing man. Don't bury your head in a newspaper or walk around on autopilot. You want to look for chance encounter possibilities. You have nothing to lose by trying to start a short dialogue. Of course, some people are rude and simply won't reply to a stranger or just want to be left alone, but the more you can engage someone, the better your odds that you'll gain something (a new idea, some useful information, a contact, or a new friend).

CONVERSATION FOLLOW-UP

Refer to the Future

When a conversation has been started, and you like the man you're talking to, how can you ensure that you'll meet again? One tactic is to refer to something in the future and see if he asks how he can contact you to follow up. For example, one woman, Cecile, was enjoying some witty banter one day with a cute man standing behind her in the take-out line at the deli. She told him a joke that she had just heard from someone at her office. Then she said, "That's the only clean joke I know. I'll save my other ones for another time." The man immediately picked up on her cue and asked how he could reach her "to hear her other jokes." Okay, not the most subtle line in the world, but it worked.

If you've referred to the future and the man doesn't pick up on your cue, you can try one of these other tactics:

- **Let it slip:** You can inadvertently divulge contact information about yourself (your last name, say, or where you work) if you want him to be able to find you later.
- **Ask for a referral:** "Do you know a good car mechanic? If you do, let me tell you how you can reach me to give me that phone number."
- **Offer to provide information:** "I just read an interesting book about this, but I can't remember the name of it. Would you like me to e-mail the title to you when I get home?"

Personal Cards

Another convenient way to continue any conversation is to have in your possession a personal card printed with your name and phone number on it. You can offer the card to select men, and also to women who might want to fix you up with someone. In the business world, you wouldn't leave the office without your business cards. In the dating world, you shouldn't leave home without a few personal cards in your purse or your pocket. This is practical, not crass. You can hand out your business cards from work if you have some, as long as they're not overtly intimidating or too far outside your brand image. If you print your own, you can do this easily at a copy store for a small fee. Just write down your name, phone number, and e-mail address, bring it into your nearest Kinko's, and a salesperson will assist you with printing choices for layout, paper color, and font style. If printed cards are a bit too formal for you, at least have a pen and small pad of nice notepaper in your purse to write down your information, should the occasion arise.

CONVERSATION RUTS

Have you ever realized that the things you *say* may also be keeping you in a rut? Think about this: What would happen if you gave a completely different answer the next time someone asked you, "What's new?" I'm not talking about replying to a new man you meet; I'm talking about replying to the people you already know. Maybe your usual reply is, "Not much" or "Same old, same old," or "What's new with *you*?" Perhaps you're more clever with your responses and you actually think of something specific to relate: "Oh, I just got a new cat. Look at this photo of him!" or "Well, I'm training to run the Chicago marathon this spring. It's hard work!" Whatever your answer may be, even if it changes from time to time, it may actually be closing doors without you knowing it.

These autopilot conversations are missed opportunities to "make a sale." If your #1 priority is finding a husband, consider framing your everyday conversations around this mission. Rather than having the same old conversation, or giving the same old answer, or even giving an answer that actually conveys something randomly new in your life, you should strategically communicate your #1 priority.

As a top salesperson will tell you, the rule is "ABC": Always Be Closing. Try to "close a sale" if you have the opportunity. For example, a girlfriend sees you at the hair salon and approaches you to say hello. She hasn't seen you in a few months and asks, "Hi! How are you?" If you are conscious of escaping your rut and turning a casual conversation into an opportunity to find a husband, you might reply: "I'm great, thanks! Since I saw you last, I have made a big commitment to find someone to share my life with this year. I would love to meet as many new men as possible. Say, do you by any chance know any single men?"

Imagine the possibilities that can result because you gave a different answer at the beginning of this conversation other than, "Fine thanks, how are *you*?"

IF OPPORTUNITY DOESN'T KNOCK, THEN OPEN THE DOOR YOURSELF

What if there's a man you've seen regularly from afar, but you don't know how to start a conversation with him? You can break out of the rut of waiting for him to talk to you first, even without bending the femininity rules once. If you've admired him for a while, he's probably not a total stranger. Maybe you've seen him in the cafeteria at your office, so you know he's employed with your company, but he has never noticed you. Or maybe he lives in your apartment building and you saw him a few times in the elevator, but you weren't alone and it seemed awkward to make small talk in front of other people. Well, here's a guerrilla marketing tactic just for these special circumstances.

You can orchestrate a legitimate reason to approach a man you've been wanting to meet. Let's think about that guy you've seen in your office cafeteria: How can you get his attention? Consider volunteering for the next charity walk-a-thon in your city. As a participant in the event, you'll be given a sponsor sign-up sheet. You'll have to roam around your office building asking people if they will sponsor you at ten cents a mile, right? So, this is an easy excuse to meet him. Hey, it's for charity!

Approach him in the cafeteria and explain what you're doing. The walk-a-thon provides much fuel for conversation: descriptions of the charity, details about the event, how many sponsors you've already collected, and lots more. If he doesn't seem interested in you after this exchange, you'll at least have one more legitimate follow-up opportunity when you return to collect his money after the event. (If he didn't sponsor you, he's not right for you anyway: What kind of man won't shell out a few dollars for charity?) But if there is still no interest on his part, well, at least you gave it a shot, you've done a good thing by raising money for charity in the process, and can now stop pining for him and move on.

If you are attracted to that man in the elevator from your apartment building, what could you do? Remember to think creatively. Maybe you can join the building's Committee to Collect Money for the Doorman's Christmas Gift. An endeavor like this would likely involve ringing everyone's doorbell in the apartment building to collect money. So you'll have to knock on his door! Try to come up with any legitimate reason (just once) to interact with someone you admire from afar. If the man doesn't *think* you've pursued him first, technically you haven't bent the rules even once. Sometimes a guerrilla marketer just has to open her own doors.

BIG CHANGES

So far we've talked about fairly easy-fix changes to your routine, such as shopping at a different store, toting conversation starters, rethinking some of your everyday answers, and creating legitimate excuses to meet men. But I'm sorry to say that you must also consider two very *big* changes to your routine. These are so big that you may be tempted to dismiss them. "Oh, I could never do *that*!" you might respond. But hear me out . . .

Your Job

Here is a simple question: Are you in a job where you have opportunities to meet interesting men? Yes or no. If the answer is no, you might consider finding a new job. Your job may be the primary cause of your rut. I realize that this is a big statement, and for many women the task will be impossible, but it's something I want you to contemplate carefully. Do you remember your answer to the three questions in Step #1, Marketing Focus—especially question number two: "Would you do *anything* to find a husband?" If your answer was honestly and truly "yes," then finding a husband trumps your job for the next 12 to 18 months.

You probably spend half of your waking hours each day at work. That's a lot of time wasted if you don't have any contact with eligible men. Assess the odds of finding a husband in your current work environment, versus the odds in new jobs that you could envision securing, given your abilities. Of course, very few jobs are a mecca for meeting hordes of eligible men, but use your judgment to assess your current situation. For example, even if you work only with women, your job may provide you with a network of people who can fix you up. Or the job may involve meeting many male clients. Or your job could send you on business trips with potential to meet new men. These are not bad situations.

But what if you work alone at your home computer or in a very small office with one or two other people and the best possibility for meeting someone new is when the Xerox repair man comes calling? Or maybe you work in a bar where you meet a lot of men, but not the right kind of men and not in the right kind of situation. Think hard about your other options. Be willing to change your job if you can find another one with more husband-hunting possibilities, even if it pays less.

I have one client who did something radical. She had such a busy job that she never had enough time for *The Program*. So she took a year off from work to focus on finding a husband. Clearly, it requires a significant amount of financial savings to be able to afford this course of action, but if you have the means, it might be worth considering. The only caveat is that if you want results by the end of your year off, you have to treat *The Program* like a full-time job. You are not "on vacation," but rather using each day to network, plan, and participate in all *Program*-esque activities.

Your Home

Do you live in a location that is conducive to meeting new men? Are you in an optimal city and neighborhood that maximize your odds of finding a husband? Think carefully about this question. Some neighborhoods are remote and keep you from meeting new people, or are too suburban to attract many singles. Some cities have notoriously bad odds for single women. San Francisco, Washington, D.C., and New York City are cities that women consistently complain about as having few bachelors. Now, if you live in one of these cities, you don't have to start packing your bags immediately, but if an opportunity arises to make a geographic change (you hear about a job in another city, or your closest friend moves and suggests you join her, or the lease on your apartment is ending soon), consider it seriously.

One woman, Kate (age 40), had lived in Manhattan for 10 years. She saw that too many single women were looking for too few single men. She saw a lot of younger women in "glossier packages," and too many women who seemed just like her. She wasn't unique. One night it simply dawned on her, as if a switch had been flipped: The odds of her meeting Mr. Right in Manhattan were not good. The lease on her apartment was ending in two months, so she took this opportunity to look at a map and decide where else she might want to live. Her first criterion was to find a place where her style and personality would be distinctive. Her second criterion was a place where she could work in a less demanding job (so she could focus on finding a husband), but still afford a decent lifestyle. She picked Minneapolis; she already had two friends (a married couple) who lived there. During the next two months, she networked like crazy to obtain as many names as possible of friends of friends who lived in Minneapolis. She quit her job and moved. It was a brave and perhaps "crazy" move because she didn't have a new job lined up yet. She had no idea if the odds were really better for single women in Minneapolis than in Manhattan, but at least she would have a whole new area to explore, and everyone she met there would be new.

As this book goes to press, Kate has been in her new city for one month. Through all the names she accumulated from friends, and friends of friends, she has gone on four dates through fix-ups and three from online dating. She says her net is cast so wide that her only requirement is "a man who knows how to use cutlery." She has met two single girlfriends who have advised her about everything from the best singles organizations to the best volunteer activities. On average, she has two job interviews per week. During one interview, she described candidly how she had moved to Minneapolis because she hoped to improve her chances of meeting more single men. The interviewer replied, "My wife is a hopeless matchmaker, and as soon as I tell her that, she'll have half a dozen men to fix you up with!" Maybe Kate was in the right place at the right time.

You have succeeded with Step #8, and can begin Step #9, if you:

1. Analyzed your routine by making three lists of where you go (and when), what you do, and who surrounds you.

2. Methodically went through your lists and made changes to each and every item, again and again.

3. Set goals for yourself to do one to three different things each day.

4. Selected a conversation starter that is consistent with your brand and now carry it with you at all times.

5. Thought about conversation ruts and made efforts to give strategic answers to casual questions.

6. Created a legitimate excuse to initiate a conversation if there is a man you admire from afar.

7. Challenged yourself to consider whether big changes in your job or home are needed in your life, and, if so, started looking for transition opportunities.

Step #9

Niche Marketing:

"Date" Women

**WHAT I LEARNED AT
HARVARD BUSINESS SCHOOL**

Niche marketing is a powerful tool in selling any product. The notion is that your product has small groups of ideal buyers who are subsets of the larger marketplace. These groups (or niches) have the most eager and willing buyers because they have certain traits that are ideally suited to what you are selling. While you would continue to sell your product to a general customer base, you might market your product more heavily to a high-potential niche. For example, some cosmetics companies offer hypoallergenic face creams, which they sell to regular customers in any department store. But some of these companies have realized that the patients of dermatologists are a perfect niche market for their products. Dermatologists have a high number of patients who are ideally suited for hypoallergenic products, especially face creams. So a few smart cosmetics companies have created a special sales force to sell directly through dermatologists to their patients.

Another example of niche marketing is this book. *The Program* really can work for anyone: women and men of all ages, and gays and lesbians. But I have chosen one niche, "women over 35 looking for husbands," for marketing the book because I believe they (you) are my best customers.

WHY "DATE" WOMEN?

Women are often an overlooked niche when you are looking for a husband. No, I'm not suggesting that you pursue "romantic" dates with women if you are heterosexual! But here's a fact: Women are more likely to fix you up on a blind date than are men. Certain women will be your target niche because they are most likely to "buy" your request for fix-ups.

So your task in Step #9 is to identify six female friends or acquaintances, take each out on a "date," and directly ask her to fix you up. It's not as simple as it sounds. This is not what you have already been doing when you've asked your friends to fix you up in the past. This is a strategic endeavor designed to systematically identify women with high potential to know single men, and get them to actively fix you up.

THE GOALS FOR YOUR "DATES"

The four goals for your female "dates" are to:

1. Let these six women know about your marriage focus.
2. Ask them explicitly to fix you up with any single men they know.

3. Brainstorm about eligible men they may know but might have overlooked.

4. Ask these women in turn to ask their friends and relatives (who may in turn ask *their* friends and relatives) to fix you up.

This last goal may be the most significant, as it starts a powerful "viral" marketing process—that is, spreading the word in marketing-speak—that may have results you could never imagine.

HOW TO SELECT YOUR "DATES"

Not just *any* woman qualifies for this step. The women should be selected carefully for your niche marketing campaign with the following five criteria in mind:

Criterion #1) Married: Married women won't (or at least shouldn't!) have their own dating agendas and be looking for the same single men. There won't be a conflict of interest.

  Note: One caveat here is not to choose a married woman who has a single sister or close single friend in your city. She may be on the lookout for her instead—unless you have very different qualities than her sister or her friend, in which case this woman meets the criterion.

Criterion #2) Happy: Happily married women usually want other people also to be happy and are more likely to be selfless enough to assist you. They won't be consumed with their own marital problems and thus can be emotionally available to concentrate on you.

Criterion #3) Well connected: Women who have large networks of friends, neighbors, relatives, co-workers (or co-workers of their husbands), colleagues on charity boards, classmates in adult education courses, or college or graduate school alumni networks are the ones best positioned to know, or know someone who knows, eligible men.

Criterion #4) Reliable: Women whom you can count upon to follow through (*not* the flighty, flaky, or too-busy ones) are those who will take your request seriously and actually make the phone calls and give your number to eligible men.

Criterion #5) Experienced at matchmaking: If you know someone who has played matchmaker before and knows the ins and outs of the process, that's all the better. Especially if she has had past successes, she'll be eager for more of the gratification that comes from having brought together two people who found happiness.

TROUBLESHOOTING

• *What if I don't know six eligible women for "dates"?*

If you're thinking to yourself, "I don't know six married, happy, well-connected, reliable, experienced matchmakers," I assure you that you know six women who fit *most* of the criteria, which is a good place to start. Think beyond your address book or Palm Pilot. Remember to ask your Mentor for help here, too. Think of women at any age (what about one of your mother's friends? or one of your adult daughter's friends?), at any stage of friendship (your college roommate from 20 years ago? someone you just met at the gym? a friend of a friend?), and in any city (your old friend in another city could be surprisingly well positioned to explore her network and find friends of friends in *your* city).

Let me give you some examples. One client from L.A., Jackie, age 58, went on a vacation with her teenage son to Hawaii last month. During her stay there at a major hotel, she became friendly with the concierge. The concierge was a young, outgoing woman in her late twenties who mentioned to Jackie that she hoped to move to L.A. the following year and study acting. Jackie had a great idea: She asked the concierge to have a quick drink with her one evening after her shift ended (a *Program* "date") to talk about L.A. Jackie gave her some contacts she had in the entertainment industry back home and offered to help her further when she relocated. Jackie then steered the conversation around to the issue of her recent divorce and how hard it is to meet eligible men. She then remarked, "In your job, you must come in contact with people all the time from L.A. If you happen to meet any single, older men who are staying here at the hotel, keep me in mind. You'd be a great matchmaker!" The concierge said she would be happy to help. The two women exchanged cards and will keep in touch, hopefully both helping each other in the future. Jackie really thought outside the box for this "date"!

Here's another example. A friend of mine, Maureen, age 39, once asked me on a "date" (via telephone) to help her find single men in her current city, Portland, Oregon. Although I live in Denver and don't know anyone who lives there, I did two things.

First, I looked in my business school alumni online database and sorted by city. I found three men who lived in Portland. I knew only one of them, who was married, but I sent him an e-mail and told him about this wonderful 39-year-old woman there who would love to be introduced to some single men. He had a single co-worker who later called Maureen for a date.

Second, I asked several friends in my own city (Denver) if they knew anyone in Portland. Most didn't, but when my mother, who was visiting me one day, overheard me asking someone on the phone about eligible men in Portland, she had an idea. She had just been with a tour group in London and had met a nice, older couple from Portland—and they had mentioned their single son in his forties. Unfortunately, their son lived in Seattle. But my mother phoned this couple anyway, and they later arranged for their son to take Maureen on a blind date the following month when he was home in Portland visiting his parents for Thanksgiving.

Well, Maureen did *not* marry either of these men, but both were attractive, interesting men with whom she had a nice evening. It gave her hope that there were still good men out there. More significantly, the man from Seattle had mentioned that he had tried out the national dating service called "It's Just Lunch" and had a good experience with the women he met in Seattle. Maureen had never heard of this kind of dating service, but a few months later when she was on Step #11, Mass Marketing, she remembered the tip from that Seattle guy and looked in the Portland phone book to find a Local "It's Just Lunch" service. So she signed up. It was expensive, but she added the cost to her Marketing Budget and hoped for the best. Her second lunch date was with a man she married about 10 months later!

This example demonstrates how niche marketing can work in ways that you'd never imagine. Maureen eventually found her husband from a tip she received on a date with a man from another city who had been set up with her by his parents who knew the mother of her niche marketing "date" (me)! What a small world we live in. Remember, it's a volume game. You never know what can result from a random introduction, chance encounter, or trying something new.

- ### *What if I'm too embarrassed to ask for fix-ups?*

  If you're thinking, "It's too awkward or embarrassing to ask six women to fix me up," then go back to Step #1, Marketing Focus, and ask yourself if you're truly committed to finding a husband. Nothing of any value is easy, so you can either take the plunge and ask away, or go back to your therapist or sympathetic old friends—who, by the way, are sick of hearing you whine! You could analyze for hours why you just couldn't get up the nerve to ask someone to fix you up or how you just aren't an assertive person, blah, blah, blah. This is wasted time and energy. Am I mean because I don't empathize with how difficult this may be for you? No. I do empathize, I really do, but I have to tell you: *"Just do it!"*

  Think of it this way. What if your house were on fire one winter night? Would you sit around and worry that it's cold outside and you can't find the perfect coat to wear? No! You'd just run outside because the house was in flames. You need to do whatever it takes to achieve the end result that you want. Just get out of the fire of introspection and self-doubt. Trust me (and all who have done it): *The Program* really works.

  For the ultra-shy single woman, if you still can't fathom asking women directly to fix you up, the next best thing is to make your pitch to six women via e-mail or a personal note. Perhaps you will be able to garner your courage if it doesn't involve a face-to-face request. This method is less personal, and may not be as effective, but it is better than skipping this step altogether.

HOW TO ASK SOMEONE TO FIX YOU UP

Asking for a fix-up is an important skill that you must master, and to do it well is not as easy as it may sound. Remember, your only goal is to get dates. You have to be very direct when it comes to asking. After you have identified your first woman for a "Step #9 date," call her to test your method. Most likely she will live in your city, and you can suggest a get-together that will appeal especially to her. Is she a "lady who lunches"? Suggest lunch. Is she an avid exerciser? Suggest meeting her at the gym. Is she Imelda Marcos? Suggest checking out the big shoe sale at Nordstrom's. While on the phone with her, you should say that you are "just calling to catch up and get together"; if you've never met her because she's a friend of a friend, you can make small talk about something you have in common. No mention here about your dating goals.

It would be rare to select someone outside your city for one of these six dates, but if you know someone uniquely positioned to help you (as I was with my friend Maureen because of my access to a large alumni database), by all means arrange a "telephone date" with her. This could be a woman who used to live in your city but has relocated, or someone who is a master networker and simply is well connected everywhere. A "date" via telephone usually can't create the same connection that can be made by spending a few hours in person together, but you can facilitate the next best thing. Before the "date," suggest a phone appointment time of 30 minutes so that she can plan ahead and hopefully concentrate on you when you call.

When you are on your "date," spend the first half of the time asking about her and her life: Be a good listener and ask her questions. She'll like that (and she'll like *you*). You are reinforcing or forging a bond. Eventually you should steer the conversation to yourself. This is where you talk about how hard it is to meet men. Provide a few sad or humorous anecdotes about your dating trials and tribulations. Gain her compassion. Then say directly, "You know, I could use your help with this. You're just the kind of person who can make a difference in my life. Do you know any single men?" While this is a very direct approach, it should also make your "date" feel needed.

She will probably ask you what kind of a man you're looking for, and as you learned in Step #4, Market Expansion, you must cast a wider net. No longer do you give her your old list of five to ten narrow criteria. You explain that you are open to a very wide range of men and are simply looking for "someone wonderful." Give her some examples that she may not normally consider: single dads, younger men, much older men, locations outside your city, or nontraditional professions.

It's likely that she will respond with a disappointing but sincere comment like this: "I wish I knew someone for you, but I just don't know any single men." Here's where you spring into action. Say to her, "Hmmm, you might not know any single men, but maybe there are some possibilities that aren't immediately coming to mind. Let's brainstorm!" Help her out by asking these types of questions, which you've dutifully prepared and customized in advance before your "date" with her:

- How about your husband's colleagues at work? His golf buddies?
- Can you think of anyone from that photography class you're taking?
- What about a single dad at your child's school?

- Did you see anyone interesting at your high school reunion last month?
- Weren't you telling me a while ago that your cousin just got divorced?
- I know you volunteer for the science museum; are there any single male volunteers?
- Would you mind asking the ladies in your book group next week if they know any nice men?
- Do you have any friends who might know single men through their jobs or networks?

You hope that her response to some of these prompts will be, "Oh yes! How could I have forgotten about that? There actually is this one single man I know . . . Let me ask him if he's still available," or "Oh, that's a great idea! I'll ask the other ladies next time I'm there . . ." If you get one lead, keep going with your prompts because you might get multiple fix-ups from one "date." But if she doesn't come up with any ideas after you've reminded her about all of the possibilities, then close the topic. Say, "Well, I'd really be grateful if you keep thinking about it over the next few months. And please ask your friends for me, too. Single women like me depend on the help of happily married women like you!"

FACING REJECTION

If your female "date" really declines to help you for no good reason—well, first of all, she's a bitch! And that's fine: She may tell you firmly that she just doesn't know anyone, or she hates playing matchmaker, or has recently failed to find someone for her other three single friends. A goal-focused woman like you will not be deterred by a rejection. Chalk it up to experience. Do not assume that your other five "dates" will respond the same way. Forge ahead. And don't be surprised if that "bitch" calls you back in six months with the startling news that she just met a wonderful single man she sat next to on an airplane who'd be perfect for you . . .

PUBLIC RELATIONS: DRESS TO DAZZLE

Just as you would on a first date with an interesting man, don't forget to dress well and look your best on these dates with your six women. Unless you're meeting her at the gym, consider having your hair professionally blow-dried for this special occasion. Spend 30 minutes applying your make-up. Select wonderful jewelry and accessories. These women need to see you as the men with whom they are going to fix you up will see you. They don't want to be embarrassed by setting up an unappealing friend with their husband's boss. And of course, they'll need to provide any potential blind dates with a description of you, so remember to advertise the "new you." Stay consistent with your personal brand in clothing choices and in conversation topics. And definitely pay for lunch. Deduct it from your Marketing Budget. "It's my treat" is a subtle hint that she can repay you in "other ways."

DATE FOLLOW-UP

Just like a world-class salesperson, a woman on *The Program* always follows up on her leads. This is vital to the success of Step #9. Remember that finding a husband is *your* #1 priority, but it is not the *raison d'être* for these six women. They have busy lives and will need reminding. If one of your "dates" tells you about a man she'd like to introduce to you, and a week passes by without a word, give her a call. Have a short and breezy phone conversation with her (or leave a voice message) to tell her that you enjoyed seeing her last week, and you can't wait to hear from Mr. X. If still another week passes, don't be shy: Send her a nice note or e-mail this time, repeating your excitement about meeting the man she mentioned. More than two follow-ups is annoying, so leave her alone after that. You're likely to hear from her eventually about this fix-up, but move on. Continue "dating" the other women in this step and don't allow her unresponsiveness to detain you. No time to waste.

CREATE OWNERSHIP

A good manager tries to give her employees a feeling of ownership in their work. In the business world, employees will be more motivated to make a project succeed if they believe that they are at least somewhat responsible for the outcome. Managers help create ownership in four ways:

1. Keeping employees in the loop of communication relevant to their project.
2. Reinforcing that the project is highly valued by the company.
3. Frequently giving employees positive feedback.
4. Not telling employees how to do their jobs.

You should apply these time-tested management lessons in the dating world for the six women you have selected in this step.

You have identified them as a target niche for all the right reasons, and now you have to maximize their potential.

In the past, what have you done? You've probably asked several of your friends if they knew anyone to fix you up with. They may have said "yes" or "no," and if "yes," have introduced you to one or two single men. And that was it. The well dried up. But if you really want to use your six women effectively, you have to create for them an ongoing feeling of ownership in them for your "project."

You have to keep them in the loop of communication. If they fix you up with someone, you must immediately call or write them a note afterward (remember those one-dollar note-cards you bought during the Ramp Up stage before starting *The Program*?), thanking them and sharing a few small details about the date. If it was a negative experience, soft-pedal the feedback so that they will still be motivated to try again. Be sure to focus on how appreciative you are that they took the time to introduce you to someone, even if it didn't work out. And if you meet a man who wasn't introduced to you by one of these six women, also keep them in the loop. You want to cultivate their support for all your dating efforts through regular communication with them.

You also want to show your appreciation in other ways for the support you receive from your six women, reinforcing how valuable they are to your quest. And you want to stay top-of-mind with them. Remember, this is the highest-potential niche that you've identified, and it could make a difference in your life. "Court" them. When appropriate, send them heartfelt birthday cards, give small thoughtful gifts (flowers, a picture frame, a scarf), and be on the lookout for ways to help *them*, too. Perhaps one of your "dates" is a residential real estate agent, and you've just learned that your neighbor is looking to buy a new house. Refer your neighbor to the agent! She'll be thrilled with the referral, and will maybe even return the favor with extra effort to find a single man for you. You are a world-class salesperson now, creating incentives and nurturing customer loyalty all in one fell swoop!

Understand that gratitude is not the same as positive feedback. Gratitude is just expressing thanks, while positive feedback is praise for a job well done. People want to feel that they are making a unique contribution if they are working on an important project. Be sure to make specific references during your expressions of gratitude that praise something special, insightful, or clever that each of your women has done.

Everyone has her own style of matchmaking. Some women will take their time and wait until a *prince* comes along before setting you up. Not just anyone is worthy of you, she thinks! Others will introduce you to *any* man they meet: "single" and "breathing" are the only criteria they use. Some will pass your number on to an eligible man, but if he doesn't call you, she won't prod. Other women will carefully craft your first meeting and want to be involved. They may want to double-date with you the first time, or host a dinner party to make the introduction, believing you'll both be more comfortable with other people around. The important thing is not to tell your "dates" how to do their job. Just be gracious and be grateful for whatever introduction method your "date" prefers, as long as the end result is that she is on your side and on the lookout for you.

You have succeeded with Step #9, and can begin Step #10, if you:

1. Went on "dates" with six qualified women.
2. Explicitly told these six women about your marriage focus, asked them to fix you up, brainstormed with them about other eligible men, and asked them to ask *their* friends to help you.
3. Dressed to dazzle on your "dates."
4. Remembered your personal brand on your "dates" and stayed consistent with your clothing style and conversation topics.
5. Followed up on all leads generated by your six "dates."
6. Made every effort to create a feeling of ownership in your "dates."
7. Concluded this step with a positive attitude despite any rejections.

Step #10

Telemarketing:

Bring Out Your Rolodex

WHAT I LEARNED AT
HARVARD BUSINESS SCHOOL

Telemarketing can be a surprisingly effective marketing tactic. Would you believe that roughly 4% of the people who are cold-called will actually buy a good product offered to them via the telephone? Most of us probably would have guessed that no one buys products via those annoying unsolicited calls. But from a business perspective, telemarketing is profitable. It costs very little for computers to dial thousands of phone numbers and to employ a small telesales force to make the sale. If the response rate is 4% (sometimes higher, depending on the product and how "qualified" the phone number is—in other words, it's the phone number of a person who has made similar purchases in the past), the company will make a profit. For the telephone sales pitch to be effective, it must be brief, be persuasive, and have a strong call to action. A good marketer would not likely use telemarketing as her *only* means of selling a product, but would certainly include this tactic in her overall marketing strategy.

WHAT IS THE TELEMARKETING TACTIC?

Okay, let me tell you right up front that you're *not* gonna like this step! But keep reading. My clients and seminar attendees always grimace when they hear what this involves. But trust me, it can yield very good results. So here it is: You are going to call everyone you know and directly ask them to fix you up with someone. And I mean call *everyone*. This includes men and women of all ages: all your family, friends, and acquaintances, in your address book, Palm Pilot, Rolodex, and school alumni directories (high school, college, graduate school, even summer camps from a million years ago). This includes selected current and former colleagues and business clients. And it includes all the professional and service people you know (Realtors, landlords, lawyers, doctors, dentists, veterinarians, hairstylists, florists, travel agents, teachers, vendors, accountants, stockbrokers, bankers, health club staff . . .), all neighbors (past and present), all members of groups to which you belong (charity, therapy, reading), and definitely any old boyfriends or men you've dated, if things ended amicably. Then call *anyone else* you've ever known!

If you are approximately 45 or older, you might have grown children, nieces, nephews, or friends' children to call. With the divorce rate so high these days, many grown children have divorced fathers just waiting to be fixed up.

And don't even limit yourself to calling people in your city. "It's a small world" is one of the truest clichés you'll ever hear. Remember the story of Maureen from Portland in Step #9,

Niche Marketing? You just never know what kind of contacts someone has in other cities.

You may have 500 people on your list. But if you have only a fraction of that number—that's fine, too. Just call everyone you know, however close or distant they are to you.

As a side note, you may be interested to hear how I created this step. Several years ago, when I was first starting to help women find husbands and I only had time to work with one client at a time, I personally made these telemarketing calls for each of my clients. I literally sat by my phone for hours and dialed everyone I knew, asking, "Do you know anyone in X city to fix up with so-and-so?" I didn't get contacts out of each and every call, but I got enough to know that it worked. One client, Ava, ultimately met her husband because of a chain of events sparked by one of my telemarketing calls. Ava lived in St. Louis, but one of the friends I called said she knew a nice single man in Los Angeles. I asked Ava if she had any plans to travel to Los Angeles soon, and she said, "No, but I'll make plans." (That's *The Program* attitude!) She called a friend of hers in Los Angeles, saying that she was coming to visit because I was fixing her up with someone there. Her friend said, "Well, as long as you're here, I have someone I'd like to introduce to you also. His name is Charles." And guess what happened? Ava married Charles one year later.

These calls can work in unforeseen ways. But you have to dial them yourself now, unless you know someone who has as much passion for finding you a husband as I did for my first few clients, and will make the calls for you . . .

TELEMARKETING GOALS

In Step #9, Niche Marketing, you asked six women on "dates" and asked them to fix you up. You spent a lot of time carefully nurturing each relationship and creating ownership. Here in Step #10, you are going to ask a *few hundred* people to fix you up. You are taking a more mass approach now, and you won't have time to focus in-depth on each person because of the sheer size of your call list.

Your goals for these calls are to:

1. Express your commitment to finding a mate.
2. Convey your genuine need for, and appreciation of, the person's help.
3. Directly ask for fix-ups.
4. Spend no more than 5–15 minutes on the phone with each person.
5. Obtain 1 blind date for every 10 telemarketing calls.

It may take some time for you to see results from these calls. The goal of obtaining 1 blind date per 10 calls means that over several months, if you have made 100 calls, you should expect to generate 10 blind dates. Remember, you are planting seeds here, so be patient. Few people will have immediate fix-ups for you, but you are broadcasting your availability. They will go about their normal lives, and as they bump into single men (which inevitably they will!), your name will hopefully spring to mind.

TELEMARKETING RATIONALE

Why go through this veritable torture? In addition to my personal success with telemarketing, this statistic says it all: "50% of people now married or living together were introduced by good friends or family members" (Edward Laumann, Ph.D., University of Chicago sociology professor). Logically, then, you have to mine for the gold in your own backyard and call everyone you know. I've heard the expression a million times in the business world: "It's not what you know, it's *who* you know." This is even truer in the dating world.

The good news is that unlike real telemarketers, you are not a complete stranger to those on your call list. You get to make "warm calls" instead of cold calls. Most of these people will be glad to hear from you. Many of them may know you're single, but they may not think or presume to fix you up. A direct call to action is needed.

Prioritize your call list so that you are first phoning people you think have the highest potential to fix you up. Five to fifteen minutes should be your target time to talk on the phone with one person. You want to accomplish maximum volume with minimum time investment.

The yield on telemarketing calls is fairly low. If a typical product in business has an average 4% yield from a cold call, it's reasonable to assume that since this is a "warm" one, you might get a higher yield. Most of my clients have averaged about a 10% yield. If you call 200 people, then, you're likely to get 20 fix-ups that trickle in over the course of the year. When was the last time you had that many (offline) blind dates? Even with a low yield, it's still worth trying this tactic because the bottom line is that it increases your odds of finding your husband. It takes only *one* man to be your husband, so even if you get only one fix-up here (worst-case scenario), that one could be all you need.

Who knows which one of these people on the other end of the receiver could introduce you to Mr. Right? It could happen on your first call or your two hundredth. It could happen through the most logical person on your list or the most random. Two of my favorite success stories resulting from this step happened to Beth, a 37-year-old living in New York City, and Joan, a 68-year-old living in Pacific Palisades, California. I asked them to tell their stories.

CASE STUDY:
BETH'S TELEMARKETING STORY

I had 172 names on my call list, which surprised me. I guessed I'd have about half that number. But when I went back and really thought about all the people I've met through the years, the quantity kept going up. Several names on my list were very well-connected people in New York, including my high-profile boss and the very social Realtor who sold me my apartment last year.

But also on my list were some random people, including Rose, my 80-year-old grandma's neighbor. My grandmother lives in a retirement community in Florida, and three years ago I had spent a long weekend visiting her. One afternoon we played cards with her neighbor Rose. Rose was probably also in her eighties, although she never told anyone her age. I met Rose for two hours, but I remembered really liking her. She was a hoot. I knew I was supposed to include *everyone* on my telemarketing list, so when I wrote down my grandma's name, for some reason

I also thought of Rose and jotted down her name, too. I figured that both these women would only know men in their eighties, but I put them on the list anyway.

Here's what happened: I called my grandmother first, gave her my spiel (even though she knew it only too well!), and before we hung up I got Rose's phone number from her. I called Rose next and told her that I was seriously looking this year for someone to spend my life with. She listened kindly and promised to keep her eyes open.

I made many other calls on my telemarketing list, and went on a few dates. But no one clicked. Three months later, I got a call from Rose. She had been talking to another lady she played bridge with, who mentioned her single 40-year-old grandson who lived nearby on Long Island. They fixed us up. I had low expectations, but we adored each other at first sight and we dated for about two months. He turned out not to be the right man for me in the end, but it just goes to show you never know where there might be potential.

CASE STUDY:
JOAN'S TELEMARKETING STORY

I called 206 names on my telemarketing list. The whole thing was completely embarrassing, even though I had a very nice reception from most of the people I spoke to. Number 203 was my old friend Helen. We had known each other quite well in high school, though I hadn't talked to her in almost ten years. She had been going through some difficult medical problems, but was on the mend. We had a brief chat on the phone, and she assured me she'd keep me in mind if she heard of any single men.

A few weeks later, Helen called me back. She had just come

back from a doctor's appointment. She told me that when she checked in at the doctor's office, she noticed a photograph behind the young receptionist's desk of a nice-looking older man. Helen asked the receptionist who it was, and the woman said "This is my father. Ever since he divorced my mother, I've been trying to help him find someone." Of course, Helen thought of me!

Helen told the young woman that she knew someone special to introduce to her father. They exchanged phone numbers and fixed me up with Jason, the man in the photo (although he was very reluctant at first). Now almost a year later that receptionist is going to be my stepdaughter (I'm engaged!). Who would have guessed that number 203 would lead me to The One?

MAKE IT YOUR BUSINESS

So let's get you started. Help yourself succeed with this process of telemarketing. Prior to dialing each phone number, think of a good opening line. Maybe offer a few pleasantries, or give information relevant to the person's interests, or ask a question that shows you remembered something about the person. Top salespeople in the business world claim that it's easy to "sell" a person right after you've made a connection with them by bringing up something you have in common.

Set daily or weekly goals for yourself and write them on your calendar. For example, if you have 200 names on your list, write "2 telemarketing calls" on your calendar every day for the next 100 days. Or you could make all your calls on Sundays by doing 15 calls for the next 14 Sundays. But at a minimum, try to make at least 5 calls per week.

I know this is hard. I wish I could give you a "Get Out of Singles Jail Free" card, but it takes hard work to find your husband in 12 to 18 months. However, the payoff is worth it.

YOUR PHONE SCRIPT

There are three things you want to do in each phone call:

1. Reinforce a connection between you and the person you are calling.
2. Convey that you need the person's help.
3. Ask for a fix-up.

Practice what you're going to say with your Mentor before making your first call.

Keeping in mind your telemarketing goals and the opportunity to advertise your personal brand, a sample call from Diane (an "Expert Gardener") could sound like this:

> Hi, Paula! It's Diane from down the street. Are those roses I recommended last spring growing well? . . . Oh, that's good to hear. I hope you don't mind that I'm calling you, but I wanted to ask for your help with something very important to me. I've decided that this is the year I am going to find a wonderful man to spend my life with, and I would really appreciate your help. It's very hard to meet new men. I'm a little embarrassed to ask, but I was wondering if you know any single men you could introduce to me?

If she draws a blank, give her a few generic prompts like: "Perhaps a relative or co-worker? Or one of your friends, or your husband's friends?" Also give some specific prompts based on your knowledge of groups or organizations to which she belongs: "Do you think one of the women in your bridge club might know a nice man?"

As you saw in Step #9, Niche Marketing, people usually don't have names of single men on the tips of their tongues. Especially when receiving a phone call like this out of the blue. So don't be discouraged when the typical response is: "Gee, I wish I did! I'd love to help but I just don't know any single men."

Here's what you say: "Well, that's okay! I hope you don't mind that I asked you . . . It's not easy getting up the courage to make a call like this. But if you wouldn't mind giving it some more thought, and maybe asking your husband or friends for me, too, I'd really appreciate it—even if you meet someone several months from now, please think of me."

If she asks you what kind of man you are looking for, you know what to say by now: "Someone wonderful! I'm open to anyone you think I might enjoy meeting."

When you cast a wider net with a response like this, the power of selection will be in *your* hands. Let others bring a wide variety of men to you, meet them all, then you decide which ones you'd like to get to know better. This is preferable to letting other people screen someone out before you've even met him.

CALL FOLLOW-UP

As described in Step #9, Niche Marketing, it's essential that you follow up on any leads generated. Bring out that journal you started in Step #7, Online Marketing, and keep a log of every outbound and inbound telemarketing call. If a woman on your list told you she has someone in mind, and you haven't heard anything further within ten days, call her to follow up. Because you are dialing hundreds of numbers, you need to keep all the correspondence organized. Format your notebook page into six columns across the top of your page like this:

TELEMARKETING JOURNAL

Date	Name	Contact Made or Message Left?	Any Leads?	Follow-Up Needed	Comments
11/20	Amy Perkins	Contact made	Will ask husband about his co-worker	Call her 11/30 to follow up	Very helpful: Husband works at IBM and has many male colleagues
11/24	Gina Ryman	Message left on machine	N/A	Call her 11/29 if she doesn't call back	N/A
12/6	Bob Regis	Contact made	Gave my number to his poker buddy, Tom Kuhn	Date for drinks arranged with Tom on 12/12	Tom is divorced with 2 daughters

You need to be very thorough with your note taking and organized with all follow-up. Help yourself stay on top of this process by not only making the notations in your notebook, but also by writing the necessary action step on your calendar for the date required (for instance, "11/29: Call Gina Ryman to follow up on message left," or "12/13: Call Bob Regis to thank him for introduction to Tom Kuhn").

YOU MAY BE WONDERING . . .

• *What if I don't know a lot of people?*
I hear this quite a bit. Maybe you've recently moved to a new city and haven't met many people yet. Maybe you live in a small town. Maybe you have led a relatively insular life. Maybe a lot of your so-called friends sided with your ex-husband after the divorce and you could *never* call them. If you've really given the call list development your best shot, thinking hard about everyone you've ever known, then don't worry if your list is small. Telemarketing will work whether you call 20 people or 200. The odds go down with smaller lists, but you can still expect a 10% response rate. If you have 20 people on your list, you might generate 2 fix-ups, and since you need only one husband, it can still pay off.

• *What if I get an answering machine?*
When you are making your telemarketing calls, you are likely to reach a lot of answering machines. Leave a brief, upbeat message asking the person to call you back, give some general times that you will be home, but don't leave any details about why you're calling except: "I have a favor to ask you." Don't launch into your request on the machine because it's less personal and doesn't engage the recipient in an effective way. You want to have a personal dialogue with each person to convey your com-

mitment and sincerity, and to brainstorm single men she might know. Talking to someone directly will always make that person feel more compelled to help you. It's easy to ignore a message on an answering machine, but harder to ignore a direct request when you're having a conversation with someone.

• *Should I call co-workers and clients?*

Yes, but probably not all of them. You'll have to use your judgment about which ones you think will be receptive to your request, and which ones will consider it awkward to mix your professional relationship with your personal life. It might be more appropriate to ask clients, for instance, after the transaction between you and them is completed. Some companies have explicit "no dating" policies among their employees, but that doesn't mean co-workers can't fix you up with someone outside the company. When in doubt, err on the side of asking more business associates rather than fewer. We're all human, and I think you'll be pleasantly surprised how supportive people from the office will be.

• *What if I don't have a home telephone number for someone on my list?*

Excuses, excuses, excuses. If you don't have a home phone number of someone on your list (a colleague, your hairstylist, and so on), go ahead and e-mail him, ask him in person, or simply call him at work and inquire whether he'd mind if you asked him a non-work-related question.

• *What if I'm too shy to telemarket?*

Many women feel they are too shy or uncomfortable to make phone calls like this. But you do what you have to do when the result is important enough to you. I like to use the analogy of childbirth in explaining how to convince you to make telemarketing calls. Childbirth is certainly no picnic, but millions of women subject themselves to this excruciating pain again and again because it's what they must endure to have the many future years of joy and happiness that result from having a child.

Telemarketing isn't as painful as childbirth, I promise—I've done both! Go back to Step #1, Marketing Focus, and ask yourself if you are truly committed to finding a husband. Being shy may be a real issue for you, but don't let it be an obstacle. The results from this step could produce years of joy and happiness with your future husband!

• *Don't I sound desperate making these calls?*

Women often feel embarrassed to make all these phone calls because they fear that the other person will think they're desperate. But imagine yourself at the other end of the receiver. What would you think of receiving a nice call from someone you knew asking for your help? I'm sure you would be happy to help if you could, and would think nothing less of the person for asking. I bet you'd even admire her for taking action and pursuing her goal. You are not desperate: you are *proactive*.

And remember, no one else but you knows how many people you're calling. Each person might assume you're calling two or three other friends, not two or three *hundred* other friends! Often it's the sheer quantity of the calls that creates the perception of desperation in your own mind, but you're the only one who knows the quantity.

Rejection is always a possibility—as it is in every step on *The Program*. So be optimistic but prepared for any kind of reaction from the people you call. The important thing is not to allow any rejections to get you down. You might get one negative reaction and 99 positive reactions, so just keep things in perspective and keep calling.

A LAST RESORT

If you are still unconvinced of the importance of this step, I'll toss you a bone at this point. If you'd really rather die alone than call hundreds of people and ask for fix-ups, I suppose you can e-mail some of them instead with the same request. I would still call your highest-priority names on the telephone, but you could e-mail the rest. This is not my preferred method because you lose a lot of the personal connection made over the telephone; your response rate will go down. But if you're completely set against calling, then asking via e-mail is better than not asking at all.

If you decide to e-mail these requests, be sure not to send a group e-mail. You must compose a message to each person individually to help her feel important, as if she alone might make a difference in your life. If you send a generic message to a group that begins "Dear Friends," you have depersonalized your request even further. The typical group mentality is that "someone else will help: I don't have to." You can, of course, cut and paste one message into each e-mail repeatedly and just personalize one or two lines.

EXPRESS YOUR GRATITUDE

As always, whenever someone you call has a lead for you of any kind, whether it's a direct fix-up with a single man or an indirect introduction to another person who may know a single man, be sure to express your gratitude. You should write a lovely and thoughtful thank-you note. Use the personal stationery that you bought during the Ramp Up stage in this book. I believe the art of the thank-you note is to be as genuine and detailed as possible. Use phrases such as "I truly appreciate your help from the bottom of my heart" or "Your thoughtfulness in introducing me to Jack was truly appreciated." Add any relevant details like, "We have a date planned for next Thursday, and I'm really looking forward to it," or "We met for coffee last Friday, and although I didn't think we had chemistry, we had a very interesting conversation and I'm really glad we met. You have a good eye for the kind of man I like."

If someone has really gone out of her way to help you—perhaps setting you up with multiple blind dates or having a dinner party for you—you should send her a small, thoughtful gift. A gift that has personal meaning—say, a book on a topic she's passionate about, or something she can use on an upcoming vacation—is ideal.

Because these notes and small gifts convey your sincere gratitude, these people are likely to repeat their kindness: They know how appreciated it was the first time. All of us love and respond to positive feedback for our efforts, and it begins to create that feeling of ownership we discussed earlier.

You have succeeded with Step #10, and can begin Step #11, if you:

1. Made a list of *everyone* you know (the longer, the better).

2. Made at least 5 calls per week.

3. Directly asked all these people for fix-ups.

4. Are keeping a detailed log of all communications in a journal.

5. Followed up on every lead generated.

6. Expressed your gratitude to everyone who helped you.

7. Obtained approximately 1 blind date for every 10 telemarketing calls.

Step #11

Mass Marketing:

Pump Up the Volume

WHAT I LEARNED AT HARVARD BUSINESS SCHOOL

Mass marketing is a strategy to reach the highest number of possible customers with your product. Examples of mass-marketing tactics include television advertising and outdoor billboards. These methods project a broad product message to millions of people. Not everyone pays attention to the message, but many people do absorb and act upon it. As a marketer, you never know exactly *which* people will respond, so you broadcast your message to a very wide market in the hope of reaching as many potential customers as possible. For example, Coca Cola is a product that appeals to a broad range of people in age, gender, race, and location. Therefore, using mass-marketing techniques such as TV advertising makes sense to reach so many diverse customers. A successful marketer tries to reach prospects through a wide variety of mass-marketing channels, thereby increasing the chance that the promotional message will reach the highest volume of people.

WHY VOLUME IS CRITICAL TO *THE PROGRAM*

Volume is one of the core principles of *The Program*. Remember, "The more times at bat, the greater chance you have to hit a home run." This is the step where you are going to pump up the volume even more. Thus far, you have progressed through ten steps that have created a strong foundation and many new opportunities to help you find a mate. You have started to create volume with online dating, changing your routine, networking with selected women, and telemarketing. But if you haven't met Mr. Right yet, it's time to pick up the pace, not slow down. You need to generate more and more opportunities to find a husband.

The mass-marketing tactic is a systematic, strategic approach to generate a variety of opportunities to meet men. Why? Because you have tried many things already and you haven't found him yet. You simply never know where Mr. Right is, so you have to look everywhere now. Achieving volume is exhausting and often discouraging, but if you're organized in your approach, you can do it successfully.

You're going to methodically try a little of *everything* here. I will help you create a very long list of opportunities to meet men—opportunities that have not yet been discussed in *The Program*. This will be a smorgasbord of every singles-related activity that exists, plus more that we'll invent. Naturally, you won't have the time or interest to literally try them all, but the concept of a mile-long list may provide you with the knowledge that you will never run out of options to meet your future husband. You will always have something new to try and look forward to. This list should always represent the hope that he might be just around the corner at the next place you try.

Even with all the strategy and planning that I advocate in this book, you can't ignore the notion of serendipity—of being in the right place at the right time. Mass marketing is the act of working harder to be in *more* places at the right time, to increase your odds.

If you've been single for a while, you are probably painfully familiar with many of the typical places where single people go to meet each other. You've probably tried several groups or locations already. But at the risk of being trite, I will provide you with an exhaustive list of all the different ideas that I've collected over the years for meeting 35+ singles. My collection comes from newspaper and magazine articles, Web sites, personal experiences, experiences of single friends, and suggestions from my seminar attendees and private clients.

Unfortunately, in this mass-marketing step, you can't always do what you enjoy. This is quite opposite of the advice you probably hear from friends and self-help authors, who say, "Do what you love, and the rest will come!" I think that if you haven't met Mr. Right by now, one reason may be that he has different interests from yours. He hasn't been in the same groups or locations with you. You remember from Step #1 in *The Program Thinking Method* that you go where the men are instead of going where you want to go. Well, now you're going to go *everywhere*.

A METHOD TO THE MADNESS

I have organized the many opportunities that I've collected to meet men into four categories:

1. Singles groups.
2. Social locations.
3. Dating services.
4. Other.

Your goal is to actively pursue one item from a different category each week. For example, the first week you select one item from Category #1, the next week you select one item from Category #2, and so forth. Continue to rotate through the four categories as many times as possible in the coming months. For extra volume, try two items from each category per week. (In the real estate business the motto is: "Location, location, location." In the dating business, keep thinking: "Volume, volume, volume!") While not everything will appeal to you, please force yourself to try items outside your comfort zone. The list you're going to devise, using this framework, should be plentiful enough to keep you busy into the next century (although of course that won't be necessary!).

THE STOCK PORTFOLIO: A LESSON IN DIVERSIFICATION

The main point about all this volume and rotating through the different categories is that you should treat your husband search like a stock portfolio by *diversifying*. Just as financial planners tell you to put your money into lots of different stocks to reduce your risk, I am telling you to mix up the areas for husband-hunting in which you invest your time, energy, and money. If one investment isn't working, it should be balanced by better results in other areas. The more options you have in your portfolio, the more choices you'll have to increase your bet on high performers and get rid of the low performers. Don't put all your eggs in one basket!

HOW TO START

First, using the guidelines that follow, you'll need to compile your own specific list of opportunities into the four categories for the city in which you live. Get four sheets of ruled paper, one for each of the four categories. You're going to fill in dozens of specific groups, locations, services, and ideas that you discover in your own city. Don't forget to include the phone number or Web site for each listing. Give yourself at least a week to compile a list that is thorough and bountiful.

CATEGORY #1: SINGLES GROUPS

Singles groups are organizations of single men and women focused on religion, sports, hobbies, volunteering, politics, social, and peer support (e.g., single parents). There are singles groups in every city, and one easy way to find them in your location is simply to use an Internet search engine such as www.google.com or www.ask.com. Enter your city name (say, "Denver") and the word "singles" to start your search. Be sure to type in nearby cities as well (you wouldn't let a hundred miles stop you from a wonderful man, right?). For example, I might type in "Denver singles" and wait for the results. Then I might type in "Boulder singles" (40 miles from Denver) and wait for the results. Then I might type in "Colorado Springs singles" (75 miles from Denver) and wait for the results.

If I repeat this process with a second search engine just to be very thorough, I would obtain an aggregate listing of more than 40 singles groups ranging from religious to sporting to business networking. Some are probably terrible; others are going to be really good. You never know until you try them. Some may be better suited for singles too young or too old for you, but by investigating each Web site or calling the phone number listed and speaking to a coordinator, you can determine which groups are appropriate for your age.

Try things you normally wouldn't consider. So you've never played tennis? Sign up for tennis lessons with a singles sporting group. So you're not much of a hiker? Try a hike with the Sierra Club. So you haven't been to church in ten years? Attend a Bible study class for singles.

Add to your list the singles groups that you already knew about before your Internet searches, and ask other single friends for more recommendations. Challenge yourself to get 50 listings in this category, if you live in or near a relatively big city, or 10–20 listings, if you live in a small one. Carry a small notepad in your purse and keep a running tab of everyone's suggestions as you go about your daily life. Ask your hairstylist and your Realtor. Ask the receptionist at your health club. Casually ask every date how he meets singles.

Many women, especially in smaller cities, complain to me that they've already tried all the singles groups, and they've never met anyone interesting. Or they say that the same people just keep showing up. First of all, things change. New singles are joining groups all the time, so don't assume the crowd is forever static, even if the same people were there for three weeks in a row. But I would challenge anyone who thinks that she has tried *every* singles group that I could find some others in her city that she has not yet tried. Keep asking for suggestions from not-your-usual crowd.

Pick up all the city magazines and free newsletters you can find to generate more ideas for your singles group list. Look at the ads in the back of these publications for upcoming events. Make it your mission to get on every group mailing list you can (churches, synagogues, art galleries, museums, chambers of commerce). These groups will usually have a few events each year (such as holiday parties or lectures), many of which are good opportunities for singles. Mark those event dates on your calendar.

And again, try new things that may stretch your comfort level with what you've done in the past. As an example, even if you have absolutely no interest in politics, try going to one political function (perhaps a campaign fund-raiser for your local congressman). Are you a Republican? Attend a Democratic rally just to see who's there. If you are a widow, consider joining a grief support group. Not only might this kind of group help with your feelings of loss, but some of my over-50 clients have told me they know many men and women who find mates after meeting in grief support groups.

Match.com currently has "Match Live" events in several cities (New York, Boston, Chicago, Los Angeles, San Francisco, and more) where singles meet offline in groups for activities such as wine tasting, improvisational acting classes, theater events, historic city tours, or Happy Hours. Check the www.Match.com Web site for schedules.

Of course, parties of all kinds would fall into this category: small dinner parties, large event parties, and other gatherings with friends. It should be rare that you would turn down any party invitation. Even if you already know everyone invited, this is an ideal time to advertise your brand.

CATEGORY #2: SOCIAL LOCATIONS

Most of you probably groan when you think of social locations, because you equate them with "the bar scene." But don't worry, I'm not going to suggest you start going to bars. If there are a few "refined" restaurant or bar establishments in your area, you can certainly attend a Happy Hour here and there. And hotel bars often host male business travelers, which can be good for casting a wider geographic net. But not a lot of appropriate older single men and women hang out in bars frequently, so let's be creative in finding other locations that are better for 35+ singles. Of course, not all of these locations are filled only with singles; they will have a mixture of singles and marrieds, but they are venues that are often conducive to chance encounters. Meeting married people is sometimes productive anyway, because they might introduce you to someone new.

Try going to:

- Bookstores
- Libraries
- Coffee shops
- Golf driving ranges
- Athletic clubs
- Sports events
- Airline travel lounges (when you're traveling)

- Antique car shows
- Technology conventions or forums

- High-visibility parks to walk your dog (or someone else's dog)

CATEGORY #3: DATING SERVICES

There are more different types of dating services available today than ever before. You can sample the new speed-dating services (such as the 8 Minute Dating and Hurry Date organizations), where you meet approximately 8 men in an hour by rotating tables when a bell rings. You can try meal-oriented dating services such as Just Lunch, Dinner for Six, or Table for Eight, where you go on several lunch or group dinner dates; video dating services such as Great Expectations, where you create your own video ad and view video ads of men who might be a match for you; or matchmaking services, where you are introduced to men known by a matchmaker. Dating services have often disappointed my clients in certain locations, but don't assume they are all bad, all the time. Ownership changes, popularity changes, and clientele changes. Investigate the dating services in your city to find out if any come highly recommended.

If you find a dating service that gets strong reviews from people you know, be sure to call the service and ask the following questions: How many years have you been in business? How many *active* members do you have? What percent of male members are in my age range? Can you provide a few references from current clients?

Dating services are rarely anybody's first choice. But think about it: These services wouldn't survive as businesses if no one ever met interesting people through them. So what have you got to lose? Nothing, except part of your Marketing Budget. Many of these services can be quite expensive—fifteen hundred to more than ten thousand dollars per year. Examine your budget, and if funds are available, try to find at least one dating service to join. Make sure you do your research and have a few strong recommendations before you make a selection.

A different and less expensive type of "dating service" should be considered: the personal ad sections of magazines and newspapers. Online dating services have largely taken over, but personal ads aren't extinct yet. They are still a viable, if smaller, resource for singles in many cities. Although you are dating online, you won't find all the eligible men there. As you can imagine, maybe because you used to feel the same way, some men feel uncomfortable in cyberspace (especially older ones). So include advertising in selected publications on your list.

Here are a few magazines that have good readership demographics for upscale, professional, affluent, 35+ singles: *New York Magazine*, *New York Review of Books*, *Boston Magazine*, *Philadelphia Magazine*, *Washingtonian Magazine*, *Los Angeles Magazine*, and *San Francisco Magazine*. Read the personal ads in these magazines, and check out other local magazines and newspapers in your area for alternative demographics, to understand which personal ad sections appeal to you. I recommend only *placing* an ad to start. Use the same guidelines from Step #7, Online Marketing, to create your ad, and if you find that you are not getting responses, then Plan B is to answer a few interesting ads posted by men.

CATEGORY #4: OTHER IDEAS

Here are several other ideas to meet men—but of course don't let your imagination be limited by my list. The possibilities are endless.

Single-Dad Spots

After age 35, there are a lot of single dads back on the dating scene. Try to think about where you might meet them. Often they have visitation nights with their children on Wednesdays, and I'm guessing not many of them can cook a decent meal. I bet you never thought that family-oriented pizza restaurants on Wednesday nights could be hot spots, but try one out. You might meet someone in the waiting area, sitting at the table next to you, or standing in line for valet parking. On weekends, single dads with younger kids might go to the zoo or a park. So you might want to take your own child, or invite your neighbor's child, or a niece or nephew, to the zoo or park.

If you're a single mom, you should also log onto www.Parents WithoutPartners.org. Not only is this an excellent organization that caters to the issues of single parents, but it is fertile ground for meeting single dads.

Teach a Class

How about *teaching* an adult education class for men? In most cities, there are adult education centers that are always on the lookout for new course material. Your topic doesn't have to be an academic one. I had one client who decided to teach a seminar she created called "Fifteen-Minute Meals for Bachelors." What a great idea. And this woman was not even a chef! She simply found eight quick-and-easy recipes from various cooking magazines and cookbooks, and created a 2-hour class for single men who didn't know how to cook and didn't want to spend a lot of time in the kitchen. She drafted a one-page course description about what she planned to teach, submitted it to her local adult education center, and soon she was standing in front of a room full of bachelors, all focused on her.

Be creative and think about the skills and hobbies you might have that could be crafted into a male-oriented class. Maybe you're a good conversationalist? You could teach a class called "Small Talk for Shy Men." Just research a few self-help books and magazine articles on this topic, and create a list of twenty-five ways to make interesting small talk at parties and at work. Not all the men attending this class may be single, but I think it would skew toward single men who are shy about meeting women.

For those who are averse to teaching, just enroll in a few classes as a student. As you learned in Step #1's *The Program Thinking Method*, you should select classes where the men are, even if you're not interested in the subject. Think beyond the walls of an adult education center, too. How about a do-it-yourself class at Home Depot? They teach deck staining, ceramic flooring, tile installation, and more. Choose a short seminar (just one or two evenings), so you won't waste too much time if there aren't any interesting men there and you're bored stiff with the material. Even if you don't meet a nice single man that night, you'll have stored up an interesting conversation topic from attending that seminar for a future social setting. If you can discuss topics such as Deck Staining you will probably stand out among a crowd of women!

Reunions, Jury Duty, Bar Mitzvahs, and Other Dreaded Events

The next time your five-year reunion cycle comes around, or you are drafted for jury duty, or invited to the bar mitzvah or wedding of your second cousin's son, think to yourself, "What an opportunity!" instead of trying to come up with a clever excuse for getting out of it. And whatever you do, don't bring a casual date to social events: You want to be free to meet and mingle with new people.

Always go to your reunions! I've heard so many stories from women who returned to their high school or college reunions, ran into someone they barely knew back then, and fell madly in love. Try to get on the reunion or alumni committees to plan social events, which will provide you with access to names you may be able to cultivate down the road. But don't stop there: Ask to accompany your friends to *their* reunions as well. Nobody likes going alone. These gatherings are a magnet for older singles.

And jury duty is an opportunity to meet eleven other men and women whom you don't know. Probably few, if any, will be single men in your age group, but remember that volume tactics are aimed at doing *anything* where you meet new people. You never know what tip someone may give you in a casual conversation that may lead to finding your husband. And those eleven other men and women on the jury all have friends, cousins, and co-workers who might be eligible men, just waiting to be fixed up with a smart woman who projects her brand and her dating priorities during courtroom recesses.

While you may hate attending family events where each and every one of your relatives feels compelled to drill you about why, why, why you haven't met a nice man yet, you still need to attend bar mitzvahs, weddings, family reunions, and other family get-togethers. You never know when a relative will see you and suddenly remember her single co-worker or the new single parent in his son's classroom.

Travel

Be open to taking trips with singles groups: ski weekends (even if you don't ski, you can learn—or just sit by the fire in the lodge!), hiking trips, art tours, or wine-tasting tours. Look at "Match Travel" on www.match.com for trips to destinations such as London, Paris, Tuscany, Alaska, Costa Rica, Cuba, or Las Vegas. There is even a big wave now (no pun intended) of singles cruises (look up www.singlescruise.com, www.cruisingforlove.com, www.singlestravelintl.com, and www.allchristiancruises.com). Don't be afraid to participate in something that involves a few days of commitment. Even if there aren't any interesting men on the trip, your risk may pay off in unforeseen ways. You could meet a friendly single woman who invites you to an event the following month, perhaps in another city, where Mr. Right is waiting for you. Who knows?

Way Out There

Every once in a while, you just have to do something totally out of character. What about: Joining the volunteer fire department? Taking a skydiving course? Becoming an emergency medical technician? Have you ever tried country-western dancing? Think of something zany. A ridiculous idea might just be your winning lottery ticket.

VOLUME GOALS

Once you have compiled a long list of opportunities in your city under each of the four categories, take out your calendar and write down specific dates when you're going to try an item in each category. Use a pen so you can't erase anything later just because you're tired. Tell yourself that *"Home"* is a 4-letter word. I don't know where your husband is, but there's only one place he's *not*: in your home. So you have to get out there.

Use the Mass Marketing Summary grid on page 211 like a menu, selecting at least one item per week. Choose the highest-potential opportunities first. You'll need to add these goals to all the opportunities that you listed in Step #8, Guerrilla Marketing, to change your routine, but fortunately some of the activities overlap. For example, having your morning coffee at a different Starbucks than usual qualifies as an activity with dual agendas: both doing something different (Step #8) and frequenting social locations that are conducive for single people to meet each other (Step #11).

You want to be very strategic and organized about how and when you diversify your portfolio of opportunities. You can create your own goals according to your Marketing Budget, the resources your city has to offer, and your amount of available time.

It's important to plan ahead to reach these goals for two reasons. First, with so many things you *can* do, this step might overwhelm you. It can leave you feeling as if there's so much to do that you end up doing nothing, or not diversifying and just doing what's comfortable. Second, all of us get busy with our daily lives, and it's too easy to procrastinate doing these kinds of activities unless you write them in ink on your calendar and commit to doing them. If you have to miss one, add it back in the next week.

MASS MARKETING SUMMARY

Category #1: *Singles Groups*	Category #2: *Social Locations*	Category #3: *Dating Services*	Category #4: *Other*
Religious	Bookstores	Speed dating	Single-dad spots
Sporting	Libraries	Lunch or dinner date services	Teach a class
Hobby	Coffee shops	Video dating	Enroll in a class
Volunteer	Golf driving ranges	Matchmaking	Reunions and other dreaded events
Political	Airline lounges	Personal ads	Travel
Peer support	Dog walking		Way out there
Social	Technology conventions or forums		
Arts	Antique car shows		
Singles events	Sports events		
Parties			

CASE STUDY:
CLAIRE'S CALENDAR PAGE

The calendar page that follows for the month of February was created by Claire, a 48-year-old single mother. Claire worked part-time as an administrative assistant in a small company in

Boston. When she planned her calendar, she integrated her on-line dating goals from Step #7, her guerrilla marketing goals from Step #8, her telemarketing goals from Step #10, and the goals she devised here in Step #11. She was extremely moti-vated to find a wonderful man, so she actually arranged much more than one high-volume activity per week. As a working mother with limited time and energy, she really had to plan ahead for these activities. By the way, her largest expenditure from her Marketing Budget was baby-sitting fees.

For example, on February 7, she went to a popular book-store, found an interesting book (in keeping with her brand), and sat in a centrally located chair. She just sat and read there for an hour, but she didn't get so engrossed in her book that no one wanted to disturb her. She kept looking up and smiling at passersby. Then on February 9, she had a cup of coffee at Star-bucks in nearby Cambridge (not her usual stop) while reading her newspaper for half an hour. Her conversation starter (a Boston Red Sox cap in keeping with her brand attribute "Sports Lover") was placed at the edge of her table. Read the remainder of Claire's entries to see what a diverse and active month she had. Claire showed me three months on her calendar, starting in February, and each was as dynamic as February. In mid-March, Claire met a man at her second speed-dating event and began a serious relationship with him. She ended up happily tossing away her April calendar.

CLAIRE'S FEBRUARY *PROGRAM* CALENDAR

Sunday	Monday	Tuesday	Wednesday	Thursday	Friday	Saturday
1 Make 15 tele-marketing calls Blind date from Match .com	**2**	**3** Grocery shop at Star Market	**4**	**5** Dry cleaners on Newbury Street	**6** Lecture at art museum	**7** Read book at large bookstore
8 Join new singles group Make 15 tele-marketing calls	**9** Coffee at Starbucks in Cambridge	**10** Blind date from Match .com	**11** Teach Web-site design class at Boston Center for Adult Education	**12**	**13** Dinner party at Belle's house	**14** Speed-dating event
15 Write personal ad for *Boston Magazine* Make 15 tele-marketing calls	**16**	**17** Match Live event (wine tasting)	**18**	**19** Lunch with new colleague (Linda)	**20** Take bus to work Blind date via Step #9	**21** Volunteer firefighter orienta-tion
22 Walk dog in Boston Commons Make 15 tele-marketing calls	**23** Business trip: arrive early at airport Red Carpet Club	**24**	**25** Dinner with my children at Pizza Den (single dads?)	**26**	**27** Happy Hour with single-parent group	**28**

REALITY CHECK

As you continue to see in this step and others, *The Program* requires a big time investment. You're comfortable with that in theory since you've decided that finding a husband is your #1 priority this year. But I would be remiss if I didn't share with you a reality check that happened to Alice, age 36, who works as a paralegal. Alice is one of the most devoted clients I've ever had on *The Program*. She frequently meets blind dates from the Internet for lunch during the workweek, she typically attends singles events or Happy Hours three nights per week, and she is constantly networking on the phone to follow up on leads from her direct-mail campaign or telemarketing calls. Recently, she met a man (Garrett) whom she hopes to marry, and has been spending most of her time with him.

But one day she called me in tears, saying that she had just been put "on notice" at work. She was on the verge of losing her job. Her supervisor complained of her long lunch hours, her suddenly careless mistakes, and her personal phone calls. Clearly, *The Program* was the culprit. My first question to her was, "If you had to lose your job or Garrett, which would you choose?" Without hesitating, she said, "My job." Luckily, she didn't have to lose either. We figured out a plan for her to talk with her supervisor, put in extra hours at work, cut back a little on her time with Garrett, and basically salvage her job. She wasn't fired, but the lesson she learned was that there can be consequences for having priorities.

TIPS FOR MASS MARKETING

Despite any reality checks, you must forge ahead, maximizing the opportunities to meet men whenever you go out. Obviously, just showing up in various places is only part of the challenge. Often women complain to me that they've already tried certain singles events or groups, but had no luck meeting anyone. I immediately ask, "Did you make the most of your time there?" My question refers to meeting men as well as meeting women with whom you can network. Here are a few more tips to maximize your opportunities:

1. **Arrive everywhere 30 minutes early:** If you are attending a singles function of any kind, always plan to arrive 30 minutes early. This allows you to be one of the first in the room and to scope out the situation. By getting settled and placing yourself in a central location early, you will have the best view of everyone who walks in the door and can have your pick of anyone on whom you want to focus. Usually most other people are new to these situations as well, so if you know the lay of the land, you have a natural conversation starter to help someone find something or understand what to do. You also have a little "quality time" with the first arrivals, so you're almost guaranteed to meet at least one new person that night.

2. **Go solo:** It is infinitely easier for a man to approach a woman and start a conversation with her if she is standing alone than to approach her if she is surrounded by her girlfriends. Men can be shy, and no one likes to face rejection in front of a crowd. Of course, you need to put safety first by not walking alone in parking lots late at night. But if you do arrive with a girlfriend, make

a pact with her that you'll immediately separate and stand alone. This may feel very uncomfortable to you, but remember, no one else is focused on your "alone status" except a single man trying to meet you, which is exactly what you want.

3. **Position yourself:** What should you do if you see a man you'd like to meet at a public place—a party, a restaurant, or a singles event—but he has not noticed you yet? You have tried to make eye contact with him, and have tried smiling at him, but neither has worked. You may need to position yourself in his line of sight, or literally position yourself in his path. Try moving to a different or closer spot in the room where he can see you better. What if he's just not wearing his glasses to appear more handsome and can't see you at a distance? Or try the old tactic of walking to the Ladies Room directly in front of him, even if it's the long way around.

4. **Start and continue the conversation:** Refer to the Conversation Starters and Conversation Follow-Up sections in Step #8, Guerrilla Marketing.

5. **Be prepared:** Just as the Boy Scout motto says. Once a conversation has been initiated, it's not always easy to keep it going when you're on the spot. Before you attend an event, brainstorm with your Mentor for some good questions to keep a conversation interesting. Depending on where you are—a party, the office, a speed-dating event—you might consider a few of these:

   • Tell me something most people would never guess about you.
   • How did you first get interested in your profession?
   • Do you have any interesting trips you'd like to take?
   • How do you know our host?
   • What was your favorite thing you did this weekend?
   • What were you like in high school?
   • Did you see the game last night?

You have been successful with Step #11, and can begin Step #12, if you:

1. Understand why volume is critical to *The Program*.

2. Built a list of approximately 100+ opportunities specific to your city, organized into four categories.

3. Integrated onto your calendar the tactics from Steps #7 through #11 for at least one month, ensuring a diversified portfolio of activities.

4. Maximized your opportunities using the five tactics provided under "Tips for Mass Marketing."

5. Followed through with the goals that you set for yourself this month.

6. Ended this step with a positive attitude and didn't get discouraged if Mr. Right is still elusive.

Step #12

Event Marketing:

Throw a Program Party!

WHAT I LEARNED AT
HARVARD BUSINESS SCHOOL

Event marketing is a great way to promote a product. A marketer can either create her own event or sponsor an existing one. An event gathers people and focuses their attention. The key is to select an event that is intriguing and projects the same image as your brand. When customers attend the event, they should make a positive connection in their minds between the event and the product, thus reinforcing the product's brand image.

For example, Evian Water sponsors a U.S. Open Tennis event every year. The brand image of Evian is "Healthy, Upscale, and Inspirational." The U.S. Open is a perfect tournament for Evian to align its brand with. It is athletic and fitness-oriented (it projects a healthy image), it attracts an upscale audience (tennis is considered an upscale sport), and it showcases the best tennis champions in the world (thus, it is inspirational). Evian places banners on the sides of the tennis court, and the players drink Evian during their water breaks, which reinforces the brand connection. Evian invites its top distributors and vendors as guests to its U.S. Open event, hosts a courtside VIP tent, and hands out Evian-logo tennis balls as gifts and prizes. It's a classic event marketing scenario.

Out of sight is out of mind, so creating an event can help keep a product top-of-mind with customers. An event is a great excuse to communicate with customers *prior* to the event to invite them; interact with them *during* the event to socialize; and follow up with them *after* the event to thank them for coming. An event is a unique opportunity to create interaction and a positive relationship with key customers and influencers.

WHAT IS A *PROGRAM* PARTY?

So you're thinking you're going to throw a party, have some wine, and chitchat about random things? No. That's what you might have done in the past, and you're still single. But I think you knew by now a *Program* step couldn't be so simple.

A *Program* Party is not just *any* party. It is a strategic, networking event to gather men and women together in a room to showcase your brand, communicate with them, and keep yourself top-of-mind. It is also a volume generator for you to bring new "customers" in the door now that you are in the latter stages of *The Program*. You may need some fresh faces and new supporters at this point. A party is perfectly timed and orchestrated now in your *Program* journey because you have been

hard at work building a network, fine-tuning your brand advertising, and getting comfortable with asking for fix-ups. This is
your night to bring it all together.

*This is also my favorite step because it is where I met my own
husband!*

PROGRAM PARTY GOALS

Of course your #1 goal is to find a husband (as always!), but
more specific party goals are to:

- Create new prospects—new men to date and new women
  who can fix you up.
- Keep yourself top-of-mind with your "customer base." Even if
  someone doesn't attend, you've made contact with that
  person through your invitation and thus provided a reminder
  that you're still available.
- Show off the "new you" (similar to a coming-out debut party).
- Inspire goodwill with other women who will benefit from
  your party, too. You'll invite old boyfriends and dates who
  didn't click with you and introduce them to other women at
  your party; hopefully, down the road these women will
  introduce you to someone else in return.

PROGRAM PARTY DETAILS

Theme

People host parties all the time, and they are usually run of the
mill. Make yours stand out from the crowd. You need a catchy
theme. Be creative and unique (but not hokey). If people think,
"Now *that* sounds like fun!" they will RSVP "yes" with enthusiasm.

If possible, make your theme consistent with your brand. One of my clients, Kelly, chose an Italian theme for her party. She had lived in Italy for 2 years, and "Italy" was part of her brand. She gave her party a catchy headline: "The Leaning Tower of Pisa Party." What did that mean? Well, it really meant nothing, except it was Italian sounding and grabbed people's attention as being "not-your-run-of-the-mill party." She served antipasto hors d'oeuvres and Bellini drinks. She had an Italian flag on the front door and handed out small packages of tricolored pasta as party favors at the end of the night.

What theme ideas can *you* create? Maybe host a Home Depot party where you invite people to paint one room in your house a new color. Everyone comes in jeans and old T-shirts to help paint the room. You provide the paint, the brushes, the rollers, and great food and drink. And give everyone a small paintbrush as a party favor.

What about throwing a party to congratulate a friend on an achievement? Or a welcome-to-town party for a newcomer? You can always have a unique holiday party, especially to celebrate one of the more obscure holidays that people usually don't observe. Perhaps a Flag Day party? An Arbor Day party? A George Washington's Birthday party? I have a friend who hired a Thomas Jefferson impersonator once for a party, and it was billed as a "Night for Historical Dialogue." Or how about a Sports party during the Super Bowl, World Series, or Stanley Cup? Perhaps an Academy Awards party?

And use what you've got! Do you already have something unique that would make a great party theme? If you have a beautiful garden outside your house, host your party outdoors and make it a "Garden Party." If you have a friend who plays classical guitar, invite her to play during your party and call it a "Celebrate Classical Music Party." One of my clients, Alyssa, worked in an art gallery, and used a new artist exhibition as the theme for her party. She invited everyone for wine and cheese and to preview the exhibit at the gallery before it opened to the public, which created excitement for her event. Be sure to think about any assets that you already have when creating your party theme.

Whatever theme you choose, make it light and upbeat. No antiwar parties, please! And take this opportunity to highlight your brand and show off any of your special talents. If you're a great cook, serve delicious food that you've prepared yourself. If you're a talented photographer, have some of your photos on display.

Invitations

Your invitations should be extended first in person or by phone, and followed up with a printed invitation by mail. This will be time-consuming, but this is not just an ordinary party. You are entertaining as an excuse to communicate with the people around you: friends, acquaintances, co-workers, ex-boyfriends, former dates, single parents of your kids' friends, and even total strangers.

Your verbal invite should encompass a short conversation to ask your guests to reserve the date. There is something specific here you need to do that can't be accomplished on a printed invitation: While you have folks on the phone or have their attention in person, take the opportunity to provide a gentle reminder that you are still looking to meet someone special this year, and encourage them to bring any of their friends to your party. Many people might not feel comfortable initiating a direct fix-up for you, but would feel comfortable casually bringing along a single friend to a big party to see what happens when the two of you meet on your own. Then they don't feel responsible if it doesn't work out. You are cleverly creating alternative avenues for fix-ups: something for everyone's comfort level.

The printed invitation should be chosen according to your theme. An Italian party invitation could be printed on Florentine paper. A Home Depot party invitation could be printed to look like those free paint chip samples given away at hardware stores. The invitations should be mailed 3 weeks prior to the party date, and should include the guest name with the suffix "and friends" on the envelope address. If you have been unable to reach someone by phone, add a handwritten note in the invitation to encourage the person to bring friends. Be sure to include an RSVP-by date so that you'll know how many people to expect. Because you have extended open invitations for guests to bring their friends, you need to plan for a possible surge in attendance.

Guest List

Your guest list requires a great deal of strategic thought. It's okay to invite your usual crowd, but make sure they understand when you extend your verbal invitation that they are highly encouraged to bring friends (male or female) who are unknown to you. But your party is really designed to invite new people who don't know you well. You are creating greater volume by reaching out to more and more people and enlisting them in your husband-hunting search. This is your chance to go through your Rolodex again and invite the insurance broker you met once during a business transaction, and your neighbor's cousin whom you met briefly last year when he was visiting next door, and the receptionist at your dentist's office with whom you've always had a pleasant exchange, and . . . keep thinking of more and more people!

Now is also the time to make any bad blind dates from your past count for something. Invite to your party all those one-date-only men you've met through fix-ups, and especially through online dating. The reason? Tell them to bring their friends. You want to get all these people in a room and see what happens. They may already know a few people at your party coincidentally because this is such a small world. Even if they don't know anyone besides you, these men will make their own connections with guests, and hopefully have a good enough time so that they will invite you to *their* next party or event.

Where

The party can be held in your home or backyard. If your space is too small or for some reason not appropriate to host a large party, think of other creative locations: perhaps a back room in a restaurant, a social hall at a church or synagogue, or an art gallery or antiques shop that might provide rental space for evening parties. Sometimes gallery or retail space is provided free because the owner will gain exposure for her products with your guests. You can even ask close friends to host the party at their home, in exchange for your undying gratitude!

Make sure that the space can accommodate large crowds and easy avenues for circulation (see the following section for more details). You have a lot of people to meet and greet that night.

Circulating

Because this party is designed as a volume booster for you, it's essential that you circulate continuously. How often have you been cornered at a party talking to one person practically the whole night and couldn't get away politely? This must not happen at your *Program* Party, so plan ahead to ensure that it doesn't. This means enlisting two or three friends (including your Mentor, if possible) as "Party Buddies" to keep you circulating. Their job is to watch your movements, make sure you aren't stuck in one place too long (not more than ten minutes), and help disentangle you from lengthy conversations.

Identify these friends in advance and call them before the party to request their assistance. Don't make light of your request: They must take this job seriously and keep watch over you during the party. The reason you need to enlist more than one friend is that no one person can be relied upon to help you every moment. You need a Plan A, Plan B, and Plan C in place. Select some of your more aggressive friends who won't hesitate to interrupt a conversation and insist that you "come into the kitchen and take care of something right away."

Ten minutes is just the right amount of time to talk with one guest or small group during the party. It's just long enough to reconnect with old friends, establish a brief rapport with someone new, and advertise your brand. To exit gracefully from a conversation after ten minutes, use one of these two tactics:

1. **Recap tactic:** Provide a brief recap of your conversation with someone to show that you were listening, and offer closure. For example, "I enjoyed talking to you about your trip to Hawaii, and it was nice to meet you [or see you again]." Then smile and

walk away. This tactic rarely hurts the person's feelings since you've indicated that you had a nice chat and didn't offer a fake, insulting excuse to leave such as, "I'm going to get a drink" or "I see someone I have to go talk to."

2. **Introduction tactic:** Ask the person with whom you are speaking, "Do you know Tom? He's really great. Let me introduce you to him." Then bring the person over to Tom, make an introduction, and let the two of them talk while you gracefully drift away and continue circulating.

Your Look

Obviously, you want to look your best. This is the time to make sure your "packaging" is perfect. Shop for something new to wear and charge it to your Marketing Budget. Your choice should be consistent with everything you learned in Step #3, Packaging, and Step #5, Branding: feminine, flattering to your figure, congruent with your brand—and no power suits! If your Mentor is available, bring her shopping with you, or at least show your outfit to her in advance of the party. Advance clothing approval from a male friend or two is also preferable. Reserve appointments earlier during the day of the party to have your hair and make-up done professionally. Think of yourself as Cinderella going to the Ball—you want to feel transformed and special, because this feeling will project the right kind of energy to your guests.

Helpers

In addition to your Party Buddies, you need a few people to help with the logistics of the party: the food, drinks, coat retrieval, ringing telephone, and even potential toilet overflow!

You have to stay focused on your party goals, and can't be distracted by logistics tonight of all nights. If you can afford to hire a professional caterer or some college students to help you, that's the ideal scenario. Otherwise, ask your closest friends (including your Mentor, if she's attending) to take 30-minute shifts during the party and perform these functions as needed. Be very clear with your helpers about what you expect them to do, and when they should do it. Consider handing them a printed list with their responsibilities in advance, so that they won't have to interrupt you during an important conversation with a question about party logistics.

Go All-Out

It can be expensive and time-consuming to plan a big party, but it is one of the best uses of your time and Marketing Budget. So go all-out. Not only will this event generate volume for you with the new people you meet that night, but hopefully it will have a ripple effect and spur other party invitations for you in the future. When deciding whether to add "this touch" or "that touch" to your party, think in terms of making a long-term investment, not in terms of saving time and money. You want to inspire your guests to feel gratitude after attending your wonderful event and to reciprocate with future party invitations and fix-ups.

MORE TIPS FOR YOUR *PROGRAM* PARTY

1. **Prepare small talk:** Because you will be circulating all night and having short conversations with many different people, you need to be armed with an arsenal of small talk. Refer back to any

lists of questions you made in Step #11, Mass Marketing, prior to attending a singles event. A list with ten topics or anecdotes that you can use for small talk will make circulating easier. Always be able to discuss the seasons' sports teams when you're single! If you're not sports-minded, start reading the sports pages in the newspaper and have a sports-oriented friend teach you the basics for small talk purposes. Also, use any interesting trivia from that fly-fishing (or other male-focused) class you may have taken last month. Think of a few stories related to the theme of the party. Maybe have a joke handy (ask your friends for suggestions if you don't know any). Be sure to invest the preparation time in advance so that circulating and being charming appear effortless.

2. **Eat beforehand:** You have a big agenda tonight, and you don't have time to sample the food yourself. Eat before the party starts, not only to save you time during the event, but to ensure that the food tastes good and that nothing gets stuck in your teeth later. And don't have more than one alcoholic drink: You need your wits about you!

3. **Stagger the arrivals:** Depending on the size of your party and the space constraints of your venue, consider staggering the arrivals of your guests. Divide your list in half (giving careful consideration to the mixture of people in each half) and give them two separate time frames for your party. For example, tell the first half that the party runs from 5:00–7:00, and tell the second half that it's from 6:00–8:00. The room will probably be quite crowded around 6:30, but staggering the arrivals will maximize your ability to connect with more people.

4. **Give a party favor:** People usually don't get party favors at adult parties (beyond some weddings and upscale charity fund-raisers), so this practice will be unique and appreciated. It's also an excel-

lent opportunity to send someone home with an object that will keep you top-of-mind for a while. Be creative when choosing a party favor that reflects your party theme and/or personal brand. Seek advice from your Mentor and other clever friends. It doesn't have to be an expensive item.

One idea I liked was from a "Stanley Cup Hockey Playoff" party: The hostess handed out hockey pucks at the end of the night. She suggested that her guests use them as paperweights, which was brilliant. Why brilliant? Because a paperweight sits on someone's desk and reminds the person about you while he or she is sitting near the phone . . . ready and able to make networking calls for you! Another good idea is from a client of mine whose brand included her profession as a "Nurse." She handed out small boxes of fluorescent-colored Band-Aids for her party favors. This was a unique idea and a practical gift (everyone uses Band-Aids at some point). This was also fun and memorable because of the bright colors.

5. **Know your guest list:** Be sure to spend an hour prior to your party reviewing your guest list. Know it cold. It can be difficult to remember names, backgrounds, and connections in a large group, so allow yourself time to study who's who and keep their details straight.

One woman I know used a party guest list quite cleverly, although not for the purposes of finding a husband; she was instead looking for a job. She was at a party in New York. She saw the names of two men on the guest list in advance. She didn't know either of them personally, but had seen photos of them in the media: Martin S., the president of a large bank corporation, and George T., a famous financier. During the party, she approached Martin S. and said, "George T. would like to say hello to you. Please wait here." Then she walked across the room and approached George T. She said, "Martin S. would like to say hello to you. Please come with me." She then brought the two men together, placed herself in the middle, and proceeded to introduce herself as they all chatted together. You've gotta love a woman with chutzpah!

6. **Create goodwill:** After reviewing your guest list, identify several introductions that you'd like to make among your guests. This includes introducing single men who are not The One for you to other single women. Also make connections between guests with similar business or personal interests. As you enable new friendships to develop between others at your party, you are creating goodwill for yourself in the future.

7. **Take a break:** Every hour, you should duck into the powder room or your bedroom to take a deep breath and check your appearance. Do you have any food stuck in your teeth? Do you need to reapply your lipstick? Maybe you need to review the guest list that you have hidden somewhere in your bedroom to remind yourself of a person's name. You may want to write yourself a note to follow up with someone after the party, if necessary. Take just two minutes alone each hour to regroup and make sure your party goals are on track.

CUSTOMER SERVICE

Party Follow-Up

Step #12 is hardly complete after the last guest leaves your party. As you know from earlier steps, a world-class salesperson always follows up on her leads. A successful party should yield at least five new contacts, male or female. There will probably be many leads to pursue after this event, and you should make a list right away of the necessary follow-ups so you won't forget anything.

While it's still fresh in your mind, spend 15 minutes later that night making a list of all the new contacts you made. Bring out your guest list and make notations next to the names: Did he bring someone new? If so, what is that person's name and background? Did she mention fixing you up with a single friend? If so, with whom and when? Did you see two guests meeting each other for the first time who seemed to bond? Was there a small group that would be ideally suited for a future dinner party or outing that you could initiate?

Write down all these connections and schedule the necessary follow-ups on your calendar: reminder phone calls in ten days to anyone who suggested a fix-up, invitations for smaller group outings for you and selected guests who connected at your party, and thank-you calls to anyone who helped you perform a hostess function during the evening.

To Pursue or Not to Pursue

If you remember the femininity guidelines from Step #3, Packaging, it is *not* recommended that you directly call a man whom you met at your party to suggest a date. Hopefully he will call you first if you made a connection with him. If not, use your party follow-up as a convenient way to break the rules once with a low-key approach. If there was one new man in particular who caught your interest, call the mutual friend who brought him that night and plan a small-group outing that includes him. In this case, your mutual friend could casually invite him along, and it won't be *too* obvious that you're interested in him. Sound like high school? That's okay. You're young at heart.

The Dating Exchange

Another idea for your party follow-up is to organize a future gathering that I call a "Dating Exchange." This capitalizes on the resources of any new single women whom you may have met at your party. The idea is that most single women know at least one single man who is not The One: ex-boyfriends, past blind dates who were nice but with whom there was no chemistry, or even single brothers or male cousins. Invite several single women to your Dating Exchange, open a few bottles of wine, and have each woman put the name of a single man into a hat. Take turns pulling names from the hat as you each get assigned a "recycled" single man from someone else in the room. The woman who wrote down the man's name initially will call him to arrange the blind date with the new woman. You can exchange names with each other later to fine-tune the matches if you draw a name that seems to be a complete mismatch for any reason, but everyone goes home that night with one new blind date. It's a creative follow-up party, and a lot of fun. The wine can be, however, an important component!

YOU MAY BE WONDERING . . .

- *How often can I have a Program Party?*

  A *Program* Party is really a tall order. If done correctly, it will take a lot of your time and energy to plan, coordinate, and execute such a feat. And it will make a dent in your *Program* Marketing Budget. So this full-scale event is not likely to come around often. Perhaps twice during 18 months is ideal.

If you know a few other people who would like to cohost a *Program* Party with you, however, you can spread out the work and cost, augment your guest list, and have additional parties.

• Can I use some of these event marketing tactics at other parties that I attend?

Absolutely. Classic event marketing tactics such as circulating, preparing small talk, creating goodwill, and follow-up are not only transferable, but they should become habit for you at all parties or gatherings.

• Do you really expect me to call a man with whom I had one bad date six months ago and invite him to my party with his friends?

Of course! *The Program* is a bold, assertive plan to find your husband. This is not a lazy summer day at the beach. You should not hesitate to make the time you spent on a bad date count for something. Think of it as a dividend earned on your time invested. You invested your valuable time preparing for that date, sitting through what turned out to be a date with Mr. Wrong, and complaining about it later to your friends. So now you can cash in on it.

Simply call him and give a cheerful hello. State right up front that you are calling to invite him to a big party that you're throwing. Don't let him wonder why you're calling: He might think you want to pursue something with him, or that you're angry if he never called back. Also, let him know right away that there will be many single women at your party, and you would be delighted if he brought several of his single male friends.

What's the worst that can happen? He declines your lovely invitation? No problem; you have many other guests on your list. He doesn't remember you? No problem; just introduce yourself again!

• *What is the ideal male-to-female ratio at a Program party?*

The ideal ratio at your *Program* Party is 60% men and 40% women. You might assume that it would be preferable to have 90% men if possible, but you want the men to have an enjoyable evening, too. They will have more fun if the ratio is close to even. Besides, they would probably leave early if there weren't enough women. Remember that you are looking to meet new women as well, not just men, because women are your best "niche" for arranging fix-ups.

You have succeeded with Step #12, and can begin Step #13, if you:

1. Strategically planned a party according to the guidelines for theme, location, invitations, circulating, your appearance, helpers, and going all-out.
2. Hosted a party.
3. Used the tips provided in this chapter to maximize your party.
4. Pursued all leads after the party with meticulous follow-up.
5. Gained at least five new contacts (male or female) as a result of your party.

Step #13

Product Life Cycle:

Recharge Yourself

WHAT I LEARNED AT
HARVARD BUSINESS SCHOOL

Products have a natural life cycle. They typically go through four stages, beginning with their *introduction*, then moving to a *growth* stage in which they gain momentum, then advancing into a *maturity* stage, and finally going into a stage of *decline*, when they might be withdrawn from the marketplace. This cycle is normal and expected, and indicates that a product has had a good run. The best products will be reintroduced as "new and improved" and begin their life cycle again. This reflects the outcome of a marketing manager's ongoing attempt to study customer patterns, make adjustments, and keep a product current. A successful marketing manager will anticipate these cyclical stages and plan for their inevitable occurrence.

WHY IT'S IMPORTANT TO RECHARGE

The Program is a marathon. You will find a husband quickly with *The Program*, but it still takes some time. You have to pace and take care of yourself, both physically and emotionally. Staying motivated may be your greatest challenge. After months of intense focus and growth, you are bound to experience a decline in energy and motivation. This is natural and expected. You have been working hard on the previous twelve steps, gaining momentum, and becoming confident in your stride. And you have just hosted your big *Program* Party. After so much effort, you are probably exhausted. But you can't look or act tired, since clearly that would not project an appealing image to a potential husband. So you need—and, indeed, deserve—a break! At this point, you should do things completely off-*Program*.

Finally, I can offer you a step you're gonna like! It's short and sweet. In Step #13, you are not going to behave as you have been in the previous twelve steps. You are going to revel in mindless, unassertive activities. You are not going to care how you look or what people think. Indulge in whatever makes you happy!

HOW TO RECHARGE

You need to recharge both physically and emotionally. Both realms are equally important to sustain the momentum you need to find a husband in the coming months.

Physically

There are many ways to recharge physically, and everyone will have her own method that works best. What makes your body feel rested and rejuvenated? Maybe you should take a vacation, either alone or with family and friends. Go someplace that inspires you: perhaps to the mountains or to the ocean. Or go to a destination spa (my personal favorite!) where you can dip into your Marketing Budget and splurge. If that's too expensive, spend a day or even an hour at a local day spa for a pedicure or a massage. Take your dog to a grooming salon! Take a long hike or run 10 miles. Take a day or two off from work and do whatever you feel like doing: sleep late, plant beautiful flowers in your garden, bake cookies, or try a new recipe from your favorite cookbook. Read a good book (but *not* this one!). Visit a local attraction you've never been to before. If there's an aquarium in your city, go and watch the soothing sea turtles and fish float by. Spend a weekend at a lovely bed-and-breakfast nearby that serves a country-style breakfast and herbal tea.

Be sure to wear your oldest and most comfortable clothes, even if they are unflattering, and certainly don't wear make-up. Don't even blow-dry your hair, for heaven's sake!

However you choose to recharge physically, make it something that has little or no chance for meeting Mr. Right. This time period should be stress-free and without agenda.

Emotionally

Use this time to recharge emotionally as well. Get some perspective on your life by making a list of everything *good* that you have. This list might include your: health, family, friends, job, children, pets, home, and anything else that you take for granted as you pursue your #1 priority of finding a husband. Really spend time here appreciating what you *do* have instead of what is missing.

While you're making lists, start another one about all the successes that you've had on *The Program*. Even if you haven't found Mr. Wonderful yet, I bet you've experienced some triumphs, big and little. Congratulate yourself on being open-minded about joining a new singles group, completing your online profile, being asked on a second date by a man you really like, not wearing all black to a party, or not crying when you got home from a terrible blind date. Write down as many items as you can remember: No deed is too trivial! When this list is compiled, ask yourself if you've made more progress in the time since you joined *The Program* than in the last five years combined. I will be shocked if your answer is no, and hope that your yes answer will help in the emotional recharging process.

Perhaps you are simply feeling disorganized now because you've been going out three or four nights each week. What you might really crave is doing a mundane task such as rearranging your closet or putting a year's worth of photos in an album.

You may also just need a good cry. There are probably a lot of pent-up emotions that you've accumulated and suppressed during *Program* steps thus far: sadness from unmet expectations with a date or boyfriend, feelings of rejection, and many nights of loneliness. Go rent a sad video (a real tearjerker!) and cry your eyes out. For me, the movie *Terms of Endearment* always requires an entire box of Kleenex. It's good for you to purge these emotions from your system before continuing on your journey. I told you in the beginning of this book that there is no psychological advice here about why you're still single—only action. But of course you are not a robot and must deal with the inevitable feelings that go along with this territory. *The Program* process is often an emotional roller coaster.

Most important, the difference between a future bride (a "*Program* woman") and a forever-single woman is that the former doesn't let her negative emotions stall her progress. She deals with these normal feelings at the appropriate place and time, then moves onward and upward!

CASE STUDIES:
HOW I RECHARGED

- **Nina, age 44:** "I couldn't afford a vacation, so I tried to turn my apartment into a tropical island resort for a weekend. I told my friends and family that I was going out of town and turned off my phone, fax, and cell phone. I made myself piña colada drinks in the blender, listened to the Beach Boys on my CD player, and watched the Travel Channel. I even put a chocolate mint on my pillow each night. I slept late, read a mystery novel, and had a relaxing vacation without leaving home."

- **Marian, age 50:** "I took 3 personal days off from work and went to visit my daughter. She's in college now, and we rarely have time for long talks like we used to. That's really what I craved. I timed my visit with her winter break, and invited her for a slumber party at a hotel near her dorm. We ordered room service and stayed up until three in the morning talking about her boyfriends, her roommate, and her plans for next semester abroad. It felt wonderful to see the beautiful girl I had created, and to know that she was happy."

- **Amanda, age 36:** "I had always wanted to learn how to scuba dive. I flew down to Florida, enrolled in a 5-day crash course, and earned my scuba certification. It was invigorating to accomplish a challenge like that. The weather was beautiful, the nights were quiet, and the ocean made all my problems seem so small. I guess you could say I saw 'a lot of fish in the sea' when I was there, but it felt great to think about cooking them instead of marrying them!"

- **Pauline, age 62:** "I went to visit my best friend in Texas for three days. She had been divorced for several years, but is now remarried to a terrific husband. She is happier than she's ever been in her life. Instead of feeling jealous that she had everything I want, I felt optimistic that if it could happen to her, it could happen to me. I saw in Texas what I know will be my life soon too, and I was inspired!"

- **Julia, age 41:** "I stayed home for three days and rented several of the saddest videos ever made. I had just ended a four-month relationship with a man whom I had definitely thought was The One. I needed a major cry. I had Chinese food or pizza delivered every night for dinner, I literally burned the T-shirt he had left in my closet, and I took an hour-long bubble bath each night. By day four, I was so sick of being around myself that I went outside and ran six miles. I got my groove back."

SOMETIMES YOU JUST HAVE TO LAUGH

The Program is serious business, as you know by now. But by Step #13, you just have to see the humor in the situation and not take yourself too seriously. I received a joke on the Internet a while ago titled "Marketing 101." It's an irreverent version of several marketing terms in *The Program*. It made me laugh, and I hope it will make you laugh, too.

Marketing 101

You see a handsome guy at a party. You go up to him and say, "I'm fantastic in bed."

That's Direct Marketing.

You're at a party with friends and see a handsome guy. One of your friends goes up to him, points at you, and says, "She's fantastic in bed."

That's Advertising.

You see a handsome guy at a party. You go up to him and get his telephone number. The next day you call and say, "Hi, I'm fantastic in bed."

That's Telemarketing.

You're at a party and see a handsome guy. You walk up to him and pour him a drink. You say, "May I?" and reach up to straighten his tie, brushing your breast lightly against his arm, and then say, "By the way, I'm fantastic in bed."

That's Public Relations.

You're at a party and see a handsome guy. He walks up to you and says, "I hear you're fantastic in bed."

That's Brand Recognition.

You're at a party and see a handsome guy. You talk him into going home with your friend.

That's a Sales Rep.

Your friend can't satisfy him so he calls you.

That's Tech Support.

You're at a party and see a handsome guy. You say, "By the way, I'm fantastic in bed—want to take me home and give it a try?" When you get to his place, you change into lingerie and climb into bed. When he makes a move, you point out that you never promised him sex.

That's Product Marketing.

You're on your way to a party when you realize that there could be handsome men in all the houses you're passing. So you climb onto the roof of one house situated toward the center of the block and shout at the top of your lungs, "I'm fantastic in bed!"

That's Spam.

WHEN TO STOP RECHARGING

While it may be tempting to stay in the cozy retreat of this step forever, at some point you must stop recharging and move on to the next step. It's very easy to drift off course, so usually I recommend spending five to seven days on this step. Take your own temperature and stay at this rest stop for the time period you really need—as long as you're making progress toward rejuvenation.

If you are wallowing for weeks on end in a depressed state, you are probably not using this step in the spirit in which it is designed. You may be slipping backward and losing hope. Talk to your Mentor and find a way to resurface.

Try to end this step with something uplifting, something to really boost your ego and your spirits. If you have a good relationship with your parents, maybe visit them and feel like their little girl again. Let them spoil you. Or maybe what would feel better instead is charging an outrageously expensive new purse to your credit card?

The transition back to reality is usually met with a groan. It's just like coming back from a wonderful vacation and thinking about returning to work the next day. Ugh. So plan ahead for this inevitable feeling. Use the last day of your recharging period as a planning day. Get out your calendar and organize your *Program* activities for the next three months. Set new weekly and monthly goals. Try to schedule a "Back on Track" lunch with your Mentor for this last day. Seeing your Mentor again, and reviewing your new goals with her, should help kick you back into gear. And if you have a favorite song that always gets your spirits soaring and your heart pumping, blast it on your CD player the next morning as you return to work.

LOSING MOTIVATION: WHAT IS A *PROGRAM* DROP-OUT?

I have worked with clients who encounter their fair share of disappointments during *The Program* and lose motivation. Even though this is perfectly normal, some women cannot rise above these setbacks and want to permanently drop out of *The Program*. Big mistake! *The Program* is clearly hard work, but the payoff of finding a wonderful husband is worth it, don't you think? I have seen so many people find happiness only after going through a difficult experience. It was actually the pain that made them strong enough to get what they wanted.

Besides, if you drop out, where will you go? I will tell you: back to the previous patterns that didn't work for you. Back to being lonely and to being resigned that you'll never meet someone. So stay with me . . . As so many women can already attest, *The Program* really works in the end!

YOU MAY BE WONDERING . . .

• *If everything is going really well for me on The Program and I don't feel like I need to recharge, should I skip this step?*

Only one person in the history of *The Program* has ever asked me this, but I thought I'd include it in this book because it made me realize that not everyone wants to stop and smell the roses. Still, the answer is no. Even if you have a date with a different man every night of the week, and more fix-ups are pouring in from your direct-mail, niche marketing, and telemarketing campaigns, you still need to take a break now. The reason is that you will definitely burn out at some point down the road from all this activity. It's better to schedule your break now than to come crashing to an emergency halt later.

• *What if my biggest emotion at this point is not fatigue, sadness, or loneliness? What if my dominant emotion is really* **anger?**

Many women tell me how utterly angry they are. "Men are jerks, they don't want a commitment, they have wasted my time . . ." And these women get mad at *The Program*, too: "Why do I have to change my packaging and behavior patterns to find a husband?" You have every right to get angry. In fact, get *really* angry. This is the time and place for it. Recharging is as much about venting your feelings of anger as it is about relaxing and crying. Find a way to let off steam. Pound your fists into your

246 | Step #13: Product Life Cycle

pillow until the feathers fly out. Go into your closet and scream as loud as you can. Whatever works for you!

I didn't create the reality out there. Yes, men have a lot of problems, and it's not fair that you should have to market yourself to find a husband. I'm just here to help you achieve your goal while working within the confines of reality.

• *How often can I come back to this step?*

Recharging is a very productive step. It helps maintain your positive attitude, which is essential to finding a husband. Come back to this step whenever you are feeling discouraged, as long as you're not spending more time *on* than *off* Step #13. Perhaps once every three or four months is reasonable. Repeat visits here are like booster shots: Get one every so often just to keep up your immunities against a decline in energy and motivation.

You have succeeded with Step #13, and can begin Step #14, if you:

1. Took a short break from *The Program*.
2. Did something off-*Program* physically and emotionally.
3. Had a good laugh, a good cry, and a fist-pounding session with your pillow.
4. Ended this step with an uplifting act, a *Program* planning day, and a "Back on Track" lunch with your Mentor.
5. Feel recharged and ready to continue with the next steps.

Step #14

Quarterly Performance Review:

Evaluate Your Results

WHAT I LEARNED AT
HARVARD BUSINESS SCHOOL

The best companies require regular performance reviews of their business to ensure optimal results. In other words, every few months managers must evaluate their strategy and reconcile their *estimated* versus *actual* performance. Inevitably, change has occurred since the original strategy was planned. Perhaps new market conditions exist, research turned out to be faulty, or costs were higher than expected. The only thing in business that is constant is *change*. Successful managers anticipate change, continually evaluate their results, and revise their action plan accordingly.

WHAT IS *THE PROGRAM*'S QUARTERLY PERFORMANCE REVIEW?

A Quarterly Performance Review is taking a hard look at what has been working for you on *The Program*, and what hasn't. The results will help you fine-tune your tactics and get *The Program* running efficiently for you. Now that you have spent time recharging in Step #13, you should have a new perspective from which to see your efforts more clearly. This evaluation process will examine the gap between what you *wanted* to happen while searching for a husband versus what *actually happened*. The last thing you need to do is waste your time and energy pursuing something that is not yielding productive results. As the saying goes, "Those who cannot remember the past are condemned to repeat it."

YOUR RESULTS

So what exactly are your results from *The Program* thus far? Let's start with the bottom line: You are either dating someone seriously or you are not.

If you are dating someone seriously, then you can skip to Step #15 right now.

If you are not dating someone seriously, then you are going to evaluate your results. You will analyze three phases:

Evaluation #1. Quantity and quality: The quantity and quality of the men you've been meeting.

Evaluation #2. Retention: Your ability to retain the men you've wanted.

Evaluation #3. *Program* **Audit:** Key areas in *The Program* steps that you will need to revisit.

EVALUATION #1: QUANTITY AND QUALITY

Let's say you own a store. There are two important components that will make your store a success: the *number* of customers you bring in (quantity), and the *type* of customers you bring in (quality). The more customers you bring in, the more likely you are to generate sales. High-quality customers spend money, while low-quality customers waste your salespeople's time and don't buy anything. Clearly, the optimal mix is to have a high number of high-quality customers come through your doors.

So in this phase, you will examine the quantity and quality of the men you have met and, based on your results, will create a revised *Program* Action Plan customized to your current situation.

Chart Your Results

Defining success with the quantity and quality of the men you've met over the last several months depends somewhat on your situation. As a rule of thumb, though, my belief is that you are achieving *Program* Quantity Success if you are getting 4 or more first dates (defined as going out with a man for an arranged in-person meeting) per month with different men. To measure your *Program* Quality Success, I will define a *high-quality man* as someone with whom you want a second date. You are achieving *Program* Quality if you'd like a second date with 50% or more of your dates (regardless of whether you actually went on a second date).

The Program Success Matrix on page 251 shows four different "shopping" experiences, which are analogous to your dating experiences. For example, if you wanted to find a beautiful vase and had fifteen minutes to shop, which outlet would be your best bet to shop? For me, I'd head straight to an upscale department store (such as Neiman Marcus, Saks Fifth Avenue, or Nordstrom's) because that's where I find a high quantity of high-quality choices. You wouldn't go to a garage sale, where you're unlikely to find a high-quality item among a small selection. Going to a flea market will increase your choices, but it would be rare to find something you really want. And while a boutique usually has high-quality items, there are usually too few choices to find exactly what you want. Remember, you've got only fifteen minutes to shop, so maximize your odds and aim for an upscale department store. You might pay a premium price, but hopefully you'll have it forever.

Which of these four squares best describes your current situation?

Square #1) Garage Sale: Low volume of men (3 dates or less per month) and low quality of men (you want a second date with less than 50%).

Square #2) Flea Market: High volume of men (four or more dates per month) and low quality of men (you want a second date with less than 50%).

Square #3) Boutique: Low volume of men (3 dates or less per month) and high quality of men (you want a second date with more than 50%).

Square #4) Upscale Department Store: High volume of men (four or more dates per month) and high quality of men (you want a second date with more than 50%).

The Program Success Matrix: *Find your square*

QUANTITY

		Low (3 dates or less per month)	High (4 dates or more per month)
Q U A L I T Y	**Low** (You want a 2nd date with less than 50% of your 1st dates)	**#1. Garage Sale**	**#2. Flea Market**
	High (You want a 2nd date with more than 50% of your 1st dates)	**#3. Boutique**	**#4. Upscale Department Store**

Revise Your Action Plan

Once you have identified your square, go to the corresponding action plan below.

Square #1: "Garage Sale" Action Plan

If you are in a Garage Sale, you are experiencing low quality and low volume. You have not had many dates (3 or fewer per month), and the ones you've had to choose from have been, to speak plainly, "junk"—not nice men, nothing in common with you, not looking for a serious relationship, they smelled bad (!), etc. You've wanted a second date with less than 50% of them.

This is the least desirable square to be in, and you need to get out of it fast. If you find yourself here, *The Program* is not working for you and we need to figure out why. Usually this situation is a result of not thoroughly completing many of the steps. I have spoken to several women in this situation. These are women who typically have attended my seminar, feel excited about all the new possibilities, but then take little action. They believe that *The Program* will magically find them a husband if they make a few small gestures toward change.

One woman e-mailed me three months after attending my seminar and found herself in a Garage Sale. She wrote, "Your *Program* doesn't work. I had my teeth whitened, chose a brand, joined a co-ed softball league, and asked three friends to fix me up. I've had only two dates in three months, and they were both terrible. I still haven't found my husband."

Well, I'd be shocked if she *had* found a husband with those few actions! What she did is better than doing nothing at all. But again, *The Program* is a comprehensive, strategic plan comprised of sequential building blocks to enact over the course of 12 to 18 months. It is not a brief series of one-off, haphazard activities.

Go back to the beginning at Step #1, Marketing Focus, and ask yourself if you are truly committed to *The Program*. You might discover that although you really thought you were committed, it turns out that the steps are too assertive or time-consuming for you, so you didn't really complete most of them. If this is the case, I suggest taking another break now. Go back to your prior life and see which is preferable: your old existence or the time-consuming, uncomfortable feelings you may experience in carrying out *Program* steps. Of course, the latter scenario is the one that can produce a husband if done correctly.

Not every single woman over 35 truly wants to find a husband. I know many women who would agree with this statement: "It would be nice if it happened, but my life is full without a husband." Still, most single women over 35 are willing to truly prioritize finding a husband. It may simply take you longer to come to terms with the hard work that is involved in this process. When you find yourself in a Garage Sale, you may suddenly realize: "I'll do anything to find a husband; just get me out of here!" Sometimes it takes "failing" to ignite the passion to succeed going forward. If this describes you, get back on the horse and restart *The Program* at Step #1. I know you can do it if you really want to get married!

You should actively revisit almost every step of *The Program*, but Steps #3 and #11 deserve your special attention. A common problem with someone who finds herself at a Garage Sale is the failure of Step #3, Packaging. Usually she hasn't been given honest feedback, and something either physical or emotional is holding her back. Go back to Step #3 and select six different people—3 men and 3 women—who can provide you with new feedback about your appearance. Practice and revise your script to ask for feedback with someone different this time around. Really ensure that you are encouraging truthful comments. Be willing and able to make the changes suggested.

Last but not least, verify that your *Program* Calendar in Step #11, Mass Marketing, meets your volume goals. Be sure to go out three or four nights per week and maintain a diversified portfolio of activities.

You can now skip to Evaluation #2, Retention Measurement, in this chapter.

Square #2: "Flea Market" Action Plan

If you are in a Flea Market, you have high volume but low quality. You have found a lot of men (4 dates per month or more), but they are mostly "junk"—not nice, nothing in common with you, not looking for a serious relationship, they smelled bad (!), or what have you. You've wanted a second date with less than 50% of them. You may be receiving many offers, but you are not interested in most of them.

This situation is complicated. Its root cause is usually having a brand that is attracting the wrong kind of men for you. For example, a woman who attended one of my seminars, Carla, e-mailed me when she found herself in a Flea Market. She attached a photo, and I could see that she was very attractive. She had chosen a brand that focused on her looks: "Model, Alabama, Sultry." She had chosen "MissAlabama" as her online screen name. This brand portrayed her as a beauty queen rather than a woman of substance. She had many men pursuing her, but they were usually shallow and attracted only to her exterior. They tended to be too aggressive physically. She mistakenly slept with a few of them, who quickly dumped her. When we evaluated her results, she realized what was going on and I helped her change her brand to reflect her artistic and spiritual side. The quality of men who approached her shifted drastically (for the better) when she started projecting her new brand: "Painter, Spiritual, Alabama."

So if the quantity of the men you're attracting is high, but the quality is low, first go back to Step #5, Branding, and ask yourself these questions:

- Is your brand shallow?
- Is your brand unique?
- Is your brand realistic about yourself?

Repeat the exercise of creating your personal brand. Even though you have probably highlighted qualities about yourself and advertised them in social situations, in communications with your six women "dates," telemarketing, and online, they may be attracting the wrong type of men.

The wrong brand can also mean that Step #11, Mass Marketing, might *seem* like it's working for you because you are pumping up volume, but you should restart this step now using your new brand. Attracting lots of low-quality men is a waste of your time.

One caveat: I often hear women lament the poor quality of the men they meet, but the root cause may not be what it seems. Perhaps the men are not *actually* low quality. Rather, the woman is just being too picky and focusing only on her "type." Being in a Flea Market may also suggest you need to revisit Step #4, Market Expansion, and ask yourself these questions:

- Have you truly accepted the reality that you could fall in love with a man who may not be the type you've always imagined?
- Did you practice dating three men who represent your wider and widest nets?
- Have you told everyone you know that you are open to many

different types and are simply looking for "someone wonderful"?

- Did you expand the age parameters of your online profile according to Step #4?

Still concerned about quality? Step #9, Niche Marketing, usually yields high-quality men because this step involves more personal fix-ups from women who know you, or know your "date," well. You should try this step again, selecting six new women to "date," or as many as you can find. This second round of "dates" may not meet all of the five criteria set forth (married, well connected, experienced matchmaker, and so on), but that's okay. Just find new "dates" who fit as many as possible. This step is worth repeating because it is the best source for higher-quality men.

You can now skip to Evaluation #2, Retention Measurement, in this chapter.

Square #3: "Boutique" Action Plan

If you are in a Boutique, you have found high-quality men, but a low volume of them. The men you've dated are actually quite decent—nice men, with some common interests, looking for a serious relationship, they smelled good (!)—but they're few and far between (3 or fewer per month). You've had some good dates, but the chemistry just hasn't been quite right for any of them to turn into a relationship. The odds are against you in a Boutique simply because you don't have many choices. Luckily, this is an easy store to escape from because *The Program* offers so many options to increase your volume.

The two steps on *The Program* that yield the highest volume are Step #7, Online Marketing, and Step #11, Mass Marketing. These are the steps to revisit at this point. Ask yourself the following questions—first, regarding online marketing:

- Did you post a unique and appealing screen name, headline, and profile on a large online dating site?
- Have you considered joining an additional online dating site for more options?
- Is your front online photo your personal best, while the back-up photos are good but realistic?
- Are you meeting face-to-face the men who e-mail you, and interest you, within two weeks?
- Are you getting the expected online dating results listed in Step #7?

Now ask yourself about your mass marketing:

- Were you out of your home three to four times per week for activities other than your job?
- Did you diversify your outings, so that you tried a little of everything?
- Did you identify several singles groups in your city and attend numerous gatherings?
- Did you go to several singles locations and look for chance encounters?
- Did you carry a conversation starter and go solo?
- Did you try a few dating services, such as speed dating or personal ads?
- Did you try other ideas such as single-dad spots, teaching a class, or something zany?

Make the necessary corrections to any of the items above that elicited "no" answers, and continue focusing on Steps #7 and #11—and any others where you have been garnering some success—until the day you meet Mr. Right.

You can now skip to Evaluation #2, Retention Measurement, in this chapter.

Square #4: "Upscale Department Store" Action Plan

If you are in an Upscale Department Store, you're in the best place: high quantity and high quality. You have a large selection (4 or more dates per month) with decent men—nice, common interests, looking for a serious relationship, they smell good (!), and so on. You appear to be doing everything right, but just haven't met Mr. Right yet. You just need to do more of the same and he will be found, even if it takes more time. Remember, there's always a little serendipity involved in being in the right place at the right time. The key is to keep going. Don't get discouraged or start doubting yourself or *The Program*.

There is one important thing you may want to watch out for. Are you beginning good relationships that repeatedly don't work out—also known as "relationship fizzle"? If so, then there may be another issue at hand. You may need advice on dating practices (which will be discussed in Step #15, Exit Strategy), or you may be attracting the wrong men in the first place with false branding. We will talk about relationship fizzle and false branding later in this chapter.

EVALUATION #2: RETENTION MEASUREMENT

Bringing in the desired high-quantity and high-quality men for a first date is only half the battle, because if the men you *want* to call you back for more dates aren't doing so, you've got a problem. You're ready for the second phase of your Quarterly Performance Review: Retention Measurement. This phase will help you evaluate whether you are retaining the men you want. So hold on to your pretty hats while I tell you about the dreaded "exit interview"!

Exit Interviews

In many companies, human resource managers conduct exit interviews after an employee has decided to quit. This is the one time when employees are usually honest about their experience with the company. On their way out the door, they can express their real opinions without the threat of management repercussion. This yields very interesting and productive data for managers about how to retain future employees.

In the dating world, an exit interview means getting feedback from men who didn't call you back. I know, this doesn't sound like fun! But the whole point of a Quarterly Performance Review is to get brutally honest feedback about how you're doing in order to improve your results in the future. I have women tell me all the time that they had a fantastic date with a man, but then he never called back. Or they had a great relationship with a man, who suddenly broke it off. You should find out why this happened because you may have a recurring pattern that is sabotaging your dates and relationships. And these men are the only ones who can give you that information. *So are you ready to hear the truth?*

The good news is that you are not going to call your former dates or ex-boyfriends yourself. You are going to ask someone to do it for you. A third person is more likely to get honest feedback than you are. This person will also act as a buffer to convey information back to you in a neutral and constructive manner. You can select your Mentor as your exit interviewer, or any friend who seems particularly outgoing, perceptive, and able to put people at ease. You can choose a male or female friend who fits the bill.

Your exit interviewer should call at least three to six men whom you liked, who have taken you on a first date or two, and then never called you back or broke things off. You should also include an ex-boyfriend or two, if possible. The selected dates or ex-boyfriends should be ones you met on *The Program* (preferably in the last 12 months), and represent a variety of personalities, situations, and sources.

How to Conduct an Exit Interview

Provide your exit interviewer with the following script, along with the names and phone numbers of your ex-dates and ex-boyfriends. You can make a copy of this script directly from the book for each man to be called, customizing the blank lines for each one.

Hi, my name is _____ [exit interviewer's name], and I am calling on behalf of _____ [your name]. Do you remember her? [Or, I'm calling on behalf of your ex-girlfriend _____.] I promise this call will only take 5 minutes of your time. I am a consultant working with _____ [your name] to help her find a special person with whom to spend her life. I know this phone call may seem unusual, but as part of my service, I conduct brief, anonymous feedback sessions with men whom my clients have dated in the past. This helps them understand what changes they can make to themselves for more successful relationships in the future. _____ [your name] values your opinion and would be very grateful if you would spend a few minutes talking openly with me. I am making similar phone calls to 5 other men, and will group all the results together so she won't know who said what. I would appreciate your complete honesty in answering these few questions:

1. How would you describe her?
2. What were her best qualities?
3. What qualities could she most improve upon?
4. Would you share with me why you decided not to pursue a relationship with her? Please be honest. She is a nice person and is looking for real help that only you can provide.
5. What advice would you give her for future dates and relationships?
6. [Insert specific questions here about any problem areas that may concern you.]

Thank you so much for your time and candor! This has been very helpful and I know will really provide some good insights for _____ [your name]. If you have any other thoughts that you'd like to share with me after we hang up, my phone number is: _____.

Exit Interview Results

Encourage your exit interviewer to take notes during her conversations, but wait to call you with the feedback until all the responses have been collected and the data has been aggregated. It will be more helpful if you know whether "only one out of five men felt this way" or "four out of five men felt this way."

This information is not always easy to handle, but will make all the difference in helping you *not* repeat mistakes of the past. Be sure to encourage your exit interviewer to be totally honest with you, and not hold anything back. As she relays the feedback to you, try to keep a neutral demeanor, even if you feel as if you've just been punched in the stomach. Otherwise, your interviewer will start to soft-pedal the feedback, and this whole process will be worthless.

Negative feedback is never easy to handle in any situation, and it's especially painful when it's so personal. But keep your eye on the long run, and know that anything you hear is only helping you achieve your goal of finding a wonderful husband. Be sure to ask your exit interviewer up front to conclude your conversation with at least three positive comments she heard about you.

I want you to listen carefully to any negative feedback and treat it seriously, but use your judgment and always take it with a grain of salt. Some men who exited your life will have many problems and issues of their own, and you will not necessarily respect their opinions. Often these men will be at fault for whatever went wrong. If only one man said you "talked too much," you should be conscious of that as you go forward, but don't assume it's a major issue. But if four out of five men said you were "not very feminine," you need to listen. It's important to be aware of how you are perceived by more than one person, even if you do not have a high regard for these men in particular.

When you have collected feedback from your exit interviews, you should have some useful information about how you have been perceived by men in the recent past. Discuss the results with your Mentor and determine which comments are valid and worth acting upon. I've heard easy-to-correct feedback for women such as "She had bad breath"; chewing a breath mint before a date was a no-brainer. But the more difficult feedback to act upon is something like "She had three children and I just wasn't ready for an instant family," or "I just wasn't attracted to her."

To address the first issue about "an instant family," of course you're not going to get rid of your kids, but maybe you can come up with a strategy like my client Gina did. She decided: "I won't mention my children, unless directly asked, until the second date. Either there will be enough chemistry between us at that point and he will be open-minded to us as a package, or he will express his reservations and I will cut my losses sooner rather than later." If Gina discovers on the second date that the man has no interest in taking on the responsibility of someone else's children, I would not consider the first date a waste of her time. Rather, she was maximizing the odds that a man would be more willing to date a single mom *after* he is attracted to her and gets to know her. Sometimes it works this way, but you have not wasted a few hours if it doesn't.

To address the second issue about him "not being attracted to you," this is just the kind of feedback that can make a difference. If a man says he wasn't attracted to you, hopefully he will provide some details about why. If the reason sounds legitimate and is something you can fix by going back to Step #3, Packaging, then by all means do it. Try not to let it hurt your feelings; use it to help you make adjustments going forward. But if he says that you "just weren't his type," then throw out that data. What is not appealing to one man may be very appealing to another.

Following common sense, then, you would generally make changes where reasonable and possible, and be aware of how you are perceived.

Relationship Fizzle

Relationship fizzle is a common retention issue, and it may not surface during your exit interviews because its root cause is quite subtle. Relationship fizzle is often due to false branding, which can occur when you select brand qualities that are more wishful thinking than reality. For example, one woman, Theresa, was originally from Iowa but currently living in Washington, D.C. She thought that the brand image "Midwestern, Down-to-Earth, Musician" was unique in her environment. It was, but unfortunately it was not totally accurate when men got to know her. In reality, she was high-maintenance and erratic. She was advertising a brand that she couldn't sustain. She was wasting time by attracting men who liked her original image, but then retreated when it proved false.

Theresa placed herself in an Upscale Department Store after her quantity and quality evaluation. She was generating high-quantity and high-quality first dates, but the real reason these relationships never led to the altar was that they were built on a faulty premise. Look honestly at your own situation; if you find yourself in a similar predicament, go back quickly to Step #5, Branding, and adjust your brand so that it rings true to who you are, while still highlighting your unique and appealing features. Theresa changed her brand to: "Passionate, Sophisticated, Musician," which was honest about her personality and began to attract men with different expectations and needs that were more suited to her personality.

EVALUATION #3: *THE PROGRAM* AUDIT

No matter which square you're in, and no matter how much valuable information you've garnered from your exit interviews, there are more areas that are worth evaluating (or "auditing") in this phase. *The Program* Audit is comprised of a checklist with eleven key areas. Ask yourself the questions on this list, and then discuss your answers with your Mentor again. If all answers below are not a resounding "yes," you need to pause and make adjustments accordingly.

The Program Audit

- **Focus:** Is your commitment to *The Program* your #1 priority? Are your words consistent with your actions?
- **Your appearance:** Did you get helpful feedback about how you look during Step #3, Packaging? Were the suggestions you collected truly honest? Did both men and women provide comments? Do you believe that you project the most feminine image possible? Is your look—clothes, accessories, et cetera—consistent with your brand?
- **Your attitude:** Even if you've had some disappointments during *The Program*, have you maintained a positive attitude?

Would strangers view you from across a room as a happy, open woman (rather than hostile and aloof)? Are you careful not to project a negative attitude with defensive comments or negative body language such as always standing with your arms crossed?

❑ **Your targets:** Have you cast a wider net since Step #4, Market Expansion? Are your targets really varied in age, looks, professions, and religions? Have you stopped ruling out stereotypes?

❑ **Your Mentor:** Does your Mentor have an active role in your endeavors? Is she adhering to the Mentor Agreement that you both signed? Is your Mentor most of what you had hoped for: a cheerleader, a sounding board, and a wise coach?

❑ **Your budget:** Did you allocate a sufficient budget in Step #1, Marketing Focus? Did the areas where you spent the most money yield the best results?

❑ **Your pet:** If you have a pet, does it simply provide companionship and act as a good conversation starter in the park (versus serve as an excuse not to venture out)? Do you spend more time pursuing new friendships with men and women than with your pet?

❑ **Mixing it up:** Are you achieving your volume goals from Step #8, Guerrilla Marketing, and #11, Mass Marketing? Do you have a "diversified portfolio" of venues that you frequent: everyday errands, singles groups, singles locations, singles events, and more?

❑ **Shyness:** If you are shy, did you find a comfortable way to ask for what you want (for example, sending e-mails in Step #10, Telemarketing, instead of making phone calls)? Are you sure your shyness isn't being misinterpreted by men as indifference?

❑ **Follow-up:** Are you consistently following up on all leads for potential fix-ups? Are you meticulously keeping track of all date-related communication (online, direct mail, telemarketing) in a journal?

❑ **Sex:** Are you waiting to have sex until you both know you are in a real relationship? Are you communicating to men that sex is related to commitment? My rule for dating and sex is explained further in Step #15, Exit Strategy, but in brief: You should not have sex with men too soon. It sends the wrong signal that you are interested in something casual.

After *The Program* Audit

After you have reflected on the results of your audit, summarize what you learned. Which items deserve more time, energy, and money? What areas have been difficult for you—and should you abandon those or try to make improvements? What do other women you know do better than you to attract men? Are there more opportunities that you could pursue? What threats or pitfalls on this audit list exist for you? How can you avoid them? Write down your goals for improvement for the next three months, but be realistic. There is nothing more demoralizing than creating goals that are not attainable.

One common denominator that I see in women who find husbands on *The Program* is a drive for constant improvement. This is as much about implementing actual change as it is about a *positive attitude* toward learning from dates and relationships that didn't work out. Try to revisit Step #14 as often as possible (every couple of months), and I'll bet your results will skyrocket.

You have succeeded with Step #14, and can begin Step #15, if you:

1. Performed the Quantity and Quality Evaluation by identifying which square you're in: Garage Sale, Flea Market, Boutique, or Upscale Department Store.

2. Revised your action plan according to the guidelines for your square.

3. Arranged your exit interviews for Retention Evaluation.

4. Evaluated the feedback from the exit interviews and made reasonable changes.

5. Performed *The Program* Audit by answering the audit questions in this chapter.

6. As a result of the audit, wrote down your realistic goals for improvement and change for the next three months.

7. Continue to cycle through *Program* Steps #1 through #14 until you are dating someone seriously with high potential to become your husband.

Step #15

Exit Strategy:

"Man"agement

WHAT I LEARNED AT
HARVARD BUSINESS SCHOOL

A good business plan for a start-up company always con-
cludes with a good exit strategy. It is understood from the
beginning that you will not manage the business forever,
so you make preparations accordingly to leave when the time is
right. You set goals for where you want to take a business, and
when those goals are attained, you get out. You move on to the
next project. Before any money is committed to a business venture up front, investors need to know how they will be com-
pensated for their risk and what kind of return on investment
(ROI) is expected.

But *how* you get out of the business is not always easy. Timing and process are everything. A savvy entrepreneur will manage the company efficiently. She will invest in research and
development for the product, cut any losses quickly, monitor
changes in the marketplace, and wait for sales to peak. At just

the right time, when her instincts tell her that profits can be reaped, she will seal the deal and exit the business.

WHAT IS "MAN"AGEMENT?

While you are working your way through the steps of *The Program*, you must have an exit strategy in place once you begin dating a man seriously. You need to focus on the *man* in *management*. In other words, when you meet a man who could be your future husband, how do you manage the process of determining if he *is* The One, and manage him toward commitment? I have identified five phases that a smart woman should move through quickly when she finds someone who could be The One.

There can be a lot of psychology to wade through here; in fact, there can be so much that entire categories of self-help books exist on the topics of dating, mate selection, and getting a man to commit. But what *I* can contribute as a businessperson on this step is to tell you how to manage the process of going from serious dating to marriage *efficiently* in order to exit *The Program*. The five phases I describe below will help you whittle down your options and close the deal. These phases reflect key management lessons from the business world, but most important, they distinguish Smart Daters from Dumb Daters.

While my broad guidelines can help you navigate the dating minefields, it is ultimately your gut instincts that will direct you to the right man.

Phase One: Keep Your Options Open

Phase One begins when you start to like one man a lot. You have been on a few dates with him, and the feeling seems to be mutual. Smart Daters at this point keep their options open for as long as possible, especially when beginning to date someone seriously. They know all too well that relationships can disintegrate suddenly and mysteriously. Dumb Daters put all their eggs in one basket. They believe that if a few dates go really well, they are on their way to the altar. They tell everyone they're "seeing someone," decline offers for fix-ups, and stop attending singles events.

The whole key to this phase is to manage your time wisely. If it turns out that the two of you aren't headed for marriage, you want to reflect on this time and know that it wasn't wasted. You should be able to look back and say that you learned something from the relationship while you kept up the fast pace of *The Program* and continued to search for other men. Just in case.

In the past (pre-*Program*), you may have wasted your time pursuing dead-end relationships. You cut yourself off from meeting new men while you tried to figure out if one man was going to be Mr. Right. This was, as they say in business, an "opportunity cost." Not that this was inherently wrong, but my guess is that the *amount of time* you took to figure it out was much too long. You probably knew within three to six months, on a gut level, if things were or were not going to work out. Maybe if you had a serious relationship when you were 22, you were too young to interpret your gut instinct. But at a later age you reached a maturity level where you knew if a man was right or wrong for you early in a relationship. You may have seen warning signs that you denied or rationalized, which confused you and prolonged the relationship. You may be single today because you wasted several years with the wrong man. But no more!

So when you start dating a man you really like, you should continue to keep your options open and not date him exclusively too soon. You should continue to pursue all your other *Program* activities with full gusto. Full speed ahead with whichever step you're on. You need Back-up Plans A, B, C, and D in case Mr. Right turns out to be Mr. Wrong.

Naturally, this is tricky. What if the man you really like says to you, "What are you doing on Wednesday night?" and the truth is you have another date or have plans to attend a singles event? I recommend that you use a vague approach and reply, "I'm going out with a friend." Most men will take the hint and not probe any further. But if he persists and asks for the specifics, you can use this line: "Are we at a stage where we can ask each other these types of questions?" The beauty of this response is that he will either back off from his questioning, which allows you to freely keep your options open, or he will express some concern and want to know who your "friend" is, which will prompt a conversation about the seriousness of your relationship.

Getting him to indicate how serious he is about you, sooner rather than later, is excellent for time management. If he gets nervous and backs off at this point, you've saved yourself a lot of wasted time with him. If he gets possessive or jealous *and* lets you know he wants to be exclusive with you, this is usually a good sign. You have just fast-forwarded through weeks or months of wondering, "Where do I stand?" (Note: Possessiveness and jealousy can be red flags in some cases. Be sure to look for his appropriate interest in exclusivity versus any inappropriate jealous behavior or instability that could lead to abuse.)

The Date/Sex Rule

This is also the time frame where you may be wondering when to have sex. *The Program* answer is to wait as long as possible. My experience is that when it comes to buying a "big-ticket item"—in this case, a wife—men are not impulse shoppers. They take longer to connect emotionally, and don't equate sex with love as many women do right away. When it comes to sex, I recommend using my "2/2" Date/Sex Rule as a guideline: You must have a minimum of 2 dates per week for a minimum of 2 consecutive months before having sex with the man you are dating seriously.

It is important to pace your relationship, even in the express lane, and let it build steadily. Couples who rush into intense relationships too soon often crash and burn. My 2/2 Rule may seem like a long time for some of you, but this is my magic formula. First, it ensures that your relationship is reasonably stable because you are regularly seeing each other over a substantial period of time. And second, it encourages him to look at you as a possible wife (a "big-ticket item") and not as one-night-stand material (an "impulse buy"). If he is looking for casual sex, the 2/2 Rule will screen him out because hopefully he will get it easier and faster elsewhere and won't wait around for you. Use your own judgment about fooling around in between kissing and sleeping together, but err on the side of less being better.

Phase Two: Finders Keepers?

Clearly, a decision to marry is not all up to him. Now that you've found him, do you want to keep him? *You* have to decide if the man you're dating steadily is right for you. You were willing to cast a wider net and be open to meeting someone who wasn't your type, at least externally. But now you should decide, or reconfirm, what's most important to you internally.

Make a short list of, at most, three important internal qualities that your future husband must possess. Perhaps there are only one or two, when it comes right down to it. You should wait until this phase to create such a list because until you're falling in love with one particular man, your list might be completely different. If I had asked you a year ago to write down a maximum of three important internal qualities, you would have struggled to narrow it down to only three. But once you're falling in love, this list completely changes. You are seeking to rule "in" rather than rule "out." Whereas once your list may have looked like this:

He Has to Be . . .
- Smart
- Funny
- Spontaneous
- Fond of children
- Self-confident
- Good communicator
- Kind
- Generous
- Religious

. . . Now that your heart is pounding and your stomach is doing flips every time you think about him, your list may look like this:

He Has to Be . . .
- Kind
- Fond of children
- Spontaneous

Maybe that's all it boils down to for you now. The rest would have been nice, but you choose love over your list.

Now, how do you screen efficiently—do it well but quickly—for these three essential qualities on your list? Maybe you already know the answers about whether he has these qualities or not, since you've already had several dates with him. But if you're not sure, then you're going to create a series of "tests" that he needs to pass. In an ideal world, say back when you were in your twenties, you'd have plenty of time to figure out whether he possesses your three must-haves. You'd date for a year or two, maybe live together, and over time you'd get your answer. But in the fast lane after 35, you have no time to waste. Smart Daters get a yes or no answer for their list ASAP! Dumb Daters sit around for months and wait for opportunities to arise where they can determine if he has the qualities they require.

To get a fast answer in business, you'd use a "back-of-the-envelope" analysis. This term means that your analysis isn't thorough and scientific, but rather a quick glance at the issues to see in which direction your answer is leaning. Picture two businesspeople sitting in a lobby, making a deal. They reach for the nearest piece of paper—say, an envelope or a cocktail napkin—turn it over, and scribble down a quick calculation of the deal value. In the dating world, you're going to create a similarly quick calculation. This involves a series of three dates (or situations) with this man to quickly learn as much as possible about whether he has each of your three must-have qualities.

For example, if your list is "Kind, Fond of Children, and Spontaneous," you could create the following three dates to test him on your three attributes over the course of a month. These tests will vary depending on your individual definition of the qualities on your list.

Date A: The "Kind" Test
- Suggest to him that he volunteer with you for a day at an elder-care home.
- Or ask him to help your friend move furniture into her new apartment.

Date B: The "Fond of Children" Test
- Ask him to come with you to baby-sit your niece all day Saturday.
- Or suggest to him that he coach your son's Little League team for 2 weeks while the coach is on vacation.
- Or take him on a picnic with your kids, or with a friend who has kids.

Date C: The "Spontaneous" Test
- Invite him for a weekend at a Bed-and-Breakfast with you, giving him one day's notice.
- Or ask him to plan something fun for tonight.

Obviously, you have to be reasonable in creating these tests. If he has a major project due at the office on Monday and needs to work all weekend preparing for it, it's unreasonable to test him on spontaneity with your Bed-and-Breakfast invitation that weekend. Likewise, if you know a relaxing weekend in the country would drive him crazy, pick another type of vacation to invite him on. Remember, you're testing spontaneity, not compatible vacation preferences. "Vacation Compatibility" would be a different item on your list, and, if you are going to test for this, it would need to be one of your top three criteria. Be sure your test accurately reflects the quality you are testing.

Due to the short and somewhat random nature of these

tests, his reactions are not necessarily deal-breakers. But they should provide some degree of insight into whether or not he possesses your must-haves. You are looking here for good directional information that will help you gain a clearer picture of him quickly.

Be sure to also ask yourself a few key questions here before you move on to the next phase. Your answers will help you gauge your internal barometer about this man. How do you feel when you're with him? Are you relaxed, comfortable, attracted, and excited about your future? Can you be honest with him about your true preferences and thoughts now (except, of course, when it comes to a marriage proposal)? Is he tolerant of your views and respectful of your opinions? Do you communicate well with each other? These are all important indicators for a successful partnership.

Phase Three:
Don't Throw Good Money After Bad

One of the classic mistakes you can make in business is to "throw good money after bad." In other words, just because you've invested some money in a project, it doesn't mean you should keep funding it if it's not producing the results you had hoped for. You have to cut your losses and look for the next opportunity. Of course, this is the same in the dating world. If you realize that Mr. Right is actually Mr. Wrong, what do you do? Maybe he flunked your tests; maybe he spent the night with his ex-wife. Maybe any of a thousand other things happened suddenly. But whatever it was, it was a deal-breaker.

Smart Daters have the discipline to end the wrong relationship and move on, even when they've invested a lot of time and emotion in it already. No matter how hard this is, they just end it. Dumb Daters see the same warning signs, and rationalize them. "Maybe he'll change," "Maybe it's not so bad," and "This is better than being alone" are the dumb things they believe.

I know what I'm advising is painful and difficult. But I want you to manage your time well so that *The Program* can work for you. And that means cutting your losses early when the situation is not right. You have to do it quickly and emphatically. It's an amputation, not a taffy pull. Call him or see him in person. Tell him this is not the right relationship for you, and give him your reasons. Then walk away. You don't give it one more try. You don't suggest therapy. You don't answer his calls. You tell your friends and family that it's over to make it real. And you don't stay friends with him if seeing this man has a negative impact on you. Remember, in the Ramp Up stage you got rid of negative triggers.

But of course you should allow yourself time to mourn, especially if you're ending an intense emotional relationship. Go immediately to Step #13, Product Life Cycle, and recharge. Take a week to cry your eyes out, erase e-mails from him, and analyze what went wrong. Then put his photos and his love tokens into the back of your closet with all the other negative triggers that you've stashed back there. It's time to pick yourself up and focus on finding the real Mr. Right. Now go back to the last *Program* step where you left off before you met this Mr. Wrong.

Phase Four: Exclusivity

What if he passed your screening test with flying colors? What if you believe he's The One and he's given you every reason to believe the feeling is mutual? Then it's time to date him exclusively. This phase should occur only after an explicit conversation with him about your relationship status. You can initiate this conversation if he hasn't done it already. By this point, if such a discussion scares him away, it means he is not going to marry you anytime soon, if ever. You should both have absolute clarity that your relationship is exclusive and on a path toward marriage. This means that you both decline dates with other people and you both take down your online profiles. You function like a real and committed couple: Your friends and family (and his friends and family) know that you're in a serious relationship. Ideally he has told you he loves you, and you've said it back. But you should never consider living with him, which serves only to delay marriage rather than accelerate it.

Living together before marriage may seem like a good idea to get to know each other better, but what usually happens is that you are both on your best behavior for the first couple of months anyway. The clock is ticking and time goes by. Technically, you're still single. Then you discover things about each other that are not ideal. But because you're not married, you may not work as hard to resolve the issues. Both of you may be too comfortable, not wanting to be single again, and may not confront the issues or bring them to resolution. He says, "Let's just see what happens."

Meanwhile, you are not looking for anyone else, you are stuck in a stagnant situation, and you wake up a year later—still single. The bottom line is that your odds are better for getting married if you don't live together first. The odds are also better for *staying* married because when problems arise, mature married couples work hard to solve them rather than give up.

A Smart Dater doesn't let the man get too comfortable with the status quo. She wants to be married, and doesn't make any moves to delay that occurrence. Smart Daters don't let down their guard. They fully understand that they are still in "selling mode," and they don't live together. Dumb Daters let down their guard, agree to live together, and let time slip away.

Being in selling mode doesn't mean that you shouldn't be yourself. It means that you stay consistent with your brand and stay the same person he has adored all along. Don't suddenly become needy and insecure because you've decided that you want to marry him, but you don't know whether he is going to propose or not.

You have to remove or negotiate any deal-breakers with him, such as religious practices, wanting babies, blending families, career or location changes, or lifestyle differences. If there are big issues looming between the two of you, the relationship usually can't move forward. Resolve or dissolve them in this phase. You don't need to be living together to accomplish this. If a deal-breaker can't be resolved, then break up (that's why it's called a *deal-breaker*!). It's tough to accept, but you should absolutely not waste any more time with him if you know something will ultimately end your relationship anyway. As you negotiate through these murky waters, remain in selling mode. Be smart about how you discuss sensitive issues and continue to highlight your brand.

I was impressed with how my client Debra negotiated her deal-breakers while continuing to highlight the attribute in her brand that her boyfriend, Matt, valued most about her: "Flexible." There were two key issues that kept coming to the surface whenever she and Matt talked about a future together: golf and religion. Matt was passionate about golf. Not only had Debra never played golf before, but she had bad childhood memories of an absent father who spent entire weekends away from her family while he golfed with his buddies. And Matt was Christian, but not very religious; Debra was Jewish, and very committed to her religion.

One night, Debra brought these two issues to the forefront with Matt. She told him that she had been thinking a lot about whether or not they were a compatible couple. She told him she cared about him very much, and wanted to suggest a compromise to resolve the big issues about which they were both concerned. She reminded him how flexible she was, how she understood his passion for golf, and would never want him to think he had to give up golf to be with her. She asked if he could agree that golf wouldn't dominate their lives, and whether he could put a limit on the amount of time he played. She asked him for a suggestion, and they decided that two days per month plus two golf trips per year with his friends would satisfy him.

In return, she asked him to be flexible on their religious differences. She asked, "If we ever have children together, would you be willing to raise them as Jewish?" After much discussion about it, he said that since she was so flexible about his golf habit, he could agree to raise the children as Jewish. The truth was that Matt cared more about golf than religion, and Debra cared more about religion than golf. They each made a compromise that allowed them to feel confident about their future together.

Currently, Debra is contemplating how to "seal the deal" and prompt Matt to propose.

Phase Five: Seal the Deal

You're in an exclusive relationship with a wonderful man and you've both come to terms with each other's baggage: Now it's a waiting game. You're waiting for him to propose.

Smart Daters won't wait forever. They create a silent deadline and stick to it. Dumb Daters wait and wait and wait, each year blowing out one more candle on their birthday cake.

Time is of the essence. If he's not going to propose, you can't afford to throw good money after bad. You must be willing to start over and invest your time and energy on someone else, despite the pain involved. You want a husband, not the anxiety you feel with an uncommitted man. You may be in a hurry to start a family, or simply tired of being single. But *he* might not be in a hurry. Your challenge is to find a balance—not pushing too hard or explicitly stating an ultimatum, but also letting him know you're not going to wait forever. You need reassurance that you both want the same things.

If the "normal" approach of letting things unfold naturally and talking about your future together hasn't happened after three or four months of exclusivity (*note:* If you are under 40, you might have a more relaxed time frame and can wait up to six months), you can try "The Catalyst Approach." It's better than issuing an ultimatum. Create a catalyst to bring the issue of marriage to a head. This is a "crisis" situation where the outcome will give you better information about whether he is or isn't going to propose. Choose your timing carefully so that he is available to concentrate on you and your so-called crisis. There are many catalyst situations that you can use for this phase, and you'll have to evaluate your own situation to find one that is legitimate for you—one plausible in your own life right now. You can exaggerate it a little bit to create a sense of urgency and a deadline. The point is to shake up his comfort level with the way things are in your cozy relationship and gain some understanding about his time frame and plans for a future together.

Below are a few suggestions for lighting a fire under him with "The Catalyst Approach." Possible catalysts include:

- The lease for your apartment will be ending soon.
- You are contemplating a job offer in another state.
- Your old boyfriend wants you back.
- A new man has asked you on a date.
- You have been invited to join your girlfriend on a 4-week trip.
- Your ex-husband wants full custody of your kids and you need to demonstrate to the court that you have a stable home environment.
- Your 40th birthday is coming up and your gynecologist has suggested you think about freezing embryos.

Find a catalyst that makes sense for you. Let's say the lease for your apartment is ending on the thirtieth of next month. Then let him know the situation and discuss your options with him. Let's see: You can renew the lease for another year, or consider buying your own studio apartment, or use this opportunity to move to California, where you've always thought about living. What's his reaction? You will learn a lot about his intentions for marrying you based on how he responds to the catalyst and advises you to proceed. If he says, "California! How great! I'll miss you, but send me a postcard . . . ," you'll have your answer. But if he says, "Please don't buy a studio apartment; it won't be big enough for the two of us," then you can assume he's thinking along the right path. Use this conversation to emphasize the date when your lease will be terminating, and that you need to make a decision about where to live before then. But never use your catalyst to give an ultimatum or coerce him to propose under duress. A commitment obtained that way usually doesn't last, or will result in an unhappy marriage down the road.

If you choose the right catalyst, you can usually gain valuable insight about his intentions toward you. If he indicates sincerely that he is very serious about you, you should ask him directly what his time frame is. If he lets you know that he needs six months or less to feel comfortable proposing, then mark your calendar and continue with this relationship. After three months, be sure to confirm the time frame with him so you can find out as early as possible if he is going to balk.

And now for the part you don't want to hear. The raw truth. If he says he is not ready for a commitment now or anytime soon, or he wants to wait a year or more to decide whether or not to get married, believe him. These words from a man over the age of 35 usually mean he's not ready for a commitment to *you*, even if he says he loves you. Thank him for not wasting your time any further and break up with him. Recharge in Step #13, then go back into *The Program* full speed ahead on the step where you left off before meeting Mr. Wrong.

THE BOTTOM LINE

These five management phases are designed with one overall strategy: to get good information *quickly*. How you navigate this zone between dating and marriage is crucial. The women with the foresight and strength to cut their losses sooner rather than later are the ones who find wonderful husbands within 12 to 18 months.

You have succeeded with Step #15, and can exit *The Program*, if you:

1. Kept your options open in Phase One.
2. Made a short list of the three most important internal qualities desired for your man, then implemented three tests accordingly in Phase Two.
3. [If you decided he is Mr. Wrong] Ended the relationship in Phase Three.
4. [If you think he could be Mr. Right] Stayed in selling mode and negotiated any deal-breakers in Phase Four.
5. Used the catalyst approach, if necessary, to prompt a commitment in Phase Five.
6. Have a ring on your finger.
7. Live happily ever after.

Press Conference:
Questions and Answers
About The Program

If a dynamic marketing campaign is greeted with enthusiasm by the public, invariably a press conference will be scheduled to answer questions that arise after the product has been in the marketplace for a while. From *The Program*'s success have come many questions that are not specifically addressed in the 15 Steps. Below are the questions most frequently asked by my clients and seminar participants, followed by my responses.

• The Program seems very contrived. Is romance dead after 35?

Romance is certainly not dead after 35: It is alive and well. *The Program* seems very contrived because it *is* contrived. Feel free to call it "strategic" if the word *contrived* isn't palatable to you. Approaching the search for a mate with a well-crafted, strategic plan may not be a scenario straight from a romance novel, but it's certainly practical. I assume you want results more than you want to believe in fairy tales. The romance comes not in the search process, but when you've found a wonderful man.

Let me put it this way. If you were looking for a job, you could call it "contrived" to put your résumé online, ask friends for leads, buy a new interview suit, and so on. But you'd do it because you'd be more likely to find a job that way than waiting for a job to cross your path spontaneously. Why is it different with trying to find a husband?

• Are you suggesting that women need a husband to be happy?

Absolutely not. This book merely provides an action plan for the subset of women who have decided they *want* a husband, but don't know how to find the right one.

• People are always asking me why I'm still single. How do I respond to that?

You simply and confidently say, "I haven't found the right person yet." You don't delve into all your baggage and analysis of the situation. You want to convey that contrary to the implication inherent in this question, there is nothing wrong with you. You just haven't met someone yet with whom you would like to spend the rest of your life.

• Do I need money and a strong network of friends to succeed in The Program? What if I don't have the resources described in many of the steps?

Everyone has some resources, even if they are limited. The most important resources you really need for success in *The Pro-*

gram are drive and creativity. Claiming not to have resources is simply an excuse not to work hard for your goal. If your *Program* Marketing Budget is very small, you just need to be super creative.

If money is scarce, you can find creative ways to meet singles that are free—churches, parks, bookstores, etc. You can focus heavily on online dating, which is the most cost-effective method for meeting the highest volume of men. Use the computer at a library or a friend's house if you don't have one available at home or at work. You can send your direct-mail campaign via e-mail, instead of buying cards and stamps. You can improve your packaging with inexpensive home beauty treatments and borrowed clothes. And so forth. Each step can be accomplished on a very small budget, but don't forget to first consider borrowing money for this project from a friend or relative. You are investing in your future, and perhaps someone who loves you will loan you money to augment your budget.

If you don't have a network of friends, what can you do? Well, what do you think a world-class salesperson would do if she had to sell a new product but didn't have any customers? She would go out and *find* customers. You can build a network of friends if you are driven to succeed in *The Program*. You start by smiling and saying hello to people around you—at work, in the elevator, standing in line at stores, wherever you are. You strike up conversations with those who respond in a friendly manner. Over time, you feel comfortable asking them to have coffee with you. You start to talk and begin a friendship. It's what you learned in kindergarten. Except then it happened over milk instead of coffee.

- ***What if I meet a man who is separated but not yet divorced? Is it okay to date him (you did tell me to cast a wider net . . .)?***

  I want you to cast a wider net for *single* men. Men are either married or divorced; married means not single, divorced means single. There is nothing in between for you except heartache and wasted time. A man who is separated is like a woman who is "sort of" pregnant: You either are or you aren't. Remember that you are playing the odds on *The Program*: The odds of a separated man getting divorced and marrying you anytime soon are very, very low.

- ***How soon after a man's divorce is it smart to date him?***

  There is no time formula to determine when a man is ready to move on after his divorce and form a successful attachment with a new woman. It depends more on the process he has gone through than on the amount of time that has passed. An ideal situation would be where the man was separated and moved out of his home long before his divorce was final, he has already been dating and has had a "transitional relationship" with another woman, and he doesn't sound raw or eager to recount all the gory details of the unraveling of his marriage on your first date. It would also be ideal if the man has figured out his own part in the marital problems, rather than solely blaming his ex-wife, and if he made reasonable steps to resolve the issues before giving up on his marriage. Even if the problems really did stem from his ex-wife, an introspective person would consider how he missed the signs. Look for red flags that show he may still be angry, vindictive, or depressed. A man who had an affair or addiction, was abusive, or abandoned his children is not a good bet.

If he has children, it is important that he and his ex-wife are dealing with custody and visitation in a mature manner, and that he is committed to being a dad. This speaks to his character, even if it is inconvenient for a new woman in his life. Make sure that you discuss sooner, rather than later, whether he even wants to be married again, as sometimes men with children are not really interested in remarrying.

Are there any divorced men out there who meet all these criteria? Well, they are probably few and far between. But use this ideal scenario to help guide your instincts about a divorced man early on, so that you don't waste precious time with someone who is not ready or able to make a commitment to you. Still, none of this is appropriate discussion for the first few dates, when you should be concentrating on forming your own connection with him. Aim to understand his divorce process sometime between dates four and eight.

• *How soon after my own divorce should I start The Program?*

When you can answer "yes" to the three Priority Questions in Step #1, Marketing Focus. Some of you may be ready to begin dating before your divorce is final. While it's unwise to start a serious relationship with a man before the final papers are signed (technically you're still married, and besides, you need time to heal), you can start the first six steps on *The Program* which will build your foundation. Then you can be ready to look for a serious relationship when the ink is dry on your divorce papers.

• *What if the man I'm dating tells me that he's not ready for a serious relationship, but he really cares about me and wants to continue dating me?*

Believe that he's not ready. And move on without him. He must not really care about you *that* much or he'd want a commitment, just like you do. Always believe what a man tells you when it involves an excuse to hold back. Whether he professes an inability to make a commitment, a lack of readiness for marriage, a lack of knowledge of how to love someone, or whatever, he is actually telling you that you're not The One for him. Don't waste your time thinking you can change him. The only way you can "change" a man is if he's in diapers.

• *You said that most of your clients who joined The Program have found husbands in 12 to 18 months. What happened to the others?*

My success rate is difficult to measure. Many women have attended my seminars around the country and joined *The Program* without keeping me apprised of their results. But I have tallied the success (and failure) over five years of my private clients and women who have corresponded with me after attending my seminar. Most of these women have married or become engaged within 12 to 18 months. They were focused, committed, and enthusiastic about *The Program*.

Among those who were still single after that time period, some found a husband in the following year. Many of them took longer because they had less time available to focus on *The Program*. Often it wasn't their fault: They were single moms struggling to find adequate child care, or women coping with an ailing parent, and one client even developed a brain tumor during her third month on *The Program*! So life goes. But many of those who have not yet found a husband simply weren't that committed to *The Program*. They didn't complete some of the steps, they performed many tasks halfheartedly, they gave up for substantial periods in between steps, or they dropped out altogether. *The Program* isn't for everyone: It works for women who are completely focused on their goal and don't give up after setbacks.

• *Can I drop in and out of The Program and still expect results?*

Yes. Many women cannot commit fully to *The Program* for a multitude of reasons, ranging from time pressure with other commitments to discouraged attitudes from hitting a pothole in the dating road. This is reality. You can absolutely drop in and out of *The Program* and still expect some results. It may, however, take longer than 12 to 18 months to find your husband if your pattern is on-again, off-again. Listen: It is better to be on *The Program* for even one day than never at all. Do what you can, when you can.

• *Is there any way to regulate the roller coaster of emotions that I go through during The Program? There are so many ups and downs!*

It is absolutely true that some weeks on *The Program* you will feel like you can conquer the world, and other weeks you will feel like the world is coming to an end. One week, you might have two dates with men you really like and three more friends offer to fix you up. Then the next week, your phone doesn't ring once, your dates didn't call back, and the fix-ups you were so excited about seem to have vanished into thin air.

The answer is patience. This means having long-term patience that *The Program* will work over the course of 12 to 18 months, and having short-term patience for a man to call you. After 35, everyone's life is so much more complex, both for women and for men. Sometimes the phone doesn't ring all week because a man you went on a date with or the men your friends passed your number to had other pressing issues. His job, travel, his own kids, a medical problem, an ailing parent, a home repair, or any number of other things could be the reason he didn't call right away.

Don't always assume the worst and let it get you down. That's why volume is so important on *The Program*: You always want many irons in the fire so that you aren't counting too heavily on any one thing.

• *I think I intimidate men because of my career success, and they are reluctant to ask me out. How do I correct that?*

You have already begun correcting the problem simply by acknowledging this early perception that men have about you, and by framing the question around something that you can correct, instead of venting hostility that you wouldn't want these men anyway. There are wonderful men out there who are initially intimidated by a woman's career success, and it doesn't necessarily mean these men should be passed over. If you are truly casting a wider net, you are open to men who are less successful than you are. You will make accommodations for the natural reaction that often occurs when men meet women who make more money than they do, or who are in higher positions of authority.

Try to ease men into seeing the "strong" you, the "career" you.

Play down your wardrobe at first. Don't "dress for success" on the first few dates with expensive jewelry, power suits, or flashy clothing and accessories that reinforce your monetary status. If you live in a much more expensive home than he does, don't invite him over until your relationship is more secure. Don't let your conversation focus heavily on your accomplishments at work. Rather, focus on mutual interests such as family, films, books, or pets (not items that signify success, such as expensive vacations).

Consider downplaying your job title when he asks you what you do for a living on the first or second date. If you are the CEO of a real estate company, you can tell him that you "sell real estate." Eventually, if you establish strong feelings for each other, your success will not deter him and you can say or wear whatever you want. But in the beginning, you just want him to get beyond any salary or job title barriers that may prevent him from knowing you for what really matters.

• *I have a male friend who adores me and would marry me in a minute. He has many good qualities, but I am not in love with him. Still, I am sick and tired of being single. Should I settle for companionship?*

The Program is about finding a wonderful husband with whom you are truly in love. It is not about settling for companionship. While marrying a man under those circumstances may sound like a good option now while you are single, it would quickly turn sour once you said "I do." I know many divorced women who tell me that as awful as it is to be single, it was worse to be married without passion. In the long run, you will regret any decision to settle for companionship. Hold out for love.

• *How do I say no to a man if I'm not interested in him?*

You do it quickly and emphatically. Remember what I said earlier about cutting your losses? The same holds true here: It's an amputation, not a taffy pull. If you've tried to decline a date with him politely once or twice and he still hasn't absorbed the message, then it's time to get very blunt. Use very clear language such as, "I'm sorry, but there is no chance at all for us. Please stop asking me." I know this is harsh, but you need to manage your time wisely and not get bogged down with distractions.

The tricky part is that you don't want to completely alienate him because . . . I think by now you know why! Of course, he might have a network of friends for you to meet. So try to round out a "harsh" rejection by telling him something positive and specific about himself that you really liked, such as his great sense of humor or kind heart. Suggest that he might be perfect for another friend of yours, and if you ever host a party in the future, you hope he'll come so that you can introduce him to someone else. If he reacts badly to this, then *c'est la vie*. There will always be a few people you're going to estrange along this path of husband-hunting. It's a jungle out there!

• *Do you have any different advice for women over 50?*

The Program is effective for women at *any* age, whether they are 35 or 105. What I see in women over 50 is simply an increased degree of the same baggage as women under 50. Their lifestyles are *more* insular, they have endured disappointments with *more* men, and they are *more* resigned that they will never find a great husband. As they become more comfortable with their friends, home, job, or grown children, their energy to change their single status wanes. The hope they had in their 30's and 40's may have dissolved because they mistakenly think, "If I haven't met him so far, how could I possibly meet him now?" Of course, this is a self-fulfilling prophecy. If you truly want to find a wonderful husband, you now have all the tools you need with *The Program*, and nothing can stop you except your attitude.

• *Should I have a baby on my own?*

If you are over 35 and feel that having your own child is extremely important to you, then yes, I think you should consider it. You need two important elements in place, however, for this decision to be successful: You need to be financially secure, and you need to have a strong network of family and friends who are willing to help you.

Having your own child may actually help you find a husband in the long run. When you meet a man after you are a mother, he will hopefully not sense an urgency from you to fast-forward the relationship because your biological clock is ticking. He may have kids of his own from a previous marriage and not want to start a family over again. You will most likely have to put *The Program* on hold for a couple of years as you focus on pregnancy and the infant stage, but it will always be waiting for you when you are ready.

If you are not yet ready to have a baby on your own, you should at least consider freezing embryos for the future. Fertility methods are advancing every day: Fertilizing your eggs with donor sperm and freezing the embryos can increase your chances of a successful pregnancy later on. Ask your doctor for advice on this procedure.

• How can finding a husband be my #1 priority if I have young children?

It is never easy to find the time or energy for dating when you have young children, especially if you work outside the home. You come home tired at night, you haven't seen your kids all day, you have to get dressed up to go out, and you are expected to be lively and charming. But if you want to be married again, you have to do what it takes. Perhaps your *Program* Calendar can't be as full as that of a woman without young children, but do as much as you possibly can. This will require a serious investment in baby-sitters.

I hear single moms complain all the time that they can't find a good baby-sitter or can't afford one. Baby-sitters are crucial to your ability to find happiness this year, and there is no excuse. If you don't have a few good sitters, devote the time to get recommendations from friends. Interview a million baby-sitters if that's what it takes to find a few you trust. You certainly need more than one on your list. If you work outside the home, your daytime baby-sitter probably won't want to stay several extra hours at night while you go out. You need other options for evening help. You may be in a situation where your ex-husband shares custody, in which case you can try to schedule your dates when your children are at his house. And that's free!

Take any baby-sitting money that you need out of your *Program* Marketing Budget: There is no better use for it. Perhaps you can barter free baby-sitting for renting a room in your house. Several women I know have hired an au pair girl for a year, as this is often the least expensive means to get maximum help. Help yourself succeed by creating a situation at home where you are available as much as possible so that *The Program* can work for you.

There are always feelings of guilt and remorse that accompany the decision to leave children at home with a baby-sitter while you are on a date or at a singles event. But remember that *The Program* is a 12 to 18 month commitment for you, and you will be there again for your children soon, as you always have been. Think of it as making a withdrawal from a bank account into which you have deposited so much time, patience, and sacrifice in the past. You've put in a lot to raise your children thus far, and it's okay to take a little out. Most important, know that you are prioritizing your children's *long-term* needs (having a happy mother and a day-to-day father) over their *short-term* needs (having you home on Saturday night to tuck them into bed).

P.S. And remember to check out *www.ParentsWithoutPartners. org* to meet those cute single dads!

• *Should I consider a long-distance relationship?*

Absolutely! Casting a wider net definitely means looking for men who may live in another city or even in another country. You can easily expand your search geographically with online dating, and also tell everyone you know that you would be very open to fix-ups with men in other locations. I even know one woman in Connecticut who met a man on vacation who lived in the Philippines, and they are now engaged. As you travel on business or vacations, or attend functions such as weddings or reunions, always be open to men in other cities.

Of course it's always harder to work out the logistics of long-distance relationships, but I know several women who found Mr. Wonderful in a faraway zip code and made it work. The key is to devote a lot of time up front to visiting each other, having long phone conversations, and exchanging long e-mails to determine if there is a strong enough connection there to pursue something serious. Long-distance relationships can drag on forever with indecision about whether one person should relocate. But if finding a wonderful husband is truly your #1 priority, you will not let a few miles and some challenging logistics hold you back.

• If I am on antidepression medication, should I tell the man I'm dating? And if so, when?

It is common these days for people to take antidepression medication, such as Prozac, Paxil, or Zoloft, when prescribed by a doctor. You should not feel any stigma or embarrassment about it, just as you would not if it were asthma or diabetes medication. Medicine is a personal matter, and you should feel comfortable in a relationship before disclosing personal information of any kind. Some women consider antidepressants "baggage" because the reason they're taking them in the first place is rooted to deep issues.

Wait long enough so that the man you're dating knows you fairly well, but not so long such that revealing something new is shocking when he thinks he knows everything about you. Usually this time period arrives between one and three months in a steady, exclusive relationship. You don't want to wait so long that it feels like you're keeping a secret. That feeling begins to emerge when you've told each other almost everything about one another, except for this one item you're deliberately holding back. A man may react negatively to this information when you finally tell him—not because you are taking the medication, but because he feels betrayed that you kept it a secret. If this happens, explain your thinking, and remember, as with anything personal, that it is your right to divulge information when you feel comfortable, not because you feel pressured.

Be prepared to answer his questions about why you started taking the medication (genetics, hormones, crisis, childhood issues), how long you've been on it, how long you plan to stay on it, and if there are any side effects that your doctor has described. If you do feel any embarrassment about taking antidepression medication, try not to project that feeling when you tell him. Try to convey an upbeat message about how much the medicine has helped you, how common it is today, and how you are willing to answer candidly any questions that he may have. And who knows—he may even surprise you by revealing that he, too, is on the same medication!

• *Is there anything you should never say to a man on a first date?*

Yes. On a first date, you should never say that you are looking for a commitment. Although a commitment is exactly what you are looking for from the right man, you don't want to scare someone away. Many women believe that to attain maximum dating efficiency, they must screen out men on the first date according to his desire for a committed relationship. I can't believe I'm going to say this, but there actually is such a thing as being *too* efficient. First dates that include heavy conversation topics often result in regret and retreat the next day by the man. Timing is everything. Pace yourself to learn about him and his intentions at a steady rate.

While we're on the subject of what *not* to do on a first date, keep these tips in mind, too: 1) Don't ask about his income, 2) Don't be a complainer, 3) Don't talk about your ex, and 4) Don't talk about your health issues. All of these are turnoffs!

- **Does The Program work for men? How about gays and lesbians?**

  Absolutely! *The Program* works for anyone who is committed to finding a mate. I have targeted this book to women over 35 because I believe they are the most receptive niche for this radical approach, but the principles hold true regardless of gender, age, or sexual preference.

- **There is so much to do on The Program! How can I not feel overwhelmed by all this?**

  First of all, it's a *good* problem to have so many things that you can do to change your single status. Before you heard about *The Program*, you probably thought there was nothing left to do. *The Program* can feel overwhelming, especially if you already have an extremely busy life with a career, children, or other responsibilities. So you have to create reasonable goals for yourself, either daily or weekly. The planning calendar shown in Step #11, Mass Marketing, should help you organize your activities. Take it one day at a time by saying for example, "Today I am going to shop at a new grocery store." That's the only thing you have to accomplish that day. Not so hard. Or take it one week at a time by saying for example, "This week I am going to get my photo taken for my online profile." That's the only thing you have to accomplish that week. Not so hard. Of course, the more you can reasonably put on your agenda, the faster you will move through the 15 Steps and find a husband. Do whatever you can as long as you avoid feeling overwhelmed to the point of inertia. The key is to get up and do *something*.

  Some women have also formed *Program* support groups in their city. If you have friends who have also joined *The Program*, or who might be interested in joining, it's a great idea to gather them together and form a support group. The group can meet weekly or monthly, and provide encouragement, feedback, resources, and networking for women just like you. Check my Web site for *Program* support groups in your area: www.Find AHusbandAfter35.com.

Epilogue:
Pay It Forward

WHAT DOES *"PAY IT FORWARD"* MEAN AFTER *THE PROGRAM*?

First of all, *congratulations*! You have finished all 15 Steps on *The Program* and are either engaged or married. You have found the man with whom you hope to spend the rest of your life. But you're not quite through yet! I want to ask you to pay it forward.

The expression *pay it forward* is the opposite of *pay it back*. When someone does a favor or good deed for you, instead of paying back the favor to that same person, you pay it "forward" to someone new in the future. Did you ever see the movie *Pay It Forward* starring Kevin Spacey and Helen Hunt? If not, you should rent the video: I loved it. In the movie, a young boy creates a pay-it-forward scheme whereby he first performs a good deed for three people, then those three people "pay it forward." They show their gratitude by performing a good deed for three new people. Then *those* nine people go out and each one performs three more good deeds, for a total of 27 people. And so on. The idea is that the exponential growth of people each helping three more people in the future could make the world a better place. A pay-it-forward movement is ignited.

The Program helped you meet your husband. Now that you have achieved your "profit," I would like to ask you to give back to your community. The people who have invested in you along the way symbolize a community of single women, and those who support them. The right thing to do is to make a donation.

When companies become profitable, they make donations to good causes and/or set up foundations. Here, your challenge is to pay it forward to three other 35+ single women by helping them find a husband just as you did. With your help, together we can start a pay-it-forward *Program* movement.

WHY SHOULD YOU PAY IT FORWARD?

Good Karma

You have received a lot of help and goodwill from so many people during your search for Mr. Right. Now it is your turn to help others who are in your former situation. Granted, you have expressed your appreciation along the way (via heartfelt words, thank-you notes, and small gifts) to those people who went out of their way to assist you, but this is about helping other single women who are still struggling to find their husband. They may be women you don't even know. It's about making the lives of others better by sharing your experiences and mentoring those who need your newly acquired *Program* expertise. Call it charity: from those who have to those who have not.

This kind of charity is simply good karma. Whether you believe in karma (spiritual goodwill) or not, believe me, it's something you don't want to mess with! Don't tempt fate by focusing inward now. You have been blessed with a wonderful husband (or husband-to-be) and are now in the enviable position to make a difference in another single woman's life. There's an old adage that says, "If you introduce three couples who get married, you reach Nirvana!"

Personal Benefits

You will gain personal benefits for your generosity. It is very rewarding to make a difference in someone's life. I believe I have done this with my seminars, private clients, and this book. Let me just say that this is priceless. When a woman beams and tells me that I have helped her find a husband whom she never thought existed, I get tears in my eyes. I honestly do. Every time. It is just extremely fulfilling, and I want you to have this feeling, too.

HOW DO YOU PAY IT FORWARD?

First, select three women over age 35 who would be good candidates for *The Program*. You may even choose women *under* 35 if they are truly committed to finding a husband and seem to be struggling. The women can be friends, relatives, colleagues, or acquaintances. If you don't know three eligible women, ask around and collect "nominations." Almost everyone knows a single woman who would love some assistance with her quest. Helping a stranger is often easier because you can be more objective and candid, and the mentoring relationship is more professional.

There are three ways that I encourage you to pay it forward. These are actions you can also take while going through *The Program*; you don't have to wait until you are a graduate. Select one, two, or three of these, based on your time and resources:

1. **Mentor:** Become a *Program* Mentor for one or more of your three beneficiaries. You can offer to provide the same helpful service as coach, cheerleader, and truth-sayer that your Mentor hopefully gave to you. If your Mentor had some deficiencies, this is your chance to do it differently.

2. **Recycle:** Similar to the Dating Exchange party in Step #12, Event Marketing, you can recycle several of your dates or ex-boyfriends who weren't The One for you. Over time, you have probably met or been fixed up with several men who had many positive qualities, but were just not right for you. With the belief that "there is someone for everyone," this is the ideal opportunity to introduce these men to any of your three women beneficiaries.

3. **Spread the word:** Tell other single women about *The Program*. Let them know there is something they can do to change their situation. You can refer women to my Web site (www.Find AHusbandAfter35.com) and encourage them to sign up and receive my free newsletter. The Web site also lists my upcoming seminars in cities across the country.

CASE STUDIES

Below are case studies about three *Program* graduates and how they paid it forward:

Cheryl

One client, Cheryl, age 51, paid it forward to her own mother. Here is her story:

> I met Ken two years ago on *The Program* and had just returned from a wonderful honeymoon with him in the Canadian Rockies. But I couldn't forget my responsibility to pay it forward. My first thought was about my mother, who is 81 years old. She has been widowed for ten years and lives in a retirement home in Charlotte, North Carolina. I knew my mother could still have many happy years ahead of her, if only she had someone to share her life with. I know she's not too old for romance.
>
> I had been telling her for a long time about my progress on *The Program*, but she scoffed at being so proactive, even when she knew that's how I had found Ken. She kept saying, "If it's meant to be for me, it's meant to be." I didn't give up, and kept hounding her to try it.
>
> I was shocked last week when Mom called to ask me to be her Mentor. I accepted with joy and will begin immediately helping her through this journey. I promised Rachel that I would send her my mother's future wedding photo when she finds a husband. With a little luck and a lot of hard work, my mother could be Rachel's oldest success story!

Laura

Another woman, Laura, age 39, paid it forward to a woman she barely knew at her local library in Seattle, Washington. Here is her story:

> I couldn't be happier! I have been married to Jim for almost a year now. As soon as we got engaged, I couldn't stop thinking

about paying it forward. I really believe in karma, and didn't want to jinx anything with Jim. I picked three women to pay it forward to. Two of them are still hunting, but one of them has already had great success.

About once a month for the last couple of years, I would stop by the library in my neighborhood to check out a good book. I love to read. There was this librarian, Greta, who would always recommend books to me. Greta looked to be about my age, maybe late thirties or early forties.

After I got engaged, I showed up at the library one day to search for a book on planning a wedding. Greta complimented me on my engagement ring, helped me find a wedding planning book, and for the first time we had a more personal conversation. She told me that she was divorced and would love to find someone, too. I knew right away that I was meant to help her, so I told Greta about *The Program*. Best of all, I told her I knew someone to fix her up with (my last date before I met Jim). This guy was a writer, so I thought he would have a lot in common with a librarian.

Greta met my "recycled" writer about three weeks later. They fell in love, and after 9 months, they are now engaged!

Regan

Another woman, Regan, age 43, paid it forward to her doctor. Here is her story:

> I was married six months ago to Peter, whom I met on Step #11, Mass Marketing. I had submitted a personal ad to *New York Magazine*, and he was the third response I got.
>
> Anyway, after the wedding, we immediately started trying to

get pregnant. At 43, I wanted some expert assistance, and found a prominent fertility specialist through a friend.

I guess I had been so preoccupied with getting pregnant that I forgot about paying it forward until I met this brilliant female fertility specialist, Dr. B. Through our appointments, I got to know a little bit about her, and I learned that she was divorced and in her mid-fifties. I didn't know how she would take this gesture, but at my next appointment I showed up with an advertisement for Rachel's seminar ("Find a Husband After 35") that was coming to town. I didn't want to be presumptuous, but I told her that *The Program* had helped me find Peter, and if she was interested, it might be helpful if she attended.

Dr. B. gave me a knowing smile, and then said that a friend of hers had attended one of Rachel's seminars last year and had told her about *The Program* already. She said she couldn't ignore two endorsements from women she liked, so she would sign up for the class.

When Dr. B gave me the amazing news that I was pregnant four months later, I was sitting in her office and started to cry. I told her I could never thank her enough for her help. She pointed to a vase of flowers on her desk and said, "Oh, but you have already thanked me! These roses are from my new boyfriend I met on Step #9. I've started to date again, thanks to you!"

Business Before Pleasure:

A Letter to You

Dear Reader,

Now that you understand the full scope and potential of *The Program*, you have all the tools you need to change your single status.

But will you try it?

I know these 15 Steps are overwhelming. Of course they are. Your emotions are all over the map: excited, scared, skeptical, nervous, hopeful . . . but hold on! You have 12 to 18 months to make it happen. That's almost 550 days to accomplish the possible. You're going to do it one day at a time by starting with Step #1. When the going gets tough, the tough get going!

Even if you haven't officially begun *The Program*, I know that you have already started to think through the possibilities. Perhaps you have been looking in the mirror and wondering: "Too much make-up? Would my hair look better longer?" Maybe you've pushed away that ice cream sundae, you've been mulling over names for a Mentor, and you've glanced through your address book for those six women "dates." Or you've suddenly started noticing newspaper articles about online dating, you're looking more closely at people in the grocery store, and you don't make your coffee at home anymore. You might be thinking about canceling your newspaper subscription, and your head is probably swimming with adjectives to define your personal brand. All around you are tall, short, fat, thin, bald, interesting-looking men you've never noticed before. Possibilities abound. Literally, your whole outlook on life is changing. Subconsciously or consciously, you are prepping yourself for *The Program*.

And trust me, you are ready.

So *now* is the time to begin at the beginning. There is a wonderful man out there for you. *And there is actually something you can do to find him.* Please don't let another day go by without taking action.

My best wishes,

Rachel

P.S. Please send me an announcement about your wedding through my Web site: www.FindAHusbandAfter35.com!

Appendix:

Online Dating Services

Here are some online dating sites you might want to consider including on Step #7: Online Marketing:

- AmericanSingles.com (for all singles)
- Amigos.com (for Spanish singles)
- AnimalPeople.com (for singles who are animal lovers)
- BlackPlanet.com (for African American singles)
- BlackPlanetLove.com (for African American singles)
- ChristianCafe.com (for Christian singles)
- ChristianSingles.com (for Christian singles)
- Craigslist.org (for all singles)
- Date-A-Doc.com (for singles who are, or are looking to meet, health-care and science professionals)
- Date.com (for all singles)
- DatingDirect.com (for all singles)
- DoggieDating.com (for pet-loving singles)
- DreamMates.com (for all singles)
- eHarmony.com (for all singles)
- Friendster.com (meet singles via friends of friends)
- Gay.com (for gay singles)
- Glimpse.com (for gay singles)
- GreatBoyFriends.com (where women make referrals for single men)

- JewishCafe.com (for Jewish singles)
- JDate.com (for Jewish singles)
- Kiss.com (for all singles)
- LargeAndLovely.com (for "plus-sized" singles)
- Match.com (largest site; for all singles)
- Matchmaker.com (for all singles)
- Meetup.com (for local interest groups of all kinds)
- MillionareMatch.com (claims to be for wealthy singles)
- MuslimMatch.com (for Muslim singles)
- Nerve.com (for "urban hipsters")
- Personals.Salon.com (for all singles)
- Personals.Yahoo.com (for all singles)
- PlanetOut.com (for gay singles)
- RightStuffDating.com (for graduates of Ivy League and other top colleges)
- SaltAndPepperSingles.com (for singles looking to date outside their race)
- SassySeniors.com (for single seniors)
- SeniorFriendFinder.com (for single seniors)
- SeniorsCircle.com (for single seniors)
- Soulmatch.com (for singles focused on religion and values)
- Tallpersonals.com (for tall singles)
- TrueBeginnings.com (for all singles)
- UDate.com (for all singles)

NOTE: There are many more niche online dating services available beyond this list. To find additional niche sites, go to www.google.com and search for your preferred group. (For example, to find additional *Jewish* dating services, type "Jewish singles" in the search box.

Acknowledgments

There are so many people who helped me create this book. I never could have done it without them. Unless you're an author, you could never in your wildest dreams imagine all that goes into this process. Thank you to:

My literary agent, Amanda (Binky) Urban of ICM, who is simply the best in the business. Her savvy guidance and instincts helped me every step of the way. And Josie Freedman, my film agent at ICM, was spectacular in selling this book to Paramount Studios.

My team at Ballantine Books, who have been great to work with. Zach Schisgal, my incredible editor, is one of the smartest, most articulate, and most patient people I've ever worked with. Kim Hovey and Gilly Hailparn are public relations dynamos who surpassed even my wildest expectations. Libby McGuire and Christine Cabello took marketing to new heights with their creativity. Kathleen Spinelli's insightful editing comments were much appreciated. Nancy Miller's wisdom and sharp editing skills never ceased to impress me. Claire Tisne's focus and energy skyrocketed this book around the world, and her story still makes me laugh about one foreign publisher who told her: "In our country, women are trying to get *rid* of their husband, not *find* one!" Rachel Bernstein and Rachel Kind were also invaluable and persistent in the subsidiary rights process, selling this book to 18 countries thus far. Gene Mydlowski has a true gift for artistic direction. Grant Neumann used every ounce of his impressive internal thesaurus to help us find a title for this book. Anthony Ziccardi's sheer determination to propel the sales of this book was magnificent. And Gina Centrello is the brilliant force at the helm who saw the potential in this book and supported it all the way.

My lawyer, Tom Baer, is phenomenal. I can't imagine where I'd be without his wise counsel.

Marilyn Fletcher, who changed my life in a 5-minute phone call. She is vivacious and wonderful, and defines what every successful woman should be.

John Solomon, who couldn't have been more supportive and instrumental in helping me navigate my new world. He always knew *everything*.

Melanie Sturm, who was the first person to say, "You should write a book!" She lit the flame that started this movement. I am so very grateful for all her support, encouragement, and insights.

Jennifer Korman, who sat across from me in a restaurant booth last year and inspired what eventually became my book proposal. Her writing knowledge and keen advice whipped this book into motion, while our hours together on the treadmill proved to be the ultimate sounding board. Her own book will take the publishing world by storm one day soon.

Stacy Preblud, whose friendship shone in that library conference room a million years ago, listening to me rehearse before my first-ever seminar. Her smart comments made all the difference. She, too, will be a renowned author one day soon.

Dr. Sue Schimmel, the intelligent and prominent psychologist who thoughtfully answered so many of my questions and is a great friend.

Sarah Thomas has defined true friendship for more than 20 years. Her trek into Manhattan to attend one of my 4-hour seminars about finding a husband (given that she is a happily married woman) was only one of a thousand gestures of friendship she has given me. Her intelligence and grace endear her to me.

Wanda Lockwood, who is my favorite stylist and wonderful friend. I am really lucky to have been the last one admitted into her "circle." Her kind heart and vivacious personality have always inspired me. And I hope my daughter grows up to be just like her amazing daughters, Rachel and Tracy.

Mari Glick, who is one of the strongest women I know. She is my incredible friend who encouraged me to pursue writing this book over dinner in Beaver Creek, and has always been my ardent supporter.

Kelly Ford Patrick, Denver's Dynamo Radio Diva, who made that first phone call to invite me as a guest on KYGO. Her support changed my path in many ways.

More friends who made a big difference: Dr. Lorraine Dugoff, who knows about everything from literary agents to fertility methods, and supported me all the way; Anne Thomas, Sara Delano, and Karen Adair, who were my fabulous friends and seminar assistants around the country; Ted Gobillot, whose insights on market research were dead-on during our snowshoeing excursion; Donna Miller, who lent me her home when I lost electricity during Denver's worst snowstorm in 90 years (only 3 weeks before this manuscript was due); Meredith Hanrahan, who believed in this book from the start; Laura Lauder, who enthusiastically e-mailed more single friends than anyone else to spread the word about my seminars, and was always so happy for me.

So many supportive friends who helped with this book by spreading the word, contributing great ideas, or always expressing excitement to hear my latest news: Regan Asnes, David Brown, Shawn Cooper, Aimee and Alan Farkas, Anita Gaylor, Lori Gobillot, Sheri Gold, Will Gold, Diana Hayden, Beth Hooper, Marc Kerman, David Korman, Gary Lauder, Patti Levine, Greg Lyss, Lisa Mintz, Tom Moore, Eileen Oakley, Meredith Oppenheim, Marianne Owen, Peggy Scharlin, Zibby Schwartz, Justyn Shwayder, Lodene Spanola, Marjorie Stonehouse, Hildi Todrin, Hilary Von Schroeter and Jon Weintraub.

My "test readers" on the final manuscript, who were very insightful. I am so appreciative to Hilary, Melanie, Susan, Chris, Wanda, Mari, and Sally.

All my incredible clients and seminar participants over the years, who have inspired me and trusted me. I am so proud of each and every one of them for harnessing the power of *The Program*.

Jonathan Fisher, of Fisher Creative in Houston, Texas, who is a creative genius and without a doubt the foremost graphic artist and Web site designer in America (www.fishercreative.com).

Harvard Business School, one of the finest academic institutions in this country. My M.B.A. degree transformed my life in so many ways, in large part due to the dynamic marketing faculty there.

Wellesley College, for building a strong foundation of confidence, academic and social skills, and alumnae support that enabled me to pursue this new career. My four years there were among the best in my life.

And my family! My fantastic mother, Eleanor Hoffman, who read every single word of my manuscript many times over, offered invaluable suggestions, and crafted more than a hundred creative title ideas. My fantastic father, Murray Hoffman, who also read every single word of my manuscript, provided countless gems of wisdom, and as always, reminded me what's most important in life. He's the world's top cardiologist who knows how to get to the "heart" of the matter. My always supportive father-in-law, Jerry Greenwald, who was the most important catalyst in gaining visibility for my book proposal and assembling an A-team for me, for which I am eternally grateful. My wonderful mother-in-law, Glenda Greenwald, gave me many stellar ideas for my seminars, including "burying your emotional bones." My dynamic sister-in-law, Holly Greenwald, whose creative market research in New York department stores should be legendary, was one of my most genuine supporters on this book from the beginning. My brother-in-law Josh Greenwald has an intelligent wit and dazzled me with clever ideas and titles. Josh also had the foresight to suggest organizational changes in my text that had enormous impact early on. My sister-in-law Stacey Greenwald is Manhattan's most beautiful architect, and made significant contributions to this book in many ways. Julie and Scott Greenwald, my sister- and brother-in-law, have great insight and perspective, and I have always admired their strength and warmth. Many others in my family have been incredibly supportive of this book, and I sincerely thank them: Hugh and Susan Hoffman (an A+ investment banker and an A+ mother), Eric and Deanna Hoffman (a top-notch research scientist and a top-notch Spanish professor), and Susan Chapman (an excellent senior legal auditor and Oliver's biggest fan).

S. H., who is fabulous in style and heart. She is one of the most generous and charismatic women I know, and her many contributions to this book made a world of difference.

Patricia, who was my lifeline every single day while I wrote this book. She is one of the greatest and most intelligent women I know, and will always be an honorary member of our family.

My adorable nieces and nephew: Emma, Greta, Eliana, Brandon, Carly, and Isabella.

My beautiful children: Max, Grace, and Oliver. Their patience with me throughout this project was truly admirable. I am so proud of them. And their suggestions for my book title kept me laughing long and hard: My favorite was *Cupid Is a Slacker!*

My husband, Brad, who is the most incredible man on this earth. Without him I would never have felt the passion to help other women find their own wonderful husbands. It brings tears to my eyes when I try to describe Brad. He is truly kind, always makes me laugh, and lives his life with integrity. He encouraged me 100% to pursue this dream of writing a book, even though it meant a dramatic change in our family life. He is my brilliant editor, devoted business manager, and the love of my life. He definitely defines "someone wonderful."

For More Information

If you would like information about:

- More tips to find a husband after 35
- How to receive Rachel's newsletter
- When Rachel will be teaching a seminar in your city
- Local *Program* support groups
- Private consulting sessions
- Rachel's story about how she met her husband

. . . please visit www.FindAHusbandAfter35.com.

RACHEL GREENWALD has an M.B.A. from Harvard Business School and a B.A. in psychology from Wellesley College. She has been featured on the *Today* show, CNN, and many other television and radio shows around the country. She is the advice columnist on MSN.com's "Love Over 40." She has conducted seminars on "How to Find a Husband After 35" to sold-out crowds all over the world. She lives in Denver with her husband and three children.

Visit her website at www.FindAHusbandAfter35.com.